THE National SABR Pastime

A Bird's-Eye View of Baltimore

Edited by Cecilia M. Tan

SABR Published by The Society for American Baseball Research

THE NATIONAL PASTIME — 2020 EDITION

Copyright © 2020 The Society for American Baseball Research

Editor: Cecilia M. Tan
Assistant Editors: King Kaufman, Keith R.A. DeCandido
Design and Production: Lisa Hochstein
Cover Design: Lisa Hochstein
Fact Checker: Clifford Blau
Proofreader: Norman L. Macht

Front cover image: Courtesy of Baltimore Orioles
Page 105: Photo of Oriole Park at Camden Yards, Copyright © Thomas Carter | Dreamstime.com

ISBN 978-1-970159-31-8 print edition
ISBN 978-1-970159-30-1 ebook edition

Society for American Baseball Research, Inc.
Cronkite School at ASU
555 N. Central Ave. #416
Phoenix, AZ 85004

Web: www.sabr.org
Phone: (602) 496—1460

Contents

Letter from the Editor

Welcome, friends, to our "virtual visit" to Charm City. A book or magazine is always that, but our need to transport ourselves through the written word to other places and times is felt quite keenly in the year 2020, when the real-life 50th SABR convention has been postponed because of the COVID-19 pandemic. Thank you to all the donors and sustainability benefactors who made this publication possible.

Even were it not for the global crisis, this would be a time of both reflection and prognostication for SABR. Big round numbers tend to inspire such thinking: 3000 hits, 500 home runs, 50 years. This summer would have been the 50th SABR annual conclave, and 2021 would be the 50th anniversary of the organization. It was a convenient fence-post error that essentially meant we could celebrate our nifty fifty-ness for two whole years.

The pandemic put the kibosh on our gathering in 2020, but in the meantime, celebrations go on. The University of Nebraska Press has published a 600-page compendium of SABR's 50 best articles—one for each year—entitled *SABR 50 at 50*. Meanwhile, SABR itself has presented a summer of "at home" presentations, including many of the panels and research presentations that would have been seen at the convention. (All are available on the SABR YouTube channel.)

One of the #SABRVirtual presentations was given by longtime treasurer F.X. Flinn, revealing a time capsule from the year 2003, when a SABR survey about "Baseball in 2020" was given to members and posted online. Remember back when the Twins, Expos, Devil Rays, and Padres were all on the chopping block? 81% of respondents felt Montreal would lose their team by 2020, and 72% felt Washington, DC, would gain one. Both things came to pass within two years: the Expos began play as the Washington Nationals in 2005.

And 40% of respondents thought major league baseball would be interrupted by some "national emergency." The six-day interruption of the 2001 season after the September 11 attacks now seems like a lifetime ago, doesn't it? The 2020 season was put on pause on March 12; Opening Day took place July 23. As I write this, two teams have had significant outbreaks of the virus, the Miami Marlins and the St. Louis Cardinals. Only time will tell whether the illness will permanently affect their lives or careers, or whether a World Series champion will ultimately be crowned.

I expect twenty years from now we'll still be writing about "what happened" during the 2020 season, no matter how long it runs. In 2020 SABR formed a Century Committee to research and memorialize events and issues in baseball from 100 years earlier. Chaired by Sharon Hamilton, over the coming decade the committee will put a spotlight on the Jazz Age and the early years of the Negro National League. Plans are also in the works to launch another survey similar to the one given in 2003, looking at baseball in 2040. We look back; we look forward.

Here in *The National Pastime*, we mostly look back. The articles are arranged roughly chronologically, beginning with the 1901 AL incarnation of the Baltimore Orioles, and wending forward to meet not only many of the usual suspects—John McGraw, Babe Ruth, Brooks Robinson,

Frank Robinson, Earl Weaver, Cal Ripken—but many whom you may not be as familiar with. Jerry Sullivan, a 3-foot-11 actor who appeared in a 1905 Eastern League game, 46 years before Eddie Gaedel. Howie Fox, the only man to return in 1954 with the newly-placed major-league Orioles after having played for the 1953 minor-league Orioles. Tom Gastall, a bonus baby whose hobby of aviation led to his demise in the Chesapeake Bay before he could complete his second season in the majors. Xu Guiyuan, the first prospect out of MLB's academies in China, signed by the Orioles. We look at not only the major leagues, but minor leagues, college-age leagues, the Class-D Potomac League, and the Negro Leagues. Tucked in these pages you will also find the major leagues' first costumed mascot, Mr. Oriole, and even a historical account of Baltimore's role in the advance of sabermetrics through the part it played in helping Retrosheet to get off the ground.

Until such time as we can raise a glass together in the hotel bar, or sing "Take Me Out to the Ball Game" in our SABR section of the stands at Oriole Park at Camden Yards, or wherever we might gather next, I hope you enjoy reading *The National Pastime* and the other great research coming from SABR. The newly revamped website is a joy to browse, the podcast with Rob Neyer is going strong, and the #SABRVirtual video archive and future SABR at Home programming all await your perusal as well.

Wait 'til next year,

— Cecilia M. Tan
Publications Director

The American League's First Baltimore Orioles

John McGraw, Wilbert Robinson, and Rivalries Created

Gordon Gattie

Professional baseball's first Baltimore Orioles played in the American Association (AA) in 1882. Another franchise of the same name played in the AA from 1883 until joining the National League (NL) for nine seasons, from 1891 through 1899, but the NL vacated four cities after the 1899 season. The following season, the Western League's owners changed the name of their organization to the American League and sought to establish the AL as a rival major league to the NL. They seized the opportunity to replace former NL franchises with AL teams in Baltimore, Washington, and Cleveland.[1] The American League's Baltimore Orioles was created as a member of the junior circuit on January 4, 1901.

Although Johnson desperately wanted a franchise in New York City, the politically powerful New York Giants successfully prevented the AL from moving there. Instead, Johnson placed a team in Baltimore and recruited John McGraw to lead the new franchise. The ballclub was incorporated as the "Baltimore Baseball and Athletic Company" and originally issued 400 shares of stock valued at $100 apiece. The initial incorporators included players McGraw and Wilbert Robinson, Justice Harry Goldman, Eutaw House proprietor Col. James P. Shannon, St. Vincent's Catholic Church pastor Reverend John D. Boland, city tax judge Conway W. Sams, and Baltimore businessmen S. Miles Brinkley and Moses N. Frank.[2]

Baltimore fans waited out two consecutive rainouts before celebrating Opening Day on April 26, 1901. The afternoon festivities included a procession of nearly 50 carriages from the Eutaw House Hotel to American League Park and pregame activities included Johnson throwing the ceremonial first pitch.[3] The Orioles won their inaugural game over the Boston Americans in front of over 10,000 fans, 10–6, led by Mike Donlin's two triples and Joe McGinnity's complete game.[4] The Orioles occupied second place during mid-May, then slumped to fourth place following a four-game losing streak.

The team endured a challenging early June. After winning their first two games that month, the Orioles

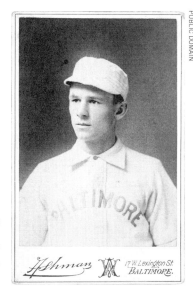

A young John McGraw, shown here in a cabinet photo portrait taken by photographer William Ashman in Baltimore between 1891 and 1894.

lost eight of their next ten contests. They fell to sixth place and 7½ games behind the league-leading Chicago White Sox following a 7–6 loss to the Milwaukee Brewers. The Orioles had built a 6–1 lead after six innings and outhit Milwaukee, 15–13, but the Brewers scored six unanswered runs, winning the 10-inning contest on a sacrifice fly following an errant throw. Frustrated with the team's ability to lose ballgames apparently within their grasp, one newspaper reporter noted, "If the defeats in themselves are becoming somewhat monotonous, the Orioles manage to have a charming variety in the methods by which they lose."[5]

Throughout the season, McGraw attempted to improve his team by recruiting players from other teams, including NL ballclubs. One of McGraw's top targets was his previous teammate and future Hall of Fame shortstop Hughie Jennings. Jennings was traded from Louisville to Baltimore in 1893 and played with the NL Orioles through the 1898 season, where he became the NL's top shortstop. Throughout June, four different ballclubs sought Jennings' services, including Baltimore, the AL Philadelphia Athletics, and the NL Philadelphia Phillies.[6] Although McGraw stated Jennings would play in Baltimore, President Johnson overrode McGraw and recognized the Athletics' claim, stating "Law and order must prevail in the American League, and the Baltimore club will not be allowed to have its own way any more than any other club. McGraw hasn't a leg to stand upon in this matter, and if he drives Jennings into the National League the Athletic club deserves some redress for which Baltimore should be held responsible."[7] McGraw rebutted Johnson's remarks, claiming Jennings hadn't been claimed when negotiations occurred, and that Johnson interfered because of his friendly relationship with Athletics owner Connie Mack. Jennings ultimately played for neither the Orioles nor the Athletics, opting for the Phillies instead. The dispute over Jennings foreshadowed future McGraw-Johnson tussles.

The next day Baltimore defeated Milwaukee, 11–4, the first of 11 consecutive wins, their longest winning streak that season. Their victories included sweeps of Detroit and Philadelphia and moved the Orioles into third place. Unfortunately, injuries to McGraw, Robinson, and other key players, along with frequent umpire troubles, led to a late season swoon and eventual fifth-place finish.[8] The Orioles struggled during early September, compiling a 4–19–2 record from August 27 through September 18, then finished the season on a high note, winning eight straight before losing the season finale; after their eighth straight win, one reporter observed, "There was nothing sensational about the game, but throughout there was the pleasant feeling of hopeful confidence."[9] Their late September streak pushed Baltimore back over the .500 mark, widening the gap between them and the sixth-place Washington Senators.

Based on their early season success, fans "confidently expected that by this time they would certainly be running neck and neck for second place and more probably fighting desperately for first."[10] The Orioles ultimately compiled a 68–65 record, 13½ games behind the pennant-winning Chicago White Sox. The Orioles led the AL with a .294 team batting average and a .353 team on-base average, while finishing third with 761 runs and 1,348 hits. McGraw, who managed and played third base before a mid-season injury, led the team with a .349 batting average and .995 OPS while pacing the AL with 14 hit-by-pitches in only 308 plate appearances; outfielder Mike Donlin led the full-season regulars with a .340 batting average and .883 OPS. Second baseman Jimmy Williams and shortstop Bill Keister each hit 21 triples and drove in over 90 runs. Baltimore's pitching staff, which had the highest average age in the league (29.0 years), attained a fourth-best 3.73 ERA, collectively struck out a league-low 271 opponents, and issued a near-league average 344 walks.

Joe McGinnity, returning to Baltimore and among those jumping from the NL to the AL, led Orioles hurlers with a 3.56 ERA, 26 wins, and 382 innings. The American League thrived during its first year as a self-proclaimed major league, and only one franchise changed locations during the off-season. (The Milwaukee Brewers moved to St. Louis and were renamed the Browns.)

The Orioles started 1902 on the right foot. On January 1, Baltimore announced they signed Joe McGinnity to a three-year deal. McGinnity had been pursued by the NL's Brooklyn Superbas; he had been assigned to Brooklyn before the 1900 season, then jumped to Baltimore before the 1901 season. As the season approached, McGraw set his everyday lineup with shortstop Billy Gilbert leading off, followed by outfielder Jimmy Sheckard, third baseman Joe Kelley, outfielder Cy Seymour, second baseman Jimmy Williams, outfielder Kip Selbach, first baseman Dan McGann, the catcher, and the pitcher.[11] The Orioles' roster experienced significant turnover during the season; only Harry Howell, Wilbert Robinson, Gilbert, Seymour, Selbach, and Williams played in at least half of Baltimore's 138 games.

Similar to their inaugural season, the Orioles planned a gala parade for Opening Day 1902. On April 23, the procession would leave the Eutaw House and travel throughout the city to the ballgrounds. There were plans for "12 mounted patrolmen and Packard's Band of 30 pieces" as well. However, unlike the previous season, no complimentary tickets were issued for Opening Day.[12] Due to a last-minute scheduling change, the Orioles opened their 1902 campaign in Boston before returning to Baltimore and hosting the Athletics for the home opener. On April 19, Baltimore carried a 6–3 lead heading into the ninth inning, scoring insurance runs during the eighth and ninth frames. Unfortunately for the Orioles, a late Boston rally resulted in four answered runs as Baltimore dropped the season opener.[13] They didn't fare better in their home opener, losing to Philadelphia, 8–1, though over 10,000 fans attended the ballgame.[14]

Baltimore endured a challenging season. Although the Orioles won four of their next six contests, they lost their next five games and slipped to seventh place. The team struggled and McGraw argued with Johnson and AL umpires while the wheels were set in motion for his eventual jump to the New York Giants. After May 2, the Orioles' highest placement for the season was fourth place; their last day in the league's upper division was June 14. However, there were reasons for hope throughout the season's first half. On May 9,

Ned Hanlon managed the 1892–98 NL Orioles, then returned to Baltimore in 1903, after the AL Orioles were replaced by New York, reestablishing a club of that name in the Eastern League.

McGraw returned from a five-game suspension, and the Orioles "played like a new team" as they defeated Philadelphia, 13–6, to end their five-game losing streak and knock the Athletics from the AL's top spot. The ballclub was praised for resurrecting the hit-and-run, Gilbert's excellent fielding was commended, and Williams homered.[15] On May 30, the Orioles swept a doubleheader from Cleveland, winning by scores of 10–7 and 12–4. The opening line from the *Baltimore Sun*'s game recap read: "It was a great day for Baltimore—a great day."[16]

Baltimore split the next four games; the last time the Orioles had a .500 or better winning percentage was on June 4. Their season started spiraling downward in late June and reached a low point on July 17, when they were forced to forfeit a game against the St. Louis Browns, the day after McGraw joined the New York Giants as manager. A few weeks earlier, on June 30, Johnson had suspended McGraw and Joseph Kelley indefinitely for their actions during the previous Saturday's ballgame against Boston. Johnson commented on McGraw's actions, "I have had time enough since I returned from the North to make a thorough investigation of this Baltimore trouble, and I am convinced that Umpire Connolly was absolutely right."[17] Robinson was named manager in McGraw's absence. Infuriated with his continued treatment by Johnson, McGraw left the AL for the Giants, where he would manage for 31 seasons and win over 2500 games.

In addition to securing McGraw, the Giants signed McGinnity, Cronin, Bresnahan, and McGann to contracts—and Kelley and Seymour jumped to Cincinnati—leaving the Orioles without enough players to field a team.[18] Johnson pieced together a roster with players

from other AL clubs—and the old Baltimore NL club[19]—so the Orioles could finish the season. The Orioles stumbled to the finish line, compiling an 8–20 record in August and 5–23 record in September, which included an 11-game losing streak.

Baltimore finished last at 50–88, 34 games behind the pennant-winning Philadelphia Athletics. Outfielder Kip Selbach, one of only three Orioles to play at least 100 games that season, lead the team in most offensive categories: plate appearances (573), runs (86), hits (161), and batting average (.320), with second baseman Jimmy Williams tallying the most triples (21), home runs (8), and best OPS (.861) on the team. McGinnity, despite leaving for New York in July, still led Baltimore hurlers with 13 wins and a 3.44 ERA, and finished second with 198⅔ innings pitched, just behind Harry Howell's 199 innings.

President Johnson successfully moved the AL Orioles' franchise from Baltimore to New York for the 1903 season.[20] In March, the American League's New York franchise was approved and commenced operations, incorporated as the Greater New York Baseball Association.[21] The rebranded New York Americans, variously nicknamed "Hilltoppers" and "Highlanders" in the press for the playing field located on elevated terrain, and "Yankees" possibly tongue-in-cheek because the ballpark was slightly north of the Giants', would use "Yankees" as the team's primary nickname starting in 1913.[22] The AL would not return to Baltimore for over fifty years, until the 1954 season when the St. Louis Browns moved east and became the second AL incarnation of the Orioles.

Though the franchise shifted from Baltimore to New York, the statistics associated with the 1901–02 Baltimore Orioles have been relegated to those of a defunct organization. The New York Yankees don't recognize the Baltimore Orioles in their official team records. Baseball-Reference.com published an article on the debate in 2014.[23] The current Baltimore Orioles trace their history from the AL charter member Milwaukee Brewers, through the St. Louis Browns and the 1953 season, to Baltimore in time for the 1954 campaign.

The 1901–02 Baltimore Orioles left a notable mark on baseball history during their short existence. Baltimore compiled a 118–153 record over their two seasons. The Orioles had only two managers in its history: Hall of Famers McGraw and Robinson, who both later managed New York-based NL teams (Robinson joining Brooklyn, where he would manage 1914–31). Their biggest hitting and pitching stars—Jimmy Williams was their best offensive player, while Joe McGinnity more firmly established his status as a top-tier major league pitcher—would shine in New York over the next five years for the Yankees and Giants, respectively. Bitterness lingered between Johnson and McGraw; the 1904 World Series wasn't played in large part because McGraw didn't want his Giants to play the AL pennant winner, spiting Johnson and his attempts to establish the AL's status as equal to the NL.

These early Baltimore Orioles should be remembered as having a key location for a major league franchise, serving a critical role in the evolution of the AL-NL relationship, and the lasting impact on New York baseball, between McGraw's tenure with the Giants, Robinson's years with the Robins (later Dodgers), and the franchise's rebirth as the New York Yankees. ■

Additional Sources

Kavanagh, Jack, and Norman Macht, *Uncle Robbie* (Cleveland, OH: Society for American Baseball Research, 1999): 11–47.

Koppett, Leonard, *The Man in the Dugout* (New York: Crown Publishers, Inc., 1993): 30–67.

Levitt, Daniel R., *The Battle that Forged Modern Baseball: The Federal League Challenge and Its Legacy* (Chicago: Ivan R. Dee Publishers, 2012).

Retrosheet: http://www.retrosheet.org/

Thorn, John (2012). The House That McGraw Built. On "Our Game" blog, https://ourgame.mlblogs.com/the-house-that-mcgraw-built-2bf6f75aa8dc.

Notes

1. Joe Santry and Cindy Thompson, "Byron Bancroft Johnson," In David Jones (Ed.), *Deadball Stars of the American League* (Dulles, VA: Potomac Books, Inc., 2006), 390–92.

2. "Ball Club Incorporation: Baltimore's American League Team With $40,000 Of Stock," *Baltimore Sun*, January 5, 1901, 6.

3. Jimmy Keenen, "April 26, 1901: Baltimore Orioles win home opener in a new major league," Society for American Baseball Research Games Project, https://sabr.org/gamesproj/game/april-26-1901-baltimore-orioles-winhome-opener-new-major-league. Accessed December 1, 2019.

4. "'Rah For Baseball," *Baltimore Sun*, April 27, 1901, 6.

5. "Orioles Ten Inning Defeat," *Baltimore Sun*, June 18, 1901, 6.

6. C. Paul Rodgers III, "Hugh Ambrose Jennings," In David Jones (Ed.), *Deadball Stars of the American League* (Dulles, VA: Potomac Books, Inc., 2006), 555–58.

7. "Hot Baseball Row," *Baltimore Sun*, June 18, 1901, 6.

8. Francis Richter (Ed.) *Reach's Official American League Base Ball Guide for 1902* (Philadelphia: A.J. Reach, 1902), 56.

9. "Can't Stop Winning," *Baltimore Sun*, September 28, 1901, 6.

10. "Baseball Ends Today," *Baltimore Sun*, September 28, 1901, 6.

11. Frank F. Patterson, "Is Ready to Play," *The Sporting News*, April 19, 1902, 3.

12. "Orioles' Opening Program," *Baltimore Sun*, April 19, 1902, 6.

13. "Orioles Lose First," *Baltimore Sun*, April 20, 1902, 6.

14. "Athletics Play Havoc With Manager McGraw's Pet Birds," *Washington Times*, April 24, 1902, 4.

15. "Win a Game At Last," *Baltimore Sun*, May 10, 1902, 6.

16. "'Twas a Great Day," *Baltimore Sun*, May 31, 1902, 6.

17. "Ban Suspends Again," *Baltimore Sun*, July 1, 1902, 6.

18. "Giants Strengthened By Sensational Deal," *Brooklyn Daily Eagle*, July 17, 1902, 11.

19. "Here's the New Team," *Baltimore Sun*, July 18, 1902, 6.

20. John Thorn, Pete Palmer, and Michael Gershman (Eds.) *Total Baseball: The Official Encyclopedia of Major League Baseball* (4th Edition) New York: Viking Press, 1995), 43.

21. Mark Armour and Daniel R. Levitt, "New York Yankees team ownership history," Society for American Baseball Research BioProject, https://sabr.org/bioproj/topic/new-york-yankees-team-ownership-history. Accessed July 7, 2020.

22. New York Yankees, History of the New York Yankees, 2018 New York Yankees Official Media Guide and Record Book, 244.

23. Mike Lynch, "1901-02 Orioles Removed from Yankees History," On "Sports Reference Blog, https://www.sports-reference.com/blog/2014/07/1901-02-orioles-removed-from-yankees-history. Accessed December 1, 2019.

Forty-Six Years Before Eddie Gaedel

Dennis Snelling

The city of Baltimore has hosted a number of historic baseball events. Although this story barely qualifies as such, it is nevertheless an interesting aside involving Jerry Sullivan, a thirty-two-year-old, three-foot-eleven stage actor who appeared in an Eastern League game in Baltimore in 1905. Forty-six years later, the St. Louis Browns famously inserted three-foot-seven Eddie Gaedel into a major league contest as a pinch-hitter. However, unlike Gaedel, Sullivan wielded a regulation bat. Not only that, he singled and scored a run. (There is no evidence Sullivan's feat inspired Bill Veeck's stunt of hiring Gaedel, or that Veeck even knew about it.)

The game in which Sullivan participated has been documented previously—with varying degrees of accuracy—standing in stark contrast to the meager facts previously published about his life. The events that conspired to bring Jeremiah David Sullivan to home plate in Baltimore began with his birth on August 12, 1873, in Low, Québec, a logging town founded by Irish immigrants.[1] Jerry's name honored his twenty-year-old brother, who drowned two months before Jerry's birth while driving logs downriver.[2]

Jerry's head and torso developed normally during infancy but his extremities did not, and doctors informed the family that their son would never reach four feet in height. Often ridiculed at school, Jerry later revealed he had learned to entertain in the classroom—his defining moment a second-grade assignment requiring the presentation of a humorous verse to classmates. Jerry was astonished when his recitation elicited laughter and approval, and he claimed to have returned to his seat "a bit wobbly."[3]

Jerry moved soon after that with his family to Wausau, Wisconsin, where physical limitations, both real and perceived, ended his schooling and limited his career options.[4] He began capitalizing on his ability to generate laughs. The local newspaper published a photograph of a teenage Jerry driving a tiny wagon pulled by a pair of goats. The wagon carried a large placard for the Mathie Brewing Company, promoting their bock beer, a strong German ale traditionally consumed by Wisconsinites each spring.[5] Buoyed by the promotion's success, Jerry left home to become an acrobat and contortionist with the Robinson Family Circus, and with a traveling medicine show hawking a "cure-all" elixir sold by Hamlin's Wizard Oil Company.[6]

During his travels throughout the US and Canada for Wizard Oil, Jerry occasionally exploited his athletic ability and comic timing in local baseball games. As early as 1892, a town team in Carroll, Iowa, drafted him to play against a female baseball squad from Denver. Sullivan stole the show, hitting a double while serving as the team's catcher. Judging his performance behind the plate "wonderful," an anonymous journalist proclaimed, "Little Jerry is a curiosity and to see him play ball is worth all the cost to attend the entire performance."[7]

When the Wizard Oil troupe visited Missoula, Montana, Jerry offered to umpire a rematch between

Jerry Sullivan as a teenager.

Missoula's town team and that of nearby Anaconda.[8] Missoula achieved its revenge, a 26–2 win, with Sullivan praised as "the best umpire that has officiated the grounds this season and was a whole circus in himself."[9] The Anacondans were so impressed they invited him to join them the next week as a player. "He can catch, throw and hit with the best of them," it was said after that contest, "and he is no slouch on the bases."[10]

In 1899, Jerry made the vaudeville circuit and demonstrated his impressive athleticism with a popular tumbling act, mixing in some comedy wrestling along the way.[11] His talent caught the attention of Gus Hill, a nationally renowned entertainer thanks to his amazing ability as a juggler of Indian clubs. Looking to expand his horizons, Hill was dipping his toes into the business end of vaudeville by forming a repertory company he dubbed the "Royal Lilliputians."[12] Jerry eagerly signed on; his signature moment involved steering a miniature fire engine pulled across the stage by a goat—an echo of his first taste of fame for Mathie Brewing. Hill then cast Sullivan in *McFadden's Row of Flats*, a farce based on the comic strip *The Yellow Kid*, and in his national touring company of *Simple Simon Simple*. In *Simple Simon Simple* he played a featured character named Mose, who made his entrance by popping out of a laundry basket in which he had hidden, a startling introduction that always surprised and delighted audiences.[13]

Jerry Sullivan also found love, marrying Helen "Nellie" Bates, a chorus girl in the *Simon* production, at City Hall in New York City the day before St. Valentine's Day 1901. Nellie's father, who had discouraged her show-business ambitions, was less than thrilled at the turn of events. When interviewed at his home in St. Louis he remarked, "About a week ago I heard my daughter was going to marry this dwarf. I was surprised, as any father would be, at such news. But… she is old enough to know her own business, and I did not attempt to prevent it."[14]

Nellie—who had adopted the stage name Helen von Deleur—said of her new spouse, "I saw him before I went on the stage two years ago and I fell in love with him at once. Then I got into the business and came into the same company last September and he fell in love with me." When asked about the height difference—Nellie was five-foot-four—she laughed, "He's mighty little for a husband, but I think it will be nice to have a husband I may pick up and shake when I feel like it."[15]

More than a decade later, the Sullivans were among several stage couples profiled in a *New York Press* article and Nellie had grown weary of the inevitable questions, tersely responding, "One day we found out we were loving one another. Then we got married. Is there anything more to say about it?"[16]

Jerry Sullivan crisscrossed the country continuously for the next several years. While in Baltimore for *Simple Simon Simple* in September 1905, he crossed paths with Buffalo Bisons manager George Stallings, the man who would lead Boston's "Miracle Braves" to a World Series title nine years later. The night before Buffalo was to play the Baltimore Orioles in a doubleheader, the notoriously superstitious Stallings spied Sullivan in a hotel lobby. He likely considered Sullivan a totem—in that era it was thought young African-American males, hunchbacks, and those with dwarfism proffered good luck. A hunchbacked little person was even better. Many sports teams employed them as human talismans.

Sullivan's experience entertaining baseball fans further aroused Stallings's interest and he invited the diminutive actor to the ballpark the next day to sit on the Bison bench. Buffalo was running out the string, giving Stallings some license, while Baltimore was only two games behind first-place Jersey City in the standings.

Jerry Sullivan, age 17, promoting the Mathie Brewing Company's bock beer.

A delighted Stallings greeted Sullivan at the ballpark, and had his new pal take part in pregame practice. As the first game was about to begin, Jerry was escorted to the coaching lines by Bisons pitcher Rube Kisinger, mostly for the comic effect of seeing Kisinger, one of the team's largest players, juxtaposed with a confidently striding Sullivan standing an inch short of four feet in height. Jerry "coached" for a couple of innings, entertaining the crowd as the Orioles jumped out to a 10–2 lead.[17]

After Buffalo's Frank McManus singled in the ninth inning, Stallings summoned a pinch-hitter for pitcher Stan Yerkes. It was normal to see a substitute in that situation—what caught everyone off-guard was his identity. It was Jerry Sullivan, carrying a bat nearly as large as he was.[18]

The umpire formally announced Jerry's entrance and the actor strutted to the plate while Baltimore pitcher Fred Burchell struggled to contain his laughter.[19] After Burchell's first pitch sailed high, he aimed the next one a little lower and Sullivan shocked everyone by swinging, looping the ball into left field as McManus ran to second.

Burchell attempted to pick-off the pint-sized baserunner. Sullivan scurried back safely, ducking between first baseman Tim Jordan's legs and sitting down on the bag. Burchell made several more pick-off attempts but Sullivan was wise and remained safely within reach of first base.

Turning his attention to the batter, Burchell surrendered a single to Jake Gettman, scoring McManus while Sullivan scampered to second, putting an exclamation point on his accomplishment by hopping affirmatively onto the base with both feet. Burchell then threw a pitch over the catcher's head and Sullivan scooted to third to great applause. Frank LaPorte, who a week later would make his major league debut with the New York Highlanders (now Yankees), lined out yet another single—adrenaline flowing, Sullivan played to the crowd in completing his circuit around the bases, punctuating his tally with an elaborately unnecessary slide into home plate.[20] Buffalo ultimately scored four runs in the inning, but it was not enough and the Bisons lost, 10–6.

Despite his 1.000 batting average, Sullivan returned to stage work. Six weeks after his baseball diversion he appeared in *Simple Simon Simple* at Broadway's West End Theatre, thereby briefly reaching the "big leagues" in his chosen profession.[21] He continued traveling the country in *Simon*, which proved especially popular in the South, and in *McFadden's Flats*, spending forty-nine weeks on the road.[22]

Jerry Sullivan in *Mutt and Jeff*.

During the summer of 1907, Sullivan braved a deadly heat wave in Philadelphia to attend the National Elks Convention. Awarded the title of "Littlest Elk," he earned a cash prize and the honor of participating in a massive parade through the city streets, accompanied, of course, by the "Tallest Elk."[23]

Around this time, twenty-two-year-old Bud Fisher created a comic strip that would alter Sullivan's life. It debuted in the *San Francisco Chronicle* sports pages on November 15, 1907, as *A. Mutt*, featuring a character Fisher had created for a previous project.[24] A few months later, "Jeff" made his first appearance as the diminutive sidekick to the long, gawky Mutt, and the two confronted a series of continual misfortunes, first connected to bad luck at the racetrack and later involving all manner of ill-fated get-rich-quick schemes.[25] Retitled *Mutt and Jeff*, King Features syndicated the strip nationwide. Gus Hill secured the rights to stage the characters in a series of musical extravaganzas—with up to six companies on the road simultaneously—and Jerry Sullivan spent the next two decades as "Jeff," performing all over North America. Bud Fisher would earn five thousand dollars a week from his creation, of which he had wisely retained ownership.[26]

Sullivan would earn much less than that. The life of a traveling vaudevillian produced notoriety, but little else. It was a vagabond existence, with most actors required to cover their own expenses.

He appeared in a few motion pictures—unfortunately among the thousands of early silent films lost over the years. When *The Court Jester* played in his hometown, the newspaper crowed, "Come and See Jerry Sullivan, a Wausau Boy."[27] A review in *Moving Picture World* said of Sullivan, "In this film the dwarf who made such a favorable impression in the fairy story *The Little Old Men of the Woods* plays a prominent part, and he does it, if anything, better than he performed his earlier task."[28] While conceding the "immortality" that film offered an actor, Sullivan, pontificating while puffing on a cigar, asserted his strong preference for the theater. "No matter what stage of perfection motion pictures reach," he insisted to a reporter, "a play by living people will always be the principal source of amusement."[29]

A final baseball reference for Sullivan appears in 1915, a three-inning pick-up game between two show business teams in New York. A recounting of the event calls him "the best player" and noted, "...his versatility has brought him much fame." [30]

As the above quotation implies, one would be hard-pressed to locate a negative review of Jerry Sullivan. Hundreds of newspapers praised him, often as a local favorite making a return visit. During a wildly popular two-week run, the *San Francisco Call* declared, "Besides being a class A 'funny' man, Sullivan is a contortionist and athlete of no mean ability."[31] His fans in Texas considered him the obvious successor to the legendary Tom Thumb.[32] More than two hundred Elks enthusiastically welcomed him to Roseburg, Oregon, with a parade through the streets of the town in which he had briefly lived.[33]

Nine-year-old Eloise Buch, hospitalized in Baltimore in March 1914 with a life-threatening illness, was perhaps Jerry's biggest fan. After she requested to see "Jeff" in person, Sullivan twice visited her and was astonished to discover she had committed many of his lines to memory.[34]

Jerry was also a prankster. Since his head and torso were normal size, one of his favorite tricks involved walking into a restaurant and requesting a booster seat. While the server was off on his mission, Jerry would take a regular seat at the table and watch with amusement when the waiter returned and searched for him in vain.[35]

Sullivan continued playing "Jeff" through the mid-1920s. However, the advent of sound in motion pictures resulted in a precipitous decline in vaudeville's popularity, and Jerry's fortunes took a sadly parallel track. He briefly returned to circus life in 1929, before joining two other little people for shows at Wonderland on

Jerry Sullivan in his mid-thirties.

Coney Island.[36] Jobs scarce, Jerry began frequenting the bar at the Circus Room of the Cumberland Hotel in New York, to ill effect.[37]

He moved into the Luna Villa, a three-story residential hotel on Coney Island, near the amusement parks where he could occasionally find odd roles, including a sideshow in which he was billed as "Jerry the Dwarf."[38] In September 1937, Sullivan was placed under arrest after drunkenly standing on a street corner and heckling a dozen members of the American Legion, shouting at them, "You're all phonies. You've never been across the seas. I could lick you."[39] The Legionnaires laughed it off, but when a police officer advised Jerry to "mind his own business or he might get hurt," Sullivan challenged the officer, culminating in a visit to the drunk tank.[40] Hauled before a judge the next morning, Sullivan gave the magistrate a military salute. Admitting having been drunk he insisted, "I'm all right now." The judge asked, "Will you be a good boy from now on?" The sixty-four-year-old replied in the affirmative and received a suspended sentence. His career as an entertainer went unmentioned.[41]

In December 1940, Sullivan attended the funeral of five-hundred-pound "Jolly Irene," a former Barnum & Bailey sideshow performer with whom he had appeared at Coney Island.[42] The marriage with Nellie was certainly all but over by this time; the Census that year listed Jerry as married, but living alone.[43]

Sullivan then disappears. He likely died before 1953; his brother William passed away that year and Jerry was not listed among the surviving siblings.[44] Sadly, Jerry Sullivan's fascinating life and considerable talents as an acrobat and comic have been almost completely forgotten—except for the day in Baltimore when he swung a baseball bat. ∎

Notes

1. World War I Draft Registration Card, Jeremiah David Sullivan, September 11, 1918.
2. "John Kelly & Mary Douglas Family History," provided by Dot Fischer, November 7, 2018.
3. *Jackson* (MS) *Daily News*, November 8, 1912, 6.
4. United States Census, 1940.
5. Janin Friend, "A Forgotten Easter Tradition," *Wausau Daily Herald*, March 31, 1983, 24.
6. *Green Bay Press Gazette*, March 21, 1893, 3. Hamlin's Wizard Oil was a "cure-all" tonic patented by a magician. As was the case with such elixirs, it consisted mostly of alcohol. Performers sang from wagons, eventually gaining popularity such that they performed in local opera houses and other stage venues, adding specialty acts such as Jerry Sullivan.
7. *Carroll* (IA) *Sentinel*, October 15, 1892, 3.
8. *Daily Missoulian*, June 16, 1895, 1; June 22, 1895, 2.
9. *Anaconda Standard*, June 17, 1895, 6.
10. *Anaconda Standard*, June 24, 1895, 3.
11. *St. Paul Globe*, December 7, 1899, 6.
12. *Buffalo Enquirer*, July 20, 1900, 5.
13. *Daily Illinois State Register*, November 5, 1900, 6.
14. *St. Louis Post-Dispatch*, February 22, 1901, 8. The attitude of Nellie's father was influenced by his wife's abandonment of the family a year earlier to pursue acting studies in Brooklyn, resulting in a divorce that made headlines in St. Louis. (*St. Louis Post-Dispatch*, November 11, 1899, 1; November 12, 1899, 8; December 7, 1899, 10).
15. *St. Louis Republic*, February 22, 1901, 1.
16. *New York Press*, December 8, 1912, 6.
17. *Buffalo Enquirer*, September 21, 1905, 10.
18. *Baltimore Sun*, September 19, 1905, 8, *Buffalo Courier*, September 19, 1905, 9.
19. *Buffalo Courier*, September 19, 1905, 9; *Buffalo Morning Express*, September 19, 1905, 9.
20. *Baltimore Sun*, September 19, 1905, 8; *Buffalo Courier*, September 19, 1905, 9; *Buffalo Enquirer*, September 21, 1905, 10.
21. *The New York Times*, October 29, 1905, 3.
22. *Montgomery* (AL) *Advertiser*, November 24, 1906, 10; *Billboard*, August 17, 1907, 33.
23. *Philadelphia Inquirer*, July 15, 1907, 5; July 18, 1907, 4. Jerry also performed at the Lit Brothers department store, with several other entertainers. (*Philadelphia Inquirer*, July 14, 1907, 5.)
24. *San Francisco Chronicle*, November 15, 1907, 8; November 16, 1907, 5; November 17, 1907, 17.
25. *San Francisco Chronicle*, March 27, 1908, 8.
26. *The Economist*, December 22, 2012; Don Markstein's Toonpedia, toonpedia.com/muttjeff.htm, accessed February 4, 2020.
27. *Wausau Daily Herald*, May 4, 1910, 8.
28. *Moving Picture World*, March 12, 1910, Volume 6, Number 10, 384.
29. *Baltimore Sun*, March 9, 1914, 4.
30. *New York Evening World*, June 28, 1915, 14.
31. *San Francisco Call*, February 10, 1913, 4.
32. *Houston Post*, October 8, 1916, 41.
33. *Roseburg Review*, March 15, 1916, 1 & 6.
34. *Baltimore Sun*, March 14, 1914, 12 & 16. Eloise recovered, eventually becoming a public health nurse. (*York Dispatch*, July 30, 1981, 42.)
35. *Asheville Citizen*, September 11, 1907, 6.
36. *Billboard*, July 27, 1929, 80.
37. *Billboard*, February 9, 1935, 65. 13
38. *Brooklyn Daily Eagle*, December 1, 1940, A13.
39. *Camden* (NJ) *Courier-Post*, September 24, 1937, 5.
40. *Brooklyn Daily Eagle*, September 24, 1937, 6; *New York Daily News*, September 24, 1937, 10. Wire services distributed the story nationally.
41. *Brooklyn Daily Eagle*, September 24, 1937, 6.
42. *Brooklyn Daily Eagle*, December 1, 1940, A13.
43. United States Census, 1940.
44. *Duluth Tribune*, December 5, 1953, 5.

Sources

Ancestry.com
California State Library
Duluth Public Library
Familysearch.com
Genealogy Bank.com
Google Books
Internet Archive
Newspapers.com
San Francisco Public Library

Babe Ruth's Half Season with the Baltimore Orioles

Gary Sarnoff

Babe Ruth began his professional baseball career in 1914 as a member of the Baltimore Orioles, a minor-league team in the International League. Long-time *Baltimore Sun* sportswriter Jesse Linthicum witnessed firsthand Ruth's 19 weeks with the Orioles. "I saw Babe Ruth hit his first home run, pitch his first game and obtain the nickname of Babe," he wrote in 1948.[1] Linthicum was at St. Mary's Industrial School in February 1914 when 19-year-old Ruth was summoned to the school's reception room to meet Jack Dunn, the owner and manager of the Orioles. A number of Ruth's school teammates and small kids from St. Mary's who idolized him accompanied him to the office. Dunn, who had never seen Ruth play, had heard plenty about the school superstar—a highly-rated pitcher and hitter, capable of playing every position. He was a left-handed thrower and a switch hitter who hit .537 in 1913. Dunn, who sought big ballplayers, liked the fact that Ruth was over six feet tall, muscular, and weighed a lean 183 pounds After Ruth accepted Dunn's contract offer without the slightest hesitation, the St. Mary's ballplayers responded like a well-rehearsed chorus. "There goes our ball club," they moaned.[2]

When Ruth and the Orioles arrived in Fayetteville, North Carolina, for spring training, Ruth made an immediate impression in the team's first intra-squad game. "The youngster landed on a fastball and circled the bases before Billy Morrisette had retrieved the hit in deep right field," a sportswriter reported.[3] Linthicum called it "a prestigious clout that sent the locals down to main street talking to themselves." As Linthicum trailed Ruth and Dunn while heading back to the hotel following the game, the writer heard Dunn say, "This Baby will never get away from me," and according to Linthicum, "Then and there Ruth acquired the nickname of 'Babe.'"[4]

Ruth began spring training as a left-handed shortstop who handled all fielding chances "with ease and grace," an observer noted.[5] The observer was also impressed when he saw Ruth fan four batters in three innings in his first pitching appearance. Ruth was noted to have terrific speed, but still needed some work: "Ruth lacks one quality of a successful pitcher: He has never had experience with fast company."[6] But when he made his first pitching start of the spring exhibition season, he looked as though he was learning when he defeated the Phillies. The next day the Orioles trailed the Phillies, 6–0, in the sixth inning when Ruth was called in from the bullpen to put out the fire. He quickly ended the inning by whiffing Eddie Matteson and Dode Paskert, and held the Phillies scoreless while his teammates chipped away at the lead and won, 7–6.

Six days later, Ruth again proved his abilities when he defeated the Philadelphia Athletics, 6–2. "Ruth, who went the full 9 innings, pitched beautifully," wrote Jesse Linthicum. "Not at any stage of the contest did he show any signs of nervousness. The Athletics paid him a big compliment by saying he is one of the best youngsters they have seen in a long time."[7] Three days later the A's got another crack at Ruth, and they were ready. "The Athletics started in on Ruth as though determined to drive the juvenile off the rubber," opined a Philadelphia sportswriter.[8] The first four Philadelphia batters reached base and the A's went on to win, 12–5. Frank Baker led the A's hitting attack by going 4-for-5. "Baker hit the ball on the nose each time and the hits shot out to the outfield like bullets," wrote Linthicum.[9] Before one of Baker's at-bats, Orioles catcher Ben Egan told Ruth about his signal to waste a pitch. When Baker came to the plate, Egan flashed the signal to Ruth, but instead of wasting one, Ruth threw the pitch over the heart of the plate, and Baker sent the ball for a long ride. Egan then went to the mound and asked Ruth why he didn't obey his signal. "I threw it waste high," Ruth answered.[10]

Undiscouraged by the powerful Athletics' rough treatment, Ruth "tossed like a million dollars" in a win over the Dodgers the following week. "In the first 5 innings, he had the visitors breaking their backs in an effort to reach his benders," penned a Baltimore sportswriter, "and when he got himself into a hole, he showed he had the necessary backbone to pull himself together."[11] In addition to striking out six, Ruth socked

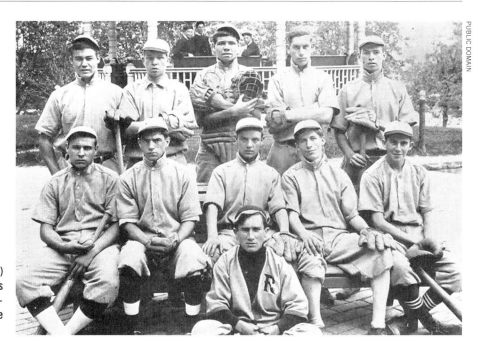

PUBLIC DOMAIN

Schoolboy Babe Ruth (with catcher's gear) pictured with his team from St. Mary's Industrial School, and three of the Xaverian brothers who ran the school (in the gazebo).

a two-run triple and hit two out of the park during batting practice. "The more I see Ruth the hitter, the more I like him," Dunn said.[12] "When batting, Ruth takes a long lunge at the ball and meets it on the nose," noted Linthicum. "He holds his bat down at the end and puts all his weight behind the swing."[13]

On April 22, Ruth blanked Buffalo in his first International League start, 6–0. He yielded 6 hits and struck out 6 while going 2-for-4 at the plate. He dropped his next game, 2–1. "Ruth pitched an excellent game," wrote Linthincum, "and should have won, 1–0. An error led to one run and a walk led to another."[14] On May 1, Ruth pitched his second win, in a relief role. With the game tied, 1–1, after nine innings, Ruth entered the game and pitched a scoreless 10th and 11th inning. In the bottom of the 11th, the Orioles had a man on first when Ruth approached the plate for his turn at bat. After taking a ball and a strike, he belted one to the left field scoreboard, far enough to allow the runner to score from first base for a 2–1 win. Ruth won his third game the next day and "again was the hero," wrote Linthicum. "His sensational work in the box and at bat stood out as the most prominent feature."[15] He struck out seven and hit a two-run triple in an 8–3 win. He upped his record to 4–1 when he hurled 11 innings in a 5–3 win at Buffalo, but then cooled off, dropping his next two decisions. On May 23, Dunn decided to start Ruth in right field and place him in the leadoff spot. Ruth had held his own as a shortstop in spring training, but Dunn was unsure about using a left-handed shortstop. The experiment was deemed a failure, as Ruth went 0-for 3. The next day Ruth was tagged for seven hits in 3⅓ innings in a

relief role. The humiliation from the first game did not prevent Ruth from coming back in the nightcap. Ruth pitched 11 innings that night for his fifth win of the season. He closed out the month of May with another win to up his season record to 6–3.

Ruth started June by splitting his first six decisions. On June 20, he didn't even make it through the second inning. He was removed after yielding back-to-back home runs, one of the two hit by a first baseman named Wally Pipp. On June 23, when Ruth blanked Toronto to win his 10th, Linthicum wrote, "Ruth pitched his most brilliant game. The youngster allowed only 5 scattered hits, 2 of which were the infield variety. He had 8 strikeouts to his credit."[16] Two days later, with the Orioles trailing, 7–0, Ruth was sent in as a relief pitcher. He held the opposition and the Orioles rallied for a 13–8 win. In his next start, Ruth allowed three runs on three hits in the first inning, but then settled down, allowing six hits in the last eight innings in a 10–5 win, his 12th of the season. On July 4, Ruth yielded two runs in the first inning. "From that point until the 7th, the visitors did not have a chance," wrote C. Starr Matthews of the *Baltimore Sun*, "for Ruth twirled like the winner he is."[17] Later in the game, Ruth smacked an RBI double to help his own cause in a 4–3 win, his 13th of the season. On July 6, Ruth won in relief to up his season record to 14–7.

With the season now at its halfway point, the Orioles were in first place and appeared to be heading for the pennant. But Dunn was losing money. Fans were flocking to see the Baltimore Federals, a new major league team. Dunn entertained the thought of moving his franchise to Richmond, Virginia, but that idea was

Joseph Lannin (left) hosts magnates of baseball Ban Johnson, John Kinley Tener, and Garry Herrmann in Boston on October 9, 1916. Lannin bought Babe Ruth from beleaguered Jack Dunn for a bargain price.

nixed by the International League, leaving him with no choice but to break up his team.

Dunn knew there would be interest for Ruth, so he offered him to his good friend Connie Mack, manager and partial owner of the Athletics. Mack was also feeling the effects of the Federal League. His attendance was down and his players were demanding new contracts mid-season, using the threat of jumping to the Federal League as leverage. "Jack, you have a great young pitcher in Ruth," Mack told Dunn, "but I can't give you what he is worth."[18]

White Sox ivory hunter George Mills, who spent time scouting Ruth and the Orioles, made a recommendation to his boss Charles Comiskey to pay $60,000 for Ruth and five other Baltimore players. Dunn was thrilled when hearing this, but no action was ever taken. Fortunately for Dunn, another financially stable team was interested.

Boston Red Sox scout Patsy Donovan came to town and stayed a while to get a good look at Ruth. When he reported back to Red Sox owner Joseph Lannin, he highly recommended the young ballplayer. On July 6, while the Red Sox were playing in Washington, Dunn traveled to Washington to meet with Lannin. Three days later, Dunn and Lannin had a long-distance phone conference to finalize the deal. Ruth and two other Orioles were sold to the Red Sox for $25,000. "If I had made the deal in 1913, I would have made twice the amount," said a disappointed Dunn.[19] And thus concluded Babe Ruth's brief season with the Baltimore Orioles. ■

Notes

1. Jesse Linthicum, *Baltimore Sun*, "Babe Ruth, 'a natural,'" August 17, 1948, 15.
2. *Baltimore Sun*, "Cree and Ruth on Job," March 11, 1914, 5.
3. *Baltimore Sun*, "Home run by Ruth feature of game," March 8, 1914, part 2, 1.
4. Jesse Linthicum, *Baltimore Sun*, "Babe Ruth,' a natural,'" August 17, 1948, 15.
5. Jesse Linthicum, *Baltimore Sun*, "Yanigans show class," March 14, 1914, 7.
6. *Baltimore Sun*, "Cree and Ruth on job," March 11, 1914, 5.
7. Jesse Linthicum, *Baltimore Sun*, "Birds beat Athletics," March 26, 1914, 5.
8. *Philadelphia Inquirer*, "Mackies make merry music meeting Ruth," Sporting Section, 1.
9. Jesse Linthicum, *Baltimore Sun*, "Baker's battng helps to defeat Dunn's Orioles," March 29, 1914, part 2, 1.
10. Jesse Linthicum, *Baltimore Sun*, "Babe Ruth, 'a natural,'" August 17, 1948, 15.
11. Baltimore Sun, "Ruth beats Dodgers," April 6, 1914, 8.
12. Jesse Linthicum, *Baltimore Sun*, "Orioles win in ninth," March 19, 1914, 5.
13. Jesse Linthicum, *Baltimore Sun*, "Baker's battng helps defeat Dunn's Orioles," March 29, 1914, part 2, 1.
14. Jesse Linthicum, *Baltimore Sun*, "Orioles lose both," April 28, 1914, 7.
15. Jesse Linthicum, *Baltimore Sun*, "Orioles divide doubleheader with Leafs," May 3, 1914, part 2, 1.
16. Jesse Linthicum, *Baltimore Sun*, "Ruth blanks Leafs," June 24, 1914, 5.
17. C. Starr Matthews, *Baltimore Sun*, "Birds and Clams split," July 5, 1914, part 2, 1.
18. Frederick G. Lieb, *The Baltimore Orioles*, (New York, G.P. Putnam's Sons, 1955), 141–42.
19. C. Starr Matthews, *Baltimore Sun*, "The rise of Babe Ruth," July 10, 1914, 5.

Demons, Colts, Giants, and Drybugs

Baseball in the 1916 Class D Potomac League

Mark C. Zeigler

Western Maryland has had a long history of organized baseball going back to the late nineteenth century.[1] Noted for its connection to the railroads to the west, and nearby coal fields that dotted the region of Allegany County, the activity of baseball became the outlet for many young men in the region, as town teams and athletic clubs became prevalent during this time period.[2]

For some, baseball became a way to get out of the coal mines. The most notable was a young man named Robert Moses Groves from Lonaconing.[3] Taking advantage of his long frame and blazing fastball, he would go on to win 300 games in the major leagues, and enshrinement into Baseball's Hall of Fame, as "Lefty" Grove.[4]

The first organized baseball clubs in Cumberland, Maryland date back to 1883, mostly amateur or town teams.[5] The local coal mines and railroads started to field organized teams in the mid-1890s. In 1906, Cumberland was accepted in the Class D Pennsylvania-Ohio-Maryland League (POM), and fielded a team called the Giants. When the Butler, Pennsylvania club folded, the franchise was moved to nearby Piedmont, West Virginia, but after three weeks, the franchise moved again to Charleroi, Pennsylvania to finish out the season. After finishing the 1906 season, the club was moved to McKeesport, Pennsylvania. Before the start of the 1908 season, the league was disbanded for financial reasons.[6]

The experience spurred interest in professional baseball in the region. In 1910, Cumberland organized a new independent club, the Colts.[7] Soon other areas, like Piedmont, joined in and played against Cumberland and other local teams in Maryland and West Virginia. After not having grounds to play on in 1912, by 1913 the Cumberland Baseball Club had a "modern baseball park in South Cumberland [built] on the Walsh property, between the N. & G. Taylor Company's tin mill and the Weber lumber yard."[8]

In 1914, a local businessman, Colonel Nelson W. Russler, a big baseball enthusiast, became the club's business manager.[9] With his savvy business sense and knack for signing quality players, Russler was influential in the establishment of the amateur Georges Creek League in 1914.[10] Based primarily in Allegany County, Maryland, the league added teams including Frostburg, Lonaconing, Midland, and the Tri-Towns of Piedmont/Westernport/Luke.

The Georges Creek League saw much success in 1914 and 1915, and the Russler-led Colts became local celebrities at South End Park, with hometown players such as Hugh Markwood, John Marean, George "Sonny" Geatz, Clarence Schafer, and the Lippold brothers, Frank and Charles.[11]

When the Class D Blue Ridge League was formed in 1915, including a team in Russler's hometown of Martinsburg, he took great interest in trying to get Cumberland admitted into the league.

However, due to travel distance from the Pennsylvania clubs in the circuit, and Sunday baseball, which was allowed in Allegany County at the time, but not in any of the current league towns, their bid went for naught.[12]

Despite the setback, Russler was determined to get Cumberland a professional baseball club in 1916. With the help of Charles Boyer, the Blue Ridge League president, Russler spearheaded a group of businessmen to garner interest in bringing pro ball to the region. Soon the Piedmont club and a newly organized team in Frostburg, Maryland applied. The minimum number of clubs to be considered was four, so Russler extended invitations to towns in Pennsylvania and Western Maryland, but with no success. Midland from the Georges Creek League was too small to draw from, but the businessmen from nearby Lonaconing gathered funds to fix up their ballfield to become the fourth club of the newly minted Class D Potomac League, calling their club the Giants.[13]

Despite the challenges to field four financially solvent teams, and a world war a continent away, Russler and Cumberland attorney Fuller Barnard Jr.—who was elected the league's president[14]—got the groundwork started to organize the Potomac League in February 1916. With much fanfare and Cumberland as its base of operations, Frostburg, Lonaconing, and Piedmont officially joined, starting play on May 3.[15]

Jake Zinnell led the Potomac League in stolen bases, and was considered one of the top players in the league.

Hebron, Maryland native Samuel Freeny attended St. Johns College while playing professional baseball for several teams in the Blue Ridge League. Upon graduating in 1917, he joined the Marines. During World War II he was taken prisoner by the Japanese and was beheaded in the Philippines.

The Colts had a rocky start before the season began, as Russler's first pick as manager, Herbert Lewis, didn't pass muster, and was released two weeks before the season began.[16] Colonel Russler quickly found a replacement in Harry Deal of Bedford, Pennsylvania, and the Colts under his guidance quickly took shape at South End Park.[17]

Russler kept a mainstay of Colts from the Georges Creek League club, with Geatz at third base; Schafer, John Marean, and newcomer Mike Koroly in the outfield; Frank Lippold behind the plate and his brother, Charley, at second base; and pitcher Jonny Stafford on the mound. Adding pitchers Eddie Price, Johnny East, and Merle Tannehill, Deal at first base, and 18-year-old local boy named George "Brindle" Long at shortstop, Russler's club was ready for Opening Day.[18]

However, after a nine-game losing streak, the dissatisfied, Russler had a revolving door of players throughout the season, until he found a lineup he was satisfied with. Among the players he was able to add to the Colts roster were pitchers Charles Dye of nearby Barton, Maryland, John "Lefty" Fike, and Virginia native Kirk Heatwole. Dye started the season with Toronto of the International League, but a hand injury led

to him requesting his release, and he soon signed with the Colts.[19] Heatwole, a rangy southpaw from the Charlottesville, Virginia area, combined with Dye to give the Colts a competitive boost.[20] Only Geatz, Schafer, and Marean began and finished the season on the Colts roster.

The Lonaconing Giants featured a local left-handed pitcher named Frank "War Horse" Muster.[21] Muster broke most of the pitching records in the Georges Creek League in 1915, and led the Giants contingent, which featured popular minor league veterans Roy "Shotgun" Keener and Joe Phillips, and newcomers Joe (Serafin) Cobb and Kenny (Mike) Knode, who both reached the major leagues.[22,23]

James McGuire started the season as the Lonaconing manager and, after losing the first five games, led the Giants to the best record, until he suddenly resigned on June 10 due to conflicts at his regular job.[24] Keener, a West Virginia native, was soon tapped to replace McGuire, and helmed the Giants until they officially disbanded on July 23 for financial reasons.[25]

Other notable Giants players were infielders Owen Flynn and John Nagle, and a local boy, pitcher John "Stub" Brown. The Lonaconing club was one of the best clubs in the league, vying for the lead with rival Frostburg Demons. Among the young Lonaconing fans was a promising 14-year-old, who idolized Muster.[26] They knew him as Bobby—the aforementioned Robert M. "Lefty" Groves.

Frostburg's club featured one of the league's better pitchers, with Somerset, Pennsylvania native R.S. "John" Baylor, and the controversial Bill Stair leading the pitching corps.[27] Stair had the league's best win percentage, but was run out of Frostburg after he was arrested and found guilty of chasing after and punching a fan on the street. That fan, a respected local businessman, did not talk kindly about the feisty Demon pitcher.[28] Pat Brophy managed the Demons, leading his club through the loss of one of their star pitchers to still finish with the best overall record when the league disbanded on August 18.[29]

Many of the players who were in the league came from the Baltimore–Washington, DC region. One was Frostburg outfielder John Salb, a Washington, DC, native, who had played previously for the Midland club in the old Georges Creek League from 1911 through 1915, and married his manager's daughter, Dorothy Dillon.[30] The Demons also featured infielders John "Shuck" Doyle and Fay Anderson, and catcher John "Sammy" Morgan.

The Piedmont club was known as the Drybugs, and though its offices were on the West Virginia side of the

Potomac River in the Tri-Towns section of Luke, they played their games on a little island on the Maryland side of the river, near Westernport, called Potomac Park.[31] The Drybugs were managed by Baltimore native Owen Harris, and featured the league's best pitcher, Ben Schaufele, another Baltimore native, who won 14 games.[32,33] The nucleus of the Drybugs roster was from the Baltimore area, including shortstop Arthur T. Smith, outfielders Frederick "Jake" Zinnell, G. C. Plaxico, and Porter Wamsley, catcher Leroy Bruff, and pitchers Tommy Verecker and E.L. Morseberger. The only homegrown regular player from the Piedmont/Westernport area on the Drybugs roster throughout the season was outfielder Don Whitworth.[34]

Top Players from the 1916 Class D Potomac League

Batting Average		Earned Run Average	
Joe Phillips, Lonaconing/Cumberland	.367	Ben Schaufele, Piedmont	1.66
Runs Scored		**Games Pitched**	
Roy Keener, Lonaconing/Cumberland	51	Ben Schaufele, Piedmont	29
Hits		**Wins**	
Roy Keener, Lonaconing/Cumberland	82	Ben Schaufele, Piedmont	14
Home Runs		**Innings Pitched**	
Joe Cobb, Lonaconing/Cumberland	6	R. S. "John" Baylor, Frostburg	207
Stolen Bases		**Strikeouts**	
Jake Zinnell, Piedmont	25	R.S. "John" Baylor, Frostburg	114
Games Played		**Win. Pct.**	
Joe Phillips, Lonaconing/Cumberland	52	Bill Stair, Frostburg (8 won, 1 lost)	.889
Fielding Percentage		**Total Chances**	
Owen Harris, Piedmont	.989	Harry Deal, Cumberland	616
Putouts		**Assists**	
Harry Deal, Cumberland	578	Arthur T. Smith, Piedmont	153
Errors			
Arthur T. Smith, Piedmont	30		

SOURCES: Lloyd Johnson and Miles Wolff, *The Encyclopedia of Minor League Baseball* 2nd edition, Baseball America, Inc., 207; Fielding Statistics from "Final Fielding Leaders," *Baltimore Sun*, August 20, 1916, 26; additional league leaders, including pitching statistics from author's extensive research on the 1916 Class D Potomac League.

AUTHOR'S COLLECTION

The Hagerstown Hubs, the 1920 Class D Blue Ridge Champions, featured two pitchers from the 1916 Class D Potomac League, Charles Dye (second from left), star pitcher for the Cumberland Colts, and Tommy Verecker (behind seated boy), who starred for the Piedmont Drybugs. Verecker also pitched one game in the Federal League in 1914.

21

1916 Class D, Potomac League Standouts

1st Baseman	Owen Harris, Piedmont	Pitcher	Ben Schaufele, Piedmont
2nd Baseman	John "Shuck" Doyle, Frostburg	Pitcher	John Baylor, Frostburg
3rd Baseman	George "Sonny" Geatz, Cumberland	Pitcher	Bill Jamison, Lonaconing
Shortstop	Arthur T. Smith, Piedmont	Pitcher	Frank Muster, Lonaconing/Frostburg
Left fielder	Ray Keener, Lonaconing/Cumberland	Utility	John Salb, Frostburg
Center fielder	Don Whitworth, Piedmont	Manager	Pat Brophy, Frostburg
Right fielder	Joe Phillips, Lonaconing/Cumberland	Umpire	Doll Derr
Catchers	Joe Cobb, Lonaconing/Cumberland;		
	Leroy Bruff, Piedmont/Cumberland (tie)		

HONORABLE MENTION: Bill Stair, Frostburg, P; Sammy Freeney, Frostburg, 1B; John Morgan, Frostburg, C; John Brown, P, Lonaconing/Frostburg; Tommy Vereker, Piedmont, P; Harry Deal, Cumberland, 1B; Charles Dye, Cumberland, P; John Herbert, Frostburg, P; Jake Zinnell, Piedmont, OF; Porter Wamsley, Piedmont, OF; Clarence Schafer, Cumberland, OF; and Mike Boyle, Frostburg, SS.

The league, however, never prospered, with Cumberland the only club able to come close to turning a profit. Lonaconing, despite having the best record, was forced to disband on July 23, leaving the league with only three clubs.[35] Despite rearranging the league schedule, the Frostburg club suffered the same fate as Lonaconing, and by August 18 had also disbanded, leaving only two clubs standing, forcing the league to disband for good.[36]

The Cumberland Colts and Piedmont Drybugs continued to field their clubs and played an independent schedule.[37] On September 24, the Drybugs played an exhibition game at Potomac Park against the National League's Cincinnati Reds, whose roster included Piedmont resident Bill "Baldy" Louden. The game featured an appearance by future Hall of Famer Christy Mathewson, which drew the largest crowd to date by the Piedmont club.[38]

In keeping his Cumberland club together through mid-September by playing an independent schedule, Russler found the club losing money for the first time, some in part from the extra salaries he paid to bring in the best players from the Lonaconing club after they disbanded in July, which included Keener, Phillips, Knode, and Cobb.[39] This dismayed the club's stockholders, and by the end of the season, all but two sold out their shares of the club, leaving Russler and George E. Jordan as sole owners.[40]

Cumberland, still itching to return to professional baseball, again applied for entry into the Class D Blue Ridge League for the 1917 season.[41] Three towns vied for the struggling Gettysburg, Pennsylvania franchise, but the league decided to keep the franchise in Gettysburg.[42]

Despite Cumberland's application being denied again, Russler's patience would soon pay off, as the Chambersburg, Pennsylvania franchise, the defending league champions, failed to pay their franchise fee by the league deadline of May 30. President James Vincent Jamison Jr. transferred the Chambersburg franchise to Cumberland.[43] Russler and the Colts were back in business, and they quickly got South End Park ready for play. Professional baseball was back in business in Cumberland.

After completing the 1917 schedule, Cumberland prepared for the 1918 season, but by that time, World War I had entered into American homes, and interest and finances dwindled in many towns in the region. Most leagues disbanded, but thanks to Russler's persistence, the Blue Ridge League was able to field four clubs to start the season as the only Class D league to play that year.[44] However, the Frederick club bowed out a week before the season was to begin, threatening to force the league to disband, until the Piedmont Drybugs came forward and quickly fielded a team as the fourth club.[45,46] Piedmont tried to bring in hometown former major league infielder Bill Louden to manage, but he was still under contract with the Saint Paul, Minnesota ball club. Instead they hired their shortstop from the 1916 team, Arthur T. "Shorty" Smith, as manager.[47] Smith, a Baltimore native, recruited many players from the Charm City region, including a former Drybugs teammate, Ben Schafeule.[48]

Like Piedmont's first entry into professional baseball in 1906, their stay in the Blue Ridge League only lasted three weeks in 1918, as the league disbanded on June 16 due to the war effort and lack of interest and finances among the other clubs.[49] Neither Cumberland nor Piedmont ever played in the Blue Ridge League again, though Cumberland did field a Class C Mid-Atlantic League club from 1925 to 1932.[50] ■

Notes

1. "Cumberland's Proposed Army Reunion," *Baltimore Sun*, June 13, 1884,
   1. "Former Cumberland Star Visits Old Battlefield," *Baltimore Sun*, September 12, 1915, 31.
2. Jim Kaplan, *Lefty Grove: American Original*, Society of American Baseball Research, 2000, 44.

3. Kaplan, 30, 39.

4. Kaplan, 275.

5. *The Baltimore Sun*, August 25, 1883, 4.

6. Pennsylvania-Ohio-Maryland League, Baseball-Reference.com. Accessed January 18, 2020. https://www.baseball-reference.com/bullpen/Pennsylvania-Ohio-Maryland_League.

7. "Won 1910 Steinweg Cup," *Cumberland News*, April 26, 1956.

8. "Will Build New Ball Park," *Washington Post*, March 2, 1913, 2.

9. "Colonel Russler Will Lead Cumberland Ball Team," *The Baltimore Sun*, January 14, 1914, 9.

10. C. V. Burns, "Sports Slants: Colts Birthplace, et al…," *Cumberland News*, September 12, 1967, 10.

11. "The Aces of 40 Years Ago," *Cumberland News*, May 12, 1955, 47.

12. *Public Opinion*, January 13, 1916, 1.

13. "Organize Baby Circuit at Cumberland Meeting," *Hanover* (Maryland) *Evening Sun*, February 24, 1916, 3.

14. Ibid.

15. "Potomac League Season Opens Tomorrow with Parade and Speeches," *Cumberland Evening Times*, May 2, 1916, 8.

16. "Manager Lewis Given His Release—Yannigans Trims Regulars 2 to 1," *Cumberland Evening Times*, April 18, 1916, 6.

17. "Deal Arrives for Practice," *Cumberland Evening Times*, April 25, 1916, 10.

18. "Mayor Koon to Toss Out First Ball at Opener," *Cumberland Evening Times*, May 2, 1916, 8.

19. "Dye Signs with Russler's Colts," *Cumberland Evening Times*, June 27, 1916, 5.

20. "Heatwole Gets a Job," *Baltimore Sun*, May 9, 1916, 10.

21. "Frank Muster, Now 90, to be Honored June 16," *Cumberland News*, June 6, 1972, 12.

22. "Joe Cobb, Minor League and Major League Statistics," Baseball-Reference.com, https://www.baseball-reference.com/register/player.fcgi?id=cobb--005jos

23. "Mike Knode, Minor League and Major League Statistics," Baseball-Reference.com, https://www.baseball-reference.com/players/k/knodemi01.shtml

24. "Jim M'Guire Resigns…," *The Baltimore Sun*, June 18, 1916, 29.

25. "Lonaconing Quits," *The Fredrick* (Maryland) *News*, July 22, 1916, 3.

26. J. Suter Kegg, "Tapping The Sports Keg," *Cumberland Evening Times*, January 12, 1960, 12.

27. "Baylor Throws Colts into White Kalsomine," *Cumberland Evening Times*, May 29, 1916, 6.

28. "Bill Stair Found Guilty of Assault," *Cumberland Evening Times*, June 27, 1916, 5.

29. Lloyd Johnson and Miles Wolff, *The Encyclopedia of Minor League Baseball* 2nd edition, Baseball America, Inc., 2007, 207.

30. "J. B. Salb Weds Miss Dillon, of Frostburg," *Washington Times*, July 26, 1911, 12.

31. Robert P. Savitt, *The Blue Ridge League*, Arcadia Publishing, 2011, 37

32. "Cumberland President is Busy Signing Players," *Baltimore Sun*, March 13, 1916, 10.

33. "Piedmont Signs Schaufele," *Baltimore Sun*, March 25, 1916, 11.

34. Donald P. Whitworth's World War I Draft Registration Card, 1917.

35. "Lonaconing Quits, League Continues," *Cumberland Evening Times*, July 24, 1916, 8.

36. "Potomac League Will Not Finish Season's Second Half," *Cumberland Evening Times*, August 14, 1916, 9.

37. "Two Teams to Stick: Cumberland and Piedmont of the late Potomac League to Play Independent Ball," *Baltimore Sun*, August 20, 1916, 26.

38. "When the Reds Play Piedmont," *Cumberland Evening Times*, September 19, 1918, 5.

39. "More Chances to Sell Ball Club: Three Towns are now after berths in the Blue Ridge League," *Gettysburg Times*, December 20, 1916, 1.

40. "Blue Ridge League Spent About $70,000 in Season," *Baltimore Sun*, December 18, 1916, 8.

41. Ibid.

42. "More Chances…"

43. "Franchise is Switched: Cumberland Gets Chambersburg's Berth in Blue Ridge," *Baltimore Sun*, July 1, 1917, 25.

44. Lloyd Johnson and Miles Wolff, *The Encyclopedia of Minor League Baseball* 1st edition, Baseball America, Inc., 1993, 148.

45. "League Sure to Continue, Says Jamison," *Baltimore Sun*, May 12, 1918, 24.

46. "Opening of Blue Ridge League Season Postponed Four Days," *Cumberland Evening Times*, May 15, 1918, 8.

47. "Must Take a Back Seat: Bill Louden Cannot Manage Piedmont Unless He is Released," *Baltimore Sun*, May 26, 1918, 24.

48. "Piedmont Pilot in Balto. After Players: Manager Smith Endeavoring to Land Pitcher Schaufele and Klingenhoffer," *Cumberland Evening Times*, May 24, 1918, 5.

49. "Blue Ridge League Closes Season Sunday," *Cumberland Evening Times*, June 15, 1918, 4.

50. Johnson and Wolff, 165, 167, 169, 171, 173, 176, 178, 180.

Baltimore's Forgotten Dynasty
The 1919–25 Baltimore Orioles of the International League

Alan Cohen

In 1920, the Baltimore Orioles were champions of the International League (IL) for the second straight year. Baltimore would win seven consecutive pennants (1919–25), and six of the championship teams are ranked in the top 35 of the 100 best minor league teams of the twentieth century by Bill Weiss and Marshall Wright.[1] (See Table 1.)

Owner Jack Dunn had survived the invasion of the Federal League by selling off some of his players and hightailing it to Richmond, Virginia, then returning to Baltimore in 1916. He would create a minor-league dynasty, locking up his best players for years during a time when the IL was exempt from the major league draft. The man who had sold Babe Ruth to the Red Sox for a bargain price had learned his lesson, placing high price tags on players desired by big-league clubs. Dunn and 11 of his players are in the International League Hall of Fame. Only one player from the dynasty years made it to Cooperstown, and there should have been more. (See Table 2). This article will discuss these eleven players and the championship seasons of which they were a part.

Jack Bentley joined the Washington Nationals (nicknamed the Senators) at the end of 1913 and, in parts of four seasons, compiled a 6–9 record in 39 games as a pitcher. He was dispatched to Minneapolis of the American Association and, on August 18, 1916, was sent to Baltimore for the balance of the season. He was formally traded by Washington to Baltimore in early 1917 and was the cornerstone as Dunn rebuilt the Orioles.

Obtained by Dunn along with Bentley was Turner Barber, who was dealt to the Cubs in exchange for outfielder Merwin Jacobson, who starred with Baltimore from 1919 through 1924. Although his services had been secured prior to the 1918 season, Jacobson spent that year in Washington, DC, doing war-related work.

Bently, during 1916, had been used at the plate as well as on the mound, and in 1917 came into his own as a hitter, batting .343. Suffering from arm trouble in 1917, he only appeared in one game as a pitcher. Baltimore improved to 88–61, finishing in third place, 2.5 games behind the league leaders.

Baltimore almost lost Bentley after the 1917 season. He was drafted by the Red Sox but entered the Army, serving with distinction in World War I. As 1919 began, he was still in France, and the Red Sox still had the rights to his services. Boston didn't need Bentley at first base, as they had Stuffy McInnis. As Boston owner Harry Frazee hadn't paid the $2,500 draft price for Bentley by February 1, Bentley returned to Baltimore.

In the abbreviated 1918 season, Baltimore continued to build. Otis Lawry, who had been obtained from the Athletics in a seven-player deal after the 1917 season, came into his own, batting .317. He played with the Orioles until midway through the 1924 season.

Eighteen-year-old Max Bishop was installed at third base in 1918. With Bentley still in Europe at the start of the 1919 season, Bishop played first base. His batting average through the season's first eight games stood at .652 with seven extra-base hits. Once Bentley returned,

Table 1. IL Orioles Teams

Year	Place on All Time Minor League Team Ranking
1921	2nd
1924	5th
1920	9th
1922	15th
1923	19th
1919	35th

Table 2. Orioles Inductees to the IL Hall of Fame

Year	Name
1948	Thomas
1950	Dunn
1952	Ogden
1954	Boley
1955	Jacobson
1956	Earnshaw
1957	Parnham
1958	Bentley, Walsh
1959	Maisel
1963	Porter
2008	Grove*

*Also inducted into the National Baseball Hall of Fame in Cooperstown.

Bishop was moved to second base, and it was at that position that he would remain for the balance of his professional career.

New faces were on the left side of the infield in 1919. The shortstop was Joe Boley, who played in the low minors in 1916 and 1917 and did not play in organized baseball in 1918. He had taken a job at a plant with work related to the war effort in 1917, and he played on the plant's semi-pro team in 1917 and 1918. One of his teammates in 1917 had been Bishop. Bishop suggested that Dunn sign Boley and the shortstop joined the Orioles in 1919.[2]

Fritz Maisel was popular with Baltimore when he played with them from 1911 through mid-1913. He was traded to the Yankees and was with them through 1917. He spent 1918 with the St. Louis Browns. His acquisition by Dunn as the team's third baseman put another stone in place.[3]

Baltimore opened at home against Rochester on April 30, 1919, with Rube Parnham pitching. The 25-year-old had gone 38–19 with Baltimore over the prior two seasons, but until January 16, 1918, was the property of the Philadelphia Athletics. He had appeared briefly, in a total of six games, with Philadelphia in 1916 and 1917. Parnham was Baltimore's top pitcher in 1919, going 28–12.

Bentley returned to Baltimore on June 21, 1919. On his first day in the lineup, he started the second game of a doubleheader against Rochester and went 3-for-5 with a sixth-inning homer.[4]

Baltimore won the IL pennant by eight games. After the season, Baltimore did not participate in the Junior World Series, which was contested that year between the champions of the American Association and the Pacific Coast League.

Late in 1919, Dunn ensured the future success of the team by signing his stars to two-year contracts. He demanded top money for his players, including a man who came on board during the 1920 season: Robert Moses "Lefty" Grove. Only 20 years old, Grove got his professional start in 1920 with Martinsburg, West Virginia in the Class D Blue Ridge League. His 1.68 ERA and 60 strikeouts in 59 innings aroused the interest of Dunn, who secured Grove's services.

Grove joined Baltimore in late June and won his first two outings. In his first appearance, on July 1, he defeated Jersey City, 9–3, in the second game of a doubleheader giving the Orioles a one and a half game lead in the league standings. He allowed five hits in the abbreviated seven-inning contest. Three days later, he defeated Reading, 8–1. He scattered seven hits, struck out eight, and, in the fourth inning, struck out the side.[5]

Another new arm in 1920 was that of Jack Ogden. Ogden was obtained from Rochester, where he had gone 10–13 in 1919. With Baltimore, he shined, and Dunn held on to him through 1927. In six of eight seasons, he won more than 20 games, and his record for the eight seasons was 191–80.

The 1920 Orioles still had Bentley, and he returned to mound duty, going 16–3 with a league-leading 2.10 ERA. He also swung a potent bat with 71 extra-base hits, 20 of which were homers, to go along with a .371 batting average. His 161 RBIs led the league.

Baltimore won its last 25 games to set an IL record. Their season's record of 110–43 barely eclipsed Toronto's 108–46 mark. In the best-of-nine JWS, Baltimore defeated American Association champion St. Paul in six games for the first of three JWS titles. Bentley's two homers won Game One, 5–3. He let his arm do the work in Game Three, winning, 9–2 to put the Birds within two games of the series win.[6] After the Saints

Babe Ruth in a borrowed New York Giants uniform, with his former owner Jack Dunn (and Giants player Jack Bentley), before the October 3, 1923, exhibition game between the Giants and the Dunn's International League Orioles. Ruth, who was a star with the Yankees by then, was enticed to play to be a gate draw. The game's proceeds went to fundraising for former Giants owner John B. Day and former manager Jim Mutrie.

BALTIMORE SUN/PUBLIC DOMAIN

The 1920 IL Orioles.

broke into the win column in Game Four, the teams traveled to Minnesota. Bentley was back on the mound, winning, 6–5, in Game Five, a triumph marred by fan hostility to umpire Otis H. Stocksdale for calling Lawry, who had bunted, safe at first in an inning where the Orioles scored the game's decisive run. In the same inning, St. Paul pitcher Dan Griner was accused of throwing a shine ball, and a further ruckus ensued.[7] The Orioles clinched the series in Game Six. Ogden pitched a 1–0 shutout and Boley's home run was the only offensive support needed.

In 1921, Dunn added pitcher Tommy Thomas. Thomas racked up 105 wins in five seasons with the Orioles before being traded to the White Sox for Maurice Archdeacon late in the 1925 season. The deal was announced on September 12, 1925, and Thomas, after spending the balance of the season with Baltimore, joined Chicago for the 1926 season.[8]

Bentley batted .412 in 141 games with 24 home runs and 120 RBI, becoming the league's first Triple Crown winner, one of only seven in its history. His batting average is the IL record. He set a league record of 246 hits that still stands and led in doubles (47), total bases (397) and slugging average (.665). The 24 homers were a league record at the time. On the mound, Bentley was 12–1 with a 2.35 ERA. Being left-handed and with these statistics, it is not surprising that he was starting to be called "The Babe Ruth of the Minors."[9]

Baltimore lost the 1921 JWS to Louisville in eight games.

The 1922 Orioles had a phenomenal record (115–52) thanks in large part to pitchers who could hit. In addition to Bentley (13–2; .351 batting average and 22 homers), the staff included Parnham (16–10; .315 batting average and six homers), Ogden (24–10; two

homers), Thomas (18–9; two homers), and Harry Frank (22–9; one homer).

Grove went 18–8 with a pair of doubles amongst his 13 hits. He remained in Baltimore for 1923 and 1924, compiling a combined record of 53–16. He made his major-league debut in 1925 with the Philadelphia Athletics, and hung around for 17 Hall-of-Fame seasons, compiling a 300–141 record for the A's and the Boston Red Sox.

Bentley hit at least 20 homers in each season from 1920 through 1922. What did he do as a pitcher? A none-too-shabby 41–6. It was his pitching that attracted John McGraw of the Giants, who obtained Bentley for $72,500. Bentley was used mostly as a pitcher by the Giants, going 40–22 from 1923 through 1925, but did manage to bat .329 with four homers, and went 5-for-12 (.417) in the 1923 and 1924 World Series.[10] In 1923, his .412 batting average (28-for-68) set the one-season mark for hitting by National League pitchers. His overall average that year was .427 as he pinch-hit on 22 occasions, going 10-for-21 with a walk.

The Orioles returned to the Junior World Series in 1922, defeating St. Paul, five games to two.

The 1923 Orioles went 111–53 and won the IL pennant by 11 games. The core of the team—Bishop, Boley, Jacobson, Lawry, and Maisel—was still around, and Bishop led the league in homers with 22. In 1921, Dunn had signed 19-year-old Dick Porter, whom he kept locked up through 1928. Porter batted .316 in 1923. It was the first of six consecutive seasons in which he batted at least .316.

Jimmy Walsh was the new first baseman in 1923 and batted .333. He was a 35-year-old veteran who had parts of six seasons in the majors, and had joined Baltimore in 1922, batting .327. It was his second go-around with Baltimore. He had been with the team from 1910 through 1912.

Grove was 27–10 with a league leading 330 strikeouts. Parnham, who had rejoined the team in 1922, was 33–7 in his last great season. In the JWS, Baltimore lost to Kansas City in nine games.

In 1924, Baltimore went 117–48 and finished 19 games ahead of Toronto. Grove's pitching (26–6) and Porter's batting (.363) led the league. The key acquisition that season was George Earnshaw. Dunn held on to Earnshaw until 1928, when the Athletics met Dunn's price of a reported $80,000. Baltimore lost to St. Paul in a JWS that took 10 games to complete, there being one tie.

In 1925, three pitchers won at least 28 games. The team's leader in wins was Thomas with 32. Earnshaw, in his first full season, won 29. Ogden won 28. Baltimore's 188 homers were tops in the league. In the JWS, Baltimore defeated Louisville in eight games.

The dynasty would yield ten inductees to the International League Hall of Fame in a steady stream of inductions between 1948 and 1963, with an eleventh, Grove, added in 2008 (after his induction to Cooperstown). Dunn's Orioles would never again have the glory of those seven great seasons. ■

Sources

In addition to Baseball-Reference.com and the sources cited in the notes, the author used:

"Bentley Goes to Red Sox: World Champions Grab Oriole First Sacker in Draft," *Baltimore Sun*, September 21, 1917, 9.

Bready, James H. *Baseball in Baltimore: The First 100 Years* (Baltimore, Johns Hopkins University Press, 1998).

Johnson, Lloyd. *The Minor League Register* (Durham, North Carolina, Baseball America, 1994).

Johnson, Lloyd and Miles Wolff. *Encyclopedia of Minor League Baseball* (Durham, North Carolina, Baseball America, 2006).

"Orioles of Old Could Probably Whip Big League Teams Today," *Salisbury Times*, April 17, 1953, 12.

Foreman, Charles J. "Orioles Mark Time Waiting for Saints," *The Sporting News*, September 30, 1920, 3.

Notes

1. Bill Weiss and Marshall Wright, *The 100 Best Minor League Teams of the 20th Century* (Parker, Colorado, Outskirts Press, 2006).
2. Darrell Hanson, "Joe Boley," SABR BioProject.
3. "Fritz Maisel an Oriole," *Baltimore Sun*, March 30, 1919, 9.
4. "Jack Bentley Rounds Out Orioles' Infield for Dash to the Pennant," *Baltimore Evening Sun*, June 23, 1919, 11.
5. "Slugging Miners are Meek Before Le:y Groves: Wins His Second Game for Orioles," *Baltimore American*, July 5, 1920, 4.
6. *The Sporting News*, October 14, 1920, 8.
7. Earl Arnold, "Wrangling and Horseplay Mark Orioles Fourth Win Over Saints, 6–5," *Minneapolis Morning Tribune*, October 14, 1920, 24.
8. "White Sox to Get Tommy Thomas from Orioles," *Baltimore Evening Sun*, September 12, 1925: 12.
9. Bill Weiss and Marshall Wright, *The 100 Best Minor League Teams of the 20th Century* (Parker, Colorado, Outskirts Press, 2006).
10. Nelson "Chip" Greene, "Jack Bentley," SABR BioProject.

Baltimore, Berlin, and the Babe

The 1936 USA Baseball Team and the Rise of Baseball's Goodwill Ambassadors

Keith Spalding Robbins

It has been noted that history is cyclical, and there is nothing new under the sun. Baseball's relationship with the International Olympic Committee is one example of beatitude realizing its fruition. Baseball was to be a medal sport for the first time at the canceled 1940 Tokyo Olympics.[1] And now some 80 years later at the 2020 Tokyo Olympics, baseball was to return, only to be postponed. The tumultuous road that baseball has taken to medal sport status traces its roots to 1936 and involves Baltimore and her most famous baseball son, George Herman Ruth.

At the XIth Summer Olympiad in Berlin, on August 12, 1936, at 8:00 PM, 21 ballplayers were introduced to the largest crowd to see a baseball game in the twentieth century.[2] One by one, each player jogged from the opposite end of the stands to the center of the huge stadium with a spotlight illuminating them in the increasing darkness. This would be the first night game for these players.[3] Adding to the drama, each ballplayer was ushered in with music played by the stadium band, the earliest examples of '"walk-up music."[4] While both teams wore the same elegant white flannels with "US" on the front and a red-white-and-blue Olympic logo shield on the left sleeve, they were distinguished by their caps and socks. This game would be between "Red Stockings" and the "Blues." The team gathered at the center of the Olympic field and gave an Olympic salute.[5]

Baseball was one of two sports officially classified as "Special Demonstrations" outside the official Olympic medal winning competitions in 1936. The uncharted path baseball took to get on that field was led by Les Mann, the controversial former player and secretary-treasurer of the American Baseball Congress and the Olympic Baseball Committee. In December 1935, the question of whether the United States would attend the Winter and Summer games held in Germany in 1936 was addressed. In a very hotly contested and divided convention, the US decided not to boycott. But on December 5, the Japanese Olympic baseball authorities decided not to send an Olympic baseball team, claiming it was too expensive to send a team overseas.[6] The Japanese did allow one official, "Frank" Matsumato from Meiji University, to travel to Berlin, where he served as an umpire.[7] In response, MLB announced at the 1935 Winter Meetings that no financial support would be given and international baseball barnstorming to Japan and other countries was banned.[8]

The issue of Japan's withdrawal was likely national pride and not money.[9] In the winter of 1935, the Wheaties All Americans, a team of college players under the leadership of Mann, Herb Hunter, and picked by Olympic Chairman Avery Brundage, and under partial sponsorship by Louisville Slugger and chaperoned by Frank Bradsby.[10] They played 15 games against Japanese collegiate teams, beating them regularly.[11] In front of 60,000 fans, they beat Waseda University, the Big Six Champion, 6–0. Yet the games were spirited and competitive. Fred Heringer, a Stanford pitcher and member of both the 1935 Wheaties and the 1936 Olympic team, noted in a 1937 interview that the Japanese players he faced were "tops in baseball, and will give anyone a run for his money."[12]

While Japanese amateur baseball supposedly did not have the funds to send a team to Berlin, monies were available for a college ball team to barnstorm across the US. From May 15 to July 1, Waseda University played 22 games, going 15–7 against college-age competition. Their coast-to-coast journey started at Stanford University (two games) and included stops at the University of Chicago (two games), Ann Arbor (one inning before the rains came), Boston, a return to Chicago, and finally Seattle and Oakland.[13] Coincidentally, the Japanese departure date was the same as the opening of the US Olympic trials.

The highlight of their barnstorming was two shutouts: Harvard (5–0) and Yale (6–0). The Yale game on June 8, 1936, made international headlines for the two-walk, 12-strikeout no-hitter by Waseda pitcher Shozo Wakahara.[14]

Meanwhile, the US Olympic Baseball leadership was selecting amateur players, attempting to find a capable opponent, and were forced to be independent and raise their own funds without support from MLB. This team needed a hero.

On February 9 and 10, 1936, newspapers around the country announced that the US Olympic Baseball team would be escorted to Berlin by baseball's greatest hero of all: The Sultan of Swat, the Bambino, Babe Ruth. Ruth was given two new nicknames: Commander in Chief of the Olympic Baseball Committee and "commandant" of the United States amateur baseball delegation.[15]

After rejecting an offer from Larry MacPhail to play for the Reds, Ruth was quoted as saying, "I'm taking a lot of interest in this Olympics baseball program."[16] *The Sporting News* of April 9, 1936, featured a photo of Ruth shaking Mann's hand.

Baltimore was chosen as the site for the trials partly due to Charm City's capable amateur baseball commissioner, Paul E. Burke, who was the Maryland state representative to the American Baseball Congress. On March 14, 1936, Mayor Howard W. Jackson made public the letter of invitation to Mann and the American Baseball Congress stating that Baltimore wanted to host the trials. And two weeks later, on March 29, *The Baltimore Sun* ran the following headline: "Babe Ruth Promises To Attend."

Tryouts were held at Gibbons Field on the campus of Mount St. Joseph. As an added benefit for the area, one or two of Baltimore's best amateurs would be selected to the team. The plan included tickets to a Washington Nationals game against the Yankees on July 5 and then the use of Griffith Stadium for a fundraiser.[17]

Mount St. Joseph, run by the Xaverian Brothers of St. Mary's Industrial School—Ruth's alma mater, was no accidental choice. This high school had an established baseball development heritage, sending numerous students to professional baseball.[18] Having empty summer dorms and a large gym and locker room, it was an ideal campus for the players.[19] They were making history, becoming Olympic baseball's first Team USA.[20]

An estimated 800 prospective ballplayers sent applications to Mann, from about a reported to 150 wound up on Gibbons Field.[21] While the trials were labeled free for all, it cost each participant a $60 admission fee. No doubt this substantial amount limited the number of attendees. Mann would later state that the fee would be refunded if a player did not make the team.[22] By Sunday, July 5, players from all corners of the country had arrived and were competing for spots on the team.[23]

Baltimore had not been the first or even the second choice for the tryouts. In the summer of 1935, the Olympic baseball committee had called for 12 regional tournaments of approved amateur teams competing to determine a national champion along with selecting a tournament all-star team.[24] After the Japanese withdrawal, an "East vs West" set of teams was proposed. Well-respected Stanford Coach Harry Wolter was to lead a West team versus an East team from the Penn Athletic Club, led by George Lang and former A's catcher Ira Thomas.[25] These earlier plans did not pan out, but would shape the tryouts in Baltimore: some of the twenty slots on the team were reserved for Penn AC ballplayers.

Three games were scheduled, two in Charm City and one at Griffith Stadium, intended to showcase the talent and serve as fundraisers for the overseas trip.[26] The two Baltimore games would feature the local sandlotters. The first, the Police Department game, was a fundraising disaster, generating a net profit of just seven dollars—significantly short of the $500 required for each self-funded or community-funded player to attend the Olympics![27] In response, Burke called for an emergency meeting of the Maryland Amateur Athletic Association to address the financial shortfall. After much deliberation, they dropped the plan to send any of Baltimore's best sandlotters to the Olympics. "Apathy of Fans Cited in Abandoning Plans" read the headline in the *Evening Sun* on the night of July 9.

A major reason for such apathy can be attributed to Baltimore's favorite son. Ruth did not attend the tryouts, and after mid-April 1936, he went silent on going to Berlin and his public support of US Olympic baseball. He was encouraged to resign his position of "Commandant" of Olympic baseball, though by whom remains unknown.[28]

Yet the retired Ruth was still making headlines. During the two weeks of the Baltimore tryouts, the Bambino was in Canada, on a golf and fishing vacation with wife Claire, daughter Dorothy, and friends.[29] News reports throughout Canada and the US documented his kindness, accessibility, and larger-than-life prowess.[30] *The Brooklyn Daily Eagle* noted that the Babe's fishing was a Ruthian event, for on the St. Mary's River he caught 21 salmon.[31] By July 9, Ruth was tracked down in Digby, Nova Scotia, coming off a round of golf at the New Pines Hotel course where he denied the Cleveland Indians had offered him a job as manager.[32] The Babe's Nova Scotia legacy lives on to this day as the Digby Pines golf course challenges its patrons to play a round "and try to drive the 11th hole like The Babe did in 1936."[33]

Ruth did help the Olympic cause in one small way by attending the farewell banquet in New York on

July 14, vigorously and confidently encouraging Jesse Owens to win the gold.[34] The Babe also participated in homecoming activities, though, when the team returned to New York. The city hastily planned a ticker tape parade and on September 4 Ruth attended the welcome home banquet sponsored by Mayor LaGuardia on Randall's Island, the site of Olympic Trials. Each Olympian, including members of the baseball team, received a special bronze medal.[35]

But while the baseball team was taking the field in Berlin, Ruth was on the links again. August 12–14, the Bambino was playing in a tournament in upstate New York at the Bluff Point Golf Resort, hosting the St. Orleans International Invitational.[36] His promises to help the 1936 Olympic team in Baltimore and Berlin went largely unfulfilled, perhaps not by his own wishes.

Dinty Dennis, the *Miami News* sportswriter who was also the assistant coach for the Olympic team, penned a scathing column on April 12, chastising MLB owners. He accused them of being hypocrites, for signing unproven minor leaguers for $25,000 but refusing to put up a few thousand for the national amateur team.[37]

Dennis was one of those who selected the team, along with college coaches Harry Wolter (Stanford), Judson Hyames (Western Michigan), Linn Wells (Bowdoin College), and Frank Anderson (Oglethorpe College), as well as Hall of Famer Max Carey and George Lang from the Penn Athletic Club. George A Lang held an executive leadership position of Mann's American Baseball Congress and was the USA delegate to the International Amateur Baseball Federaion.[38]

While the team was to be limited to 20 players, 21 were finally chosen, and of those, 16 were associated with the Baltimore trials. The other five came from the Penn Athletic Club, holdovers from the early proposal to send the Penn AC team. Of the 16, only two had no direct connection to the coaches in Baltimore: Paul Amen from Nebraska and Grover Galvin Jr. from Rockford, Iowa. Seven of the players were known by Mann and Carey from either the 1935 Wheaties (Les McNeece, Fred Heringer, Ron Hibbard, and Tex Fore, with Rolf Carlsten an alternate who did not go to Japan) or one of their baseball school sessions (Herm Goldberg and Dow Wilson). Lin Wells picked his team captain and best rival respectively: Bill Shaw and Clarence Keegan, who both were their team's best hitters. Wolter picked the west coast players: Gordon Mallatratt, Fred Heringer, Ike Livermore (all from his Stanford 1933 team), and Dick Hanna (from the 1936 Stanford team), and rivals Tom Downey from USC and

Bill Sayles from Oregon. Hyames was also the coach to Ron Hibbard, who was the Western Michigan center fielder and team captain. Finally, Anderson picked a rival, University of Georgia football and baseball star Henry Wagnon.

Like the Baltimore sandlotters, the Penn AC had financial issues. They were initially allocated to send a whole team. Although the club's membership came from top families of Philadelphia, including the Shibe family, and the team staged a benefit game against Connie Mack's A's, they were thousands of dollars short. While their goal was $5000, they raised a total of $2611, and sent only five players.[39] Only four of those were found in the box scores from their games that summer: infielders Rolf "Swede" Carlsten, Earnest Eddowes, and pitchers Carson Thompson and Charles Simons.[40] Two special player exemptions to the "strictly amateur" rules were given for Carlsten and the fifth player listed: Curtis Myers.

Carlsten had attended the University of Pennsylvania where he had starred in football and baseball, and had later bumped arround both the Orioles' farm teams (York, Wilkes-Barre, Cumberland), and the Canadian Football League—from which league he was subsequently bannned when his professional baseball career was uncovered. He ended up the starting second baseman for Penn AC and would be "rechristened" an amateur for the Olympic team.[41]

The exception made for Myers is even more curious. He was the 21st player added to the supposed 20-man roster, and unlike the other four, he does not appear in any of the numerous Penn AC box scores in the years leading to the Olympics; moreover, a check with the Penn AC Archives did not find him there either. The only note was linked to a semi-pro team in Camden (NJ), the Morgan AC. Yet in the Olympic records, he is listed as being a member of the Penn AC. He was a rather successful college baseball pitcher with a career record of 8–4 coached by former A's legend and Hall of Fame pitcher Charles, "Chief" Bender. However, Myers was more than just a ballplayer. Although the fact is not mentioned in any newspaper account of the team, he was also Lieutenant Curtis A. Myers of the US Navy, and had transferred landward to the Philadelphia Naval Yard in summer 1935. Adding to the espionage picture his home was listed as Hartford, Connecticut. His naval record included serving on various ships in the capacity of executive officer, being involved in naval aviation, and having received a Master's Degree in Paris, France.[42] He played baseball at the Naval Academy, graduating in 1927 making him the oldest member on the team and the one who

Golf Magazine deemed that Babe Ruth was "once America's most famous golfer." Ruth was hitting the links while the Olympic trials were being held in Baltimore.

had been out of the sport the longest time. Thus the question was, what was he really up to in Berlin?

Another player of note was the Baltimore tryout catcher, who played left field in the game. His name on the Berlin scoreboard was the very German-sounding "Harold Goldbergh." In reality, he was Herm Goldberg, the only Jewish player on the team. His baseball legacy is vital to understanding how we today view the team and its moral mission some eighty years later.

Although the Olympic exhibition game had two official scorers—including the father of AP sports, Alan J. Gould—no box score seems to exist, just a line score. The game lasted seven innings and ended on a walk-off home run by McNeece. The final score was 6–5. The AP went on to report, "Only a handful in the vast crowd had any idea who was playing or cared who won."[43]

The 1936 Berlin games were not about sports, but something more heinous and disturbing: the propagandization of sport for an immoral regime's social, political, and cultural agenda symbolic of military conquest. The games were part of the great deception as noted by their stated purpose in the Official XIth Olympiad Report: "Sporting and chivalrous competition awakens the best human qualities. It does not sever, but on the contrary, unites the opponents in mutual understanding and reciprocal respect. It also helps to strengthen the bonds of peace between the nations. May the Olympic Flame therefore never be extinguished."[44]

The other sport besides baseball that held a Special Demonstration in 1936 was gliding. Only countries within the specter of the ambition of Nazi Germany's influence were allowed to participate: Germany, Austria, Italy, Switzerland, Bulgaria, and Yugoslavia. Moreover, these gliding teams were housed not at the Olympic village but at the German Air Force Aviation Academy in Gatow. The official report confirmed the role of the Luftwaffe with the following: "all arrangements for the comfort and lodging of the group were under the supervision of Air Sport Leader Gerbrecht, who had been assigned to this task by the Reich Air Sport Leader."[45]

Not surprisingly, the German Air Command ranked the performances and gave out awards.[46]

On July 28, 1936—a mere three days before the opening Olympic ceremonies—Winston Churchill warned that the rising strength of the German Air Force was perilous, stating, "We are in danger as never before...."[47] With military conscription in place, gliding introduced German youth into the basics of flight and thus the tactics of air combat. Gliding had become the militarization of sport in its rawest, most unrepentant form. Gliding was elevated to a cultural statement and iconographic descriptor of the nation of Germany in much the way baseball was for the United States, the only two nations to feature Special Demonstration sports.

Was the need to better witness the rise of the Luftwaffe and their pilots' training skills and its material growth the reason why Lt. Curtis Myers was on the team?

The contentious debate about participation in the Games focused on whether sending a team was a de facto agreement with the German Regime's propaganda and thus an acceptance of their global ambitions. The words of the German Olympic Organizing Committee verified such concerns: "a mighty all-enveloping educative ideal which rises above the limits of time and the confines of national frontiers, aiming at physical, mental and moral perfection."[48]

The elimination of both those national borders and those humans deemed not physically, mentally, or morally perfect was the evil behind the propaganda façade. Years later, Goldberg recalled, "They were telling us…they were getting ready for war, although they didn't call it that. They just called it the 'preparation of Germany for expanding its borders.'"[49] This deception of their true ambitions was hidden in plain sight, and sadly undiscerned by many of the ballplayers—and other Olympians as well. Les McNeece, the Red Stocking's second baseman and the one who hit the game-winning inside-the-park home run, years later noted to a reporter, "When all the Olympic teams marched into the Stadium, there were thousands of Nazi SS Troops lining the road. We thought they were honoring us."[50]

Standing against this immoral ambition on display at the Games would give rise to many heroes, none greater than Jesse Owens, who thwarted Hitler's desire to prove Aryan superiority by winning four gold medals and setting three world records. When contrasted with the other demonstration sport of "Gliding," staged by the Luftwaffe High Command and featuring future fighter and bomber pilots, baseball represents the pastime of peace This was a team of goodwill ambassadors. Goldberg, the left fielder from Brooklyn, gave the lessons of baseball a most eloquent voice: "I learned to live with the competition, to lose when I had to lose without crying about it. To win when I could win with joyousness and to share with my teammates."[51]

And whether your teammate was Jim Creighton, Bill Mazeroski, Joe Carter, or Les McNeece, the shared experience's age-old stanza goes:

"And then Home with Joy."[52] ∎

Notes

1. Pete Cava, "Baseball in the Olympics," *Citius, Altius, Fortius (Journal of Olympic History 1997)*, Vol. 1, #1, Summer 1992, 9-16. M.E. Travaglini, "Olympic Baseball: Was es Das?" *The National Pastime* #5, Vol. 4 #2, Winter 1985, 46–55.

2. *Report of the American Olympic Committee, Games of the XIth Olympiad Berlin, Germany; IVth Olympic Winter Games Garmisch-partenkirchen Germany*, ed. Frederick W. Rubien, American Olympic Committee (New York, 1936). The actual aUendance number is still in doubt to this day. The general agreement is in excess of 100,000 with the official US American Olympic Team Report stating it at 125,000. In totalitarian Germany of that day the costs of not filling the stadium would have been higher than the ticket price of 1DM.

3. Stanford's famous Sunken Diamond did not get lights until 1996; in Philadelphia, Shibe Park did not get lights until 1939. To this day two college baseball diamonds have no lights: University of Pennsylvania and Bowdoin Colleges' Pickard Field. https://www.baseball-almanac.com/stadium/st_shibe.shtml. https://gostanford.com/sports/baseball. https://www.facilities.upenn.edu/maps/locations/meiklejohn-stadium-murphy-field. https://athletics.bowdoin.edu/information/facilities/files/baseball.

4. "The Complete History of the Walk-Up Song," MLB.com, https://www.mlb.com/cut4/the-complete-history-of-the-walk-up-song

5. Paul Amen, diary journal entry of August 12, 1936, Baseball Hall of Fame File.

6. "Japan Cancels Baseball Trip," *Hawaii Tribune-Herald*, December 7, 1935, 4.

7. Travaglini, 53.

8. *Chicago World-Telegram*, December 12, 1935.

9. Sayuri Gutherie-Shimizu, *Transpacific Field of Dreams: How Baseball Linked the United States and Japan in Peace and War*, University of North Carolina Press, 2012, 169.

10. Leslie Mann, *Baseball Around the World: International Amateur Baseball Federation*, Self-published, Springfield Massachusetts, Springfield College Library, 6.

11. "Scalzi Back from Tours," *The Huntsville Times*, February 3, 1936, 3. Scalzi was the shortstop for the Alabama Crimson Tide and a 1935 Wheaties All American.

12. Interviewed by *Corvallis Gazette Times*, September 17, 1937.

13. "Waseda Has Fine Record for Invasion," *Honolulu Advertiser*, July 7, 1936, 11.

14. "Japanese Pitcher Allows Yale No Hits and No Runs," *Boston Globe*, June 9, 1936, 21. Some west coast newspapers erroneously reported this as a perfect game.

15. *The Sporting News*, April 9, 1936, 8. Advertisement of the American Baseball Olympic Committee.

16. "Babe Ruth rejects offer to play ball with Reds," *Scranton Republican*, March 10, 1936, 16.

17. "St. Joe Selected," *Baltimore Evening Sun*, June 26, 1936, 35.

18. "Cahill May Join Senators Today," *Baltimore Evening Sun*, June 9, 1915, 9. Other players mentioned include Bill Morrisette, Lewis Malone, Rube Meadows, and Dave Roth. Malone and Morrisette were on the 1915 A's roster, the year after Connie Mack began his first great sell-off.

19. Now it's the site of a turf multipurpose field enclosed by a track, called Pleyvak Field.

20. "Baseball Amateur Aces Are Gathering for Olympic Tryouts," *Boston Globe*, July 1, 1936, 24.

21. McIver, Stuart B., *Touched by the Sun, The Florida Chronicles, Volume 3.* Chapter 2, An Olympian Homer, 14. Chapter on Les McNeece.

22. *Bennington Evening Banner*, May 23, 1936, p. 4.

23. "Here from Four Corners of Nation to Seek Olympic Places," *Baltimore Sun*, July 5, 1936, 18.

24. "District Baseball Stars Get Olympic Games Try," *Pittsburgh Press*, July 9, 1935, 26. *The Sporting News* of August 1, 1935, included a team application.

25. "West vs East," *Reading* (PA) *Times*, February 3, 1936, 14.

26. Jimmy Keenan, "July 8, 1936: Baltimore Police Tame the US Olympic Baseball Team," SABR. https://sabr.org/gamesproj/game/july-8-1936-baltimore-police-tame-olympic-baseball-team

27. Keenan, "Baltimore Police Tame US Olympic Baseball Team."

28. "Dinty's Dugout Chatter," Column. *Miami News*, April 12, 1936, 11.

29. "Beware, Poor Fish." *New York Daily News*, July 3, 1936, 195.

30. *Saskatoon Star-Phoenix* July 6, 1936. The Babe visited Alfred Scadding at a Halifax hospital.

31. *The Brooklyn Daily Eagle*, July 10, 1936, 17.

32. "Ruth Denies He was Offered Job as Indians' Pilot," *Chicago Tribune*, July 10, 1936, 25.

33. https://www.digbypines.ca/hotel-info/history. Babe Ruth played a round of golf there.

34. http://jesseowensmemorialpark.com/wordpress1/1936-olympics-in-berlin.

35. *New York Daily News* and *Brooklyn Union Times*, various stories September 3 and 4, 1936.

36. "Ruth Gets 70 in Trial Round," *South Bend Tribune*, August 14, 1936, 28.

37. "Dinty's Dugout Chatter," Column. *Miami News*, April 12, 1936, 11.

38. See note 10, page 8. Lang was noted as Vice President of the USABC and the USA delegate to the International Association Baseball Federation.

39. "Pennac Nine Needs $3000—Or Else—They'll Stay Home," *Philadelphia Inquirer*, July 10, 1936.

40. "Athletics Upset Pennac Clubbers in Olympic Tilt," *Philadelphia Inquirer*, July 7, 1936.

41. Given the issues with Jim Thorpe being stripped of his Olympic medals for playing semi-pro baseball its most curious that both Les Mann and the ever watchful and controlling Avery Brundage would allow a banned-in-Canada professional on the Olympic team, but they did.

42. Before World War II, newspapers published officers' orders and ship movements. Lieutenant Myers was found approximately every 20 months with new orders. By 1935 he was in the Philadelphia Navy Yard.

43. "100,000 See Baseball Tilt," *Baltimore Sun*, August 13, 1936.

44. *The XIth Olympic Games Berlin, 1936. Official Report: Organisationskomitee Für Die Xi. Olympiade Berlin 1936*, E. V. Wilhelm Limpert, (Berlin) 1937. Vol 6, 6. This stated is aUributed to the dictator of the German state.

45. *XIth Olympic Games Berlin*, 1936, 1100.

46. Listed in the both Berlin Olympics and the US Olympic Committee reports.

47. *XIth Olympic Games Berlin*, 229.

48. *XIth Olympic Games* Berlin, 4.

49. Josh Chetwynd and Brian A. Belton, *British Baseball and the West Ham Club*, McFarland & Co., 2006, 127.

50. McIver, 15.

51. National Holocaust Museum Oral History files for Herman Goldberg http://collections.ushmm.org/search/catalog/irn504462.

52. Thomas Newberry, "Base-Ball," *The Little Pocket-Book*, 1787 Worcester Edition, (Isaiah Thomas: Worcester, MA) 43.

George Scales and the Making of Junior Gilliam in Baltimore, 1946

Stephen W. Dittmore, PhD

Spring training for the Baltimore Elite Giants of the Negro National League began April 1, 1946, at Sulphur Dell in Jim Gilliam's hometown of Nashville. A brief story in the *Nashville Tennessean* about the Nashville Cubs, previously the Black Vols, beginning practice alongside the Elite Giants indicated "James Gilliam" would be returning to the Nashville team at third base.[1] The Cubs ostensibly served as a minor-league affiliate of the Elites. With established veterans around the Elites infield, the 17-year-old Gilliam likely figured to be nothing more than organizational depth for owner Tom Wilson's clubs.

During camp, however, Gilliam caught the eye of George Scales, Baltimore's former manager and current road secretary. George Louis Scales (sometimes listed as George Walter Scales[2]) was born August 16, 1900, in Talladega, Alabama. In his 33 years in the Negro Leagues, Scales played all four infield positions as well as the outfield and served several years as a manager. He was a steady hitter who in 743 games amassed a .312 average with 59 home runs and 502 runs batted in.[3] Bill James ranked Scales as the third-best second baseman in Negro Leagues history in his *New Bill James Historical Baseball Abstract*, describing him as a power hitter who "was both fast and quick, but tended to put on weight (he was called 'Tubby')."[4]

Scales broke into professional black baseball in 1919 as a member of the Montgomery Grey Sox. On April 2, 1938, he found himself at Wilson Park in Nashville, site of spring training for the Elites, assuming the role of player-manager following a stint with the New York Black Yankees.[5] In 1946, Scales served as the team's road secretary, with Felton Snow as manager.

By all accounts, Scales was a knowledgeable manager, well-liked by players. Long-time Elites shortstop Tommy "Pee Wee" Butts, a perennial Negro League all-star, said, "Scales was a little hard on you, but if you'd listen you could learn a lot. …Scales could get what he needed out of you."[6]

Scales would get plenty out of Gilliam that spring. "Well, it's true, I'm the one gave Junior Gilliam his chance. I forced them to play him," Scales said decades later. "Gilliam was a kid had come up from Nashville with the team as a third baseman. The manager had a friend he brought up to play second, but that guy was nothing. So I went to Vernon Green, the owner, and said, 'Make that man put Gilliam on second,' and he did, and that was it."[7]

The "nothing" player was presumably Frank Russell, who was mentioned as the projected starter in the *Baltimore Evening Sun*.[8] Russell, also a former Black Vol, played second base for the Elite Giants in 1943 and 1944, but shifted to third base in 1946. He would bat only .182 in 55 at-bats that year.[9]

During spring training in 1946, Scales was watching the right-handed-hitting Gilliam flail at curveballs thrown by right-handed pitchers. "I couldn't do anything with curveball pitchers," Gilliam recalled in 1953. "I figured I'd lay back and wait for the fastball, but the pitchers in the Negro National League were smarter than me. They just threw me curves."[10]

Having seen enough, Scales is purported to have yelled, "Hey, Junior, get over on the other side of the plate."[11] At 45 years old, Scales was old enough to be Gilliam's father, and the moniker fit. Jim Gilliam was now Junior Gilliam.

Gilliam's version of the exchange with Scales, however, suggested it was more like advice than a command. According to Gilliam, Scales approached him one day and asked, "You ever hit left-handed?"

"When I was a kid," Gilliam replied. "I broke my right arm when I was 12 but I still played with the other fellows. I'd hold my bat in my left arm and the other one, it would be in a cast."

"Then why not try it that way?" Scales said. "You're not going any place this way."[12]

"This way" was a reference to his unofficial position in his first season with Baltimore: right-handed-hitting utilityman. "George told me that if I'd learn to switch-hit, I'd never go through life as a utilityman,"[13] Gilliam said, smiling, to Bob Hunter for a 1964 *Sporting News* story. Ironically, Gilliam would be remembered as just that—a utilityman, appearing at every position except pitcher, catcher, and shortstop in his 14-year career with the Brooklyn and Los Angeles Dodgers.

If anyone in the Negro Leagues could mentor Gilliam on how to hit a curveball, it was Scales. Negro Leagues star and Hall of Famer Buck Leonard said, "George Scales knew how to hit it to a T! Josh Gibson knew it to a T. They hit a curveball farther than they hit a fastball. I saw George Scales hit a curveball four miles!"[14]

The transition to switch-hitting, while ultimately successful, was not easy. "When I first got over there I was afraid I couldn't duck," Gilliam remembered. "The first thing a switch-hitter's got to know is to duck. But by the end of 1946 I was making the full switch all the time and I found I was able to follow the curve."[15]

Butts believed Gilliam was actually a better hitter from the left side than the right. "Right-handed he was stronger, but he wouldn't get as many hits," Butts said. "When Scales switched him over, that's when Junior started hitting."[16]

Gilliam was added to the Elites roster and assigned to room with Joe Black. It was as unlikely a pairing as possible. Gilliam was a 17-year-old who had not graduated high school. Black was 22, had served in the military during World War II, and was on his way to earning a degree from Morgan State University. Gilliam was quiet and reserved. Black was outgoing and gregarious.

Neither man could have predicted how intertwined their lives would become. They would compete together with the Elites from 1946 to 1950. Their contracts would be purchased together by the Dodgers, and they'd spend part of 1951 together as teammates with Brook-lyn's Triple-A affiliate, the Montreal Royals. Black would join the major-league club in 1952 and win National League Rookie of the Year, which Gilliam would win in 1953. The two developed such a close friendship that Gilliam would become godfather to Joe's son, Chico.

While Black might be credited with helping Gilliam grow from a teenager into a man, it was Scales's instruction that transformed him into a legitimate baseball player. "Gilliam was a little fellow, very fast, didn't have the strongest throwing arm, but quick," Scales said years later. "And he wanted to play, that was the main thing."[17]

Gilliam's only known appearance in the first half of the 1946 Negro National League season occurred on Sunday, May 26, against the New York Cubans, when he entered a 4–4 game late at second base. No play-by-play exists for the bottom of the ninth, but the box score lists Gilliam as going 0-for-1. Luis Tiant Sr., throwing in his 16th season for the Cubans, pitched the ninth inning. It's not known how Gilliam was retired.[18] At the age of 17 years, seven months, and nine days, Gilliam had made his Negro National League debut.

Apparently thinking Gilliam was still too young, the Elites turned to two Negro Leagues veterans on June 4 to settle the infield, signing Sammy Hughes to play second and Willie Wells to play third. Hughes, recently released from the Army, was a Negro Leagues veteran, having played since 1930, mostly with Baltimore. Wells, who had begun the 1946 season with the New York Black Yankees, had made his rookie debut in 1924.

The Elites jumped out to a fast start in the second half, opening with a 4–1 record to occupy first place in

The Baltimore Elite Giants. In the front row, Tubby Scales is on the far left, Junior Gilliam is fourth from the left, and Henry Kimbro is in front on the far right.

NOIR TECH / LARRY LESTER

Jim "Junior" Gilliam would win the National League Rookie of the Year award in 1953 with the Brooklyn Dodgers, but in 1946, at the age of 17, he had debuted in the Negro National League with the Baltimore Elite Giants.

the NNL. The team was paced by center fielder Henry Kimbro, hitting in the third spot and batting .366. Butts occupied the two hole, sporting a .313 batting average. Midseason signee Wells was batting .344 in the cleanup spot.[19]

Kimbro, a fellow Nashville native, also took it upon himself to mentor Gilliam. "Henry was a great leadoff man for the Elite Giants," Gilliam recalled in 1964. "He told me the one thing I must learn was the strike zone. He wouldn't swing at a ball an inch off the plate. That's when I learned I couldn't get good wood on a bad pitch."[20]

As the 1946 season continued, it was clear the 35-year-old Hughes' skills were diminished. Scales approached Gilliam with the idea of focusing only on second base, rather than utility. "We got to have a second baseman to go with Butts," Scales said. "Sammy was all right, but the Army took it out of his legs. He can't get around. You try it, Junior."[21]

Butts told John Holway for his book *Voices From the Great Black Baseball Leagues*, "(Gilliam) really liked third base, but George Scales said, 'No, you'd make a better second baseman.' And I think he did. They said he had a weak arm, but he really could get rid of the ball and make those double plays. He wouldn't stumble over the bag. Sometimes I'd say he wouldn't even touch it."[22]

Gilliam finally cracked the starting nine on July 16, lining up at second base and batting eighth with his friend and roommate Black on the hill.[23] Gilliam went 0-for-3 with a sacrifice against Cubans pitcher Dave Barnhill. Gilliam's name would not appear again in a box score until August 18, when, starting at shortstop to spell Butts, he went 1-for-3 with a double and a run scored against the Newark Eagles. His double, his first known Negro Leagues hit, came off Charles England, who surrendered all 12 Elites hits in 7 ⅔ innings that day.[24] England's entire Negro Leagues career consisted of two games started, in which he allowed 17 hits and 13 runs in 9 ⅔ innings.[25]

Gilliam soon became a fixture in the Elites lineup at second base, replacing Hughes, who would retire at season's end. Gilliam started at second on August 27 against Tiant and the Cubans, batting second, a spot in the order that would become quite familiar to him over his career, and went 2-for-5.[26] On September 2, he posted a 2-for-4 performance with a triple and an RBI in a 6–1 loss to the Homestead Grays.[27]

The highlight of 1946 for Gilliam occurred on September 13 as the Elites downed the Cincinnati Clowns of the Negro American League, 10–6. The *Baltimore Sun* wrote the next day that "Johnny Washington, Junior Gilliam, and Hem (sic) Kimbro were the big guns for the victors."[28] Gilliam went 4-for-5 with a double, a stolen base, and two runs scored. The reference to "Junior" in the September 14 *Baltimore Sun* article is the first known appearance in print of the nickname Scales bestowed upon Gilliam.

Four days after the end of the season, Gilliam turned 18. He had batted .304 in 46 at-bats for the Giants in 1946.[29] Despite the limited playing time Gilliam received, Bob Luke concluded in his book on the Elite Giants, "Other than Gilliam's and Butts's performances, neither the Elites as a team nor any individual players had much to cheer about."[30]

Junior Gilliam's baptism into professional baseball was shaped by many great black players who never had a shot at the major leagues. To quote Negro Leagues star Ted Page, "George Scales made Junior Gilliam."[31] ∎

Notes

1. "Barnett Pilots Nashville Cubs," *Nashville Tennessean*, March 31, 1946.
2. Some sources such as the Negro Leagues Museum list his middle name as Walter, but his 1918 draft card appears to bear his signature: George Louis Scales.
3. "George Scales," Seamheads, accessed January 4, 2020, https://www.seamheads.com/NegroLgs/player.php?playerID=scale01geo.
4. Bill James, *The New Bill James Historical Baseball Abstract*, (New York: The Free Press, 2001), 183.
5. Bob Luke, *Baltimore Elite Giants*, (Baltimore: The Johns Hopkins University Press, 2009), 39.

6. John Holway, *Voices From the Great Black Baseball Leagues: Revised Edition*, (New York: Da Capo Press, 1992), 333–34.

7. "George Scales: The Rifle Arm of Negro Professional Baseball," *Black Sports*, May 1973, 32.

8. "Zapp New Elite Bat Star," *Baltimore Evening Sun*, April 11, 1946.

9. "Frank Russell," Seamheads, accessed January 4, 2020, https://seamheads.com/NegroLgs/player.php?playerID=russe01fra.

10. "Meet Junior Gilliam! International League's 1952 MVP," *Our Sports*, June 1953, 57.

11. Martha Jo Black and Chuck Schoffner, *Joe Black: More Than a Dodger*, (Chicago: Chicago Review Press, 2015), 107.

12. "Meet Junior Gilliam!"

13. Bob Hunter, "Gilliam: Unsung, Unhonored—and Unsurpassed," *The Sporting News*, April 4, 1964, 3.

14. Holway, *Voices*, 274.

15. "Meet Junior Gilliam!"

16. Holway, *Voices*, 335.

17. "George Scales: The Rifle Arm of Negro Professional Baseball," *Black Sports*, May 1973, 32-33.

18. "Elite Giants Defeated by N.Y. Cubans, 7–4," *Baltimore Sun*, May 27, 1946.

19. "Elite Giants defend loop lead against Cuban foe," *Baltimore Evening Sun*, July 16, 1946.

20. Hunter, "Gilliam: Unsung," 3.

21. "Meet Junior Gilliam!"

22. Holway, *Voices*, 335.

23. "Elite Giants defeat New York Cubans, 5–3," *Baltimore Sun*, July 17, 1946, 15.

24. "Elite Giants down Newark team twice," *Baltimore Sun*, August 19, 1946, 13.

25. "Charles England," Seamheads, accessed January 4, 2020, https://www.seamheads.com/NegroLgs/player.php?playerID=engla01ch.

26. "New York Cubans top Elite Giants by 5–1," *Baltimore Sun*, August 28, 1946, 14.

27. "Homestead Grays beat Elite Giants' nine, 6–1," *Baltimore Sun*, September 3, 1946, 19.

28. "Elite Giants defeat Cincinnati nine, 10–6," *Baltimore Sun*, September 14, 1946, 11.

29. "1946 Baltimore Elite Giants," Seamheads, accessed January 26, 2020, https://seamheads.com/NegroLgs/team.php?yearID=1946&teamID=BEG&tab=bat

30. Luke, Baltimore Elite Giants, 103.

31. "George Scales: The Rifle Arm."

Summer College Baseball in Maryland

Bill Hickman and Bruce Adams

EMERGENCE OF SUMMER COLLEGE BASEBALL

For more than a century, summertime baseball has been a significant part of the lives of young Marylanders. Over the decades, this has evolved from pickup games to town teams and then to amateur leagues. In the middle of the twentieth century, formal leagues with strict eligibility rules emerged. The focus of this article is on summer baseball leagues for college-age players in the Baltimore and Washington regions over the past century, and the impacts of these leagues on the development of future professional players.[1] Teams from the Baltimore and Washington franchises have won 39 of the 75 titles at the iconic All American Amateur Baseball Association (AAABA) championship played each year at Johnstown, Pennsylvania, with 68 Baltimore alumni and 67 Washington alumni making it to the major leagues.[2]

AMATEUR BASEBALL IN BALTIMORE

Baltimore amateur baseball was flourishing in the middle of the twentieth century, with more than a hundred teams playing in the region. The roots of that mid-century activity may be traced back to two leagues of the early 1900s.

The first league, founded in 1909, was the Maryland Amateur Baseball League.[3] At least one of its teams featured players from Washington College.[4] The league did not last, but re-emerged in 1930 and continued as a major force in Baltimore baseball until 1947.[5]

In 1918, the Baltimore Amateur Baseball League was formed. It lasted continuously through the proliferation of leagues in the Baltimore area in mid-century.[6] Started as a league for age 18 and under, the BABL barely touched upon the college age group, but as it evolved, it became more specialized in developing the talents of the older youths. For instance, by 1929, the Homestead Club in that league was featuring an ace pitcher from Loyola College.[7]

In the maturation process of amateur baseball around Baltimore, the leagues found they needed a superstructure of associations above them. In 1936, two rival associations united to form the Maryland Amateur Baseball Association.[8] This association became the canopy under which the amateur leagues thrived. In 1944, the Baltimore Amateur Baseball League came under the aegis of this association. The association oversaw three clusters of leagues that year: Junior Leagues (7 leagues with 45 teams), Intermediate Leagues (7 leagues with 52 teams), and Unlimited Leagues (4 leagues with 33 teams).[9]

THE IMPACT OF WALTER YOUSE

To bring the reader forward into the second half of the century in Baltimore amateur baseball, it's necessary to introduce two important figures: Dominic Leone and Walter Youse. Leone was a future Baltimore City Councilman who had experience managing local sandlot teams. He and two of his brothers owned a café and tavern in South Baltimore. In 1952, Dom Leone's team, which would become a famous winning team as Leone's Café, got its start in the Riverside No. 1 League.[10] The following year, the team moved to the age 16–18 Monumental League under the Maryland Amateur Baseball Association, and dominated with talented players like Al Kaline.[11] Kaline's final heroic act as an amateur was tying a game for Leone's in Gambrills, Maryland, just before reporting to the Detroit Tigers.[12]

Not long after the beginning of Leone's Café, Youse arrived to take over the helm of the team. He became manager in 1956, and before he was through, would earn legendary status. Youse said about Dom Leone: "You had to be happy working for a man like Dominic. He just didn't sponsor the team; he had the welfare of the players at heart. He helped the boys who played for us in a lot of ways, including getting jobs."[13] Dominic, Vince, and Tony Leone were elected to the AAABA Hall of Fame in 2006.[14]

Youse was not only an amateur baseball coach in Baltimore, but a long-time scout with the Orioles, Angels, and Brewers. He briefly managed amateur teams prior to World War II and then became a minor league manager for three teams after the war. He was a successful summer baseball manager of the American

Legion Westport Post No. 33 from 1948 through 1955.[15] He coached the Calvert Hall High School team beginning in 1953 and stayed through 1958, but he diverted his summers to coaching Leone's in 1956.[16] Before he was through, the Leone's squad would run through a series of sponsors, and be known also as Johnny's and Corrigan's.[17]

As reported in the *Baltimore Sun*, "Youse's run of success with 20-and-under summer league teams starting with Leone's in 1956 and ending with the Maryland Orioles in 2001 is unmatched. He is the winningest amateur coach in Maryland history."[18]

For the first ten years, Youse was his team's manager, but after that, he called himself the general manager. Nevertheless, as renowned Baltimore sportswriter Jim Henneman put it, "There was no question about who was running the show." Although Youse was in civilian clothes, he was always on the bench or in the dugout and gave every sign and made every critical in-game decision.[19] Youse's longest-serving field manager was iconic high school coach Bernie Walter.[20]

Teams run by Youse won 46 consecutive Baltimore city titles and a record 19 titles in the AAABA competition in Johnstown, Pennsylvania.[21] In total, Youse's teams won more than 3,000 games and lost fewer than 500.[22] Bobby Ullman, a former assistant to Youse, called him "the Babe Ruth of amateur baseball."[23]

More than fifty of Youse's players rose to become major leaguers.[24] These included Dave Boswell, Phil Linz, Ron Swoboda, Jim Spencer, Butch Wynegar, and Reggie Jackson.[25] When Jackson arrived under Youse's tutelage, he seemed to be headed for a football career. For the freshman team at Arizona State (ASU), Reggie had caught seven passes for 98 yards and had rushed for 161 yards at 7.7 yards per carry. ASU baseball coach Bobby Winkles directed Jackson to Leone's for the summer.[26] When Youse saw him in a workout, he couldn't believe his eyes. He compared Reggie's speed and power to that of Mantle at age 19.[27] He took him on as that summer's project and was rewarded by the star leading the team to another trip to the AAABA tournament. The scouts attended the tournament in droves, and watched the young slugger put on a power display that launched his baseball career.[28]

Reggie Jackson respected Youse's toughness, saying, "He was a tough cookie to convince. If I hit a ball 450 feet, he'd want to know why it wasn't 500. Yeah, old Walter was a toughie, but I owe a lot to him."[29]

Walter Youse was inducted into the AAABA Hall of Fame in 1998, and died in 2002. The successor team in the Leone's/Johnny's/Corrigan's franchise was called the Maryland Orioles.[30] It was managed by Dean

1946 Griffith League Championship Game on the Ellipse.

Albany, also a scout for the Baltimore Orioles.[31] In 2005, the team would be renamed Youse's Maryland Orioles in honor of the legend.[32] The Albany-led Orioles won nine additional AAABA crowns, and Albany himself was inducted into the AAABA Hall of Fame in 2009.[33] In achieving this success, Albany's team had to make two adjustments. First, he noticed that Griffith League competition in the AAABA tournament fared better when they used aluminum in tournament play, because after using wood all summer they could generate greater bat speed when switching to aluminum. So the Maryland Orioles started using wooden bats in 2000. Second, his team had done well in the past with mostly local players and only a few from out of the area, but would have to change. Stated Dean Albany: "Once the Griffith League teams started recruiting out of town players, we had to follow to stay competitive."[34]

DOWN THE ROAD IN THE NATIONAL CAPITAL REGION: CLARK C. GRIFFITH LEAGUE

The National Capital City Junior League, established in 1945, gave many of the most talented young players in the greater Washington area an opportunity to showcase their skills on the Ellipse behind the White House. From its inception, Clark C. Griffith, owner of the Washington Nationals (commonly called the Senators), supported the league. Upon his death in 1955, the league was renamed in his honor.[35]

Griffith's nephew Calvin, who had taken over the Senators upon his uncle's death, had a son named

Clark. Clark II illustrated the amateur league's popularity while describing one night when his team was playing for the 1959 Griffith League championship and the Senators were playing at Griffith Stadium. "At our game, we've got people standing four rows deep all around the outfield, the baselines, behind the backstop, people everywhere. As I'm leaving…, a guy yells at me, 'You know, Clark, you guys outdrew your dad's team tonight!' I looked around and thought, 'Wow, we probably did.'"[36]

In the late 1960s, the league moved its games off the Ellipse to Northern Virginia in part because of the deteriorated field conditions.[37] In 1993, the Griffith League took the step that moved it from a league of mostly local players to the upper ranks of summer collegiate baseball when it decided to follow the lead of the Cape Cod League and switch from the aluminum bats used in high school and college to wooden bats used in professional leagues. League president Mike McCarey explained to *The Washington Post*: "The premier leagues in the country use wood, and we wanted to step up…. Our function is to get kids with a lot of talent the opportunity to showcase that talent before the scouts. Professional scouts like wood because it gives you an idea of bat control, bat speed."[38]

The Griffith League was a charter member of the AAABA in 1944.[39] The Washington franchise won the AAABA national championship ten times: Marx Jewelers (1947), Federal Storage (1956, 1960, and 1962), Reston Raiders (1986), Prince William Gators (1997), and Arlington Senators (1998, 1999, 2001, and 2002). Legendary Griffith League Managers Joe Branzell (1995) and Chuck Faris (2004) as well as Coach Jake

Jacobs (2003) have been inducted into the AAABA Hall of Fame.[40]

Marylanders Steve Barber (Takoma Park/Orioles), Tom Brown (Silver Spring/Senators), Jim Riggleman (Rockville/Nationals Manager), Steve Schmoll (Rockville/Dodgers), and Mark Teixeira (Severna Park/Yankees) are among the 67 Griffith League alumni who made it to the major leagues.[41] Derek Hacopian, who managed the Bethesda Big Train to the 2004 league championship and played in the league during his All American college career, is one of more than 250 Griffith League alumni to play in the minor leagues.[42]

While most Griffith League teams were based in Virginia, the Griffith League did have Maryland-based teams, especially in its last decade, including Baltimore Pride, Bethesda Big Train, Germantown Black Rox, Silver Spring-Takoma Thunderbolts, and Southern Maryland Battlecats. The Griffith League played its last season in 2009 after some of its teams moved to the Cal Ripken Collegiate Baseball League.[43]

NEWCOMER IN WASHINGTON-BALTIMORE REGIONS: CAL RIPKEN COLLEGIATE BASEBALL LEAGUE

The Bethesda Big Train and Silver Spring-Takoma Thunderbolts joined the Clark Griffith League in 1999 and 2000 supported by nonprofit organizations dedicated to providing community-based baseball on the model of the Cape Cod Baseball League. After the 2004 season, the two teams joined with College Park Bombers, Maryland Redbirds, Rockville Express, and Youse's Maryland Orioles to establish the Cal Ripken Collegiate Baseball League named to honor former Baltimore Orioles manager Cal Ripken Senior. All six

2000 AAABA Champion Maryland Orioles with General Manager Walter Youse (center) and Manager Dean Albany (standing far left second row).

GREG PAUL

of the teams in the inaugural season were based in Maryland. The new wooden bat league expanded eligibility from the AAABA's 20 years old and under to include all players with college eligibility remaining.

The inaugural 2005 regular season turned into a battle of champions with the 2004 Griffith champion Big Train edging the 2004 AAABA champion Youse's Orioles by one game. Big Train and Thunderbolts were declared co-champions when the championship game was rained out. Three different teams won the championship the next three years: Thunderbolts, Youse's Orioles, and Rockville Express. For the next ten seasons, the league championship games were Big Train versus Redbirds. Big Train captured the crown five times. Redbirds won four in a row 2012–15. The teams were declared co-champions in 2018. The Redbirds left the league after the 2018 season, and Big Train captured its eighth league championship in 2019.[44]

In 2019, the league's fifteenth season, the league established a Hall of Fame. In addition to Cal Ripken Senior, MLB All Stars Brett Cecil (2005 Thunderbolts /Blue Jays, 2013) and Brian Dozier (2006 Big Train/ Twins, 2014) represented in the inaugural class the two dozen Ripken League alumni who have made it to the major leagues.[45]

Two of the league's most successful managers were part of the inaugural class. Big Train manager Sal Colangelo has led his team to nine regular season titles and eight league championships with a regular season record of 434 wins and 177 losses for an eye-popping winning average of .710.[46] Dean Albany, co-founder of the Ripken League, captured nine AAABA titles in his roles as manager and general manager of Youse's Maryland Orioles. Bruce Adams, the sixth member of the inaugural class, co-founded the Ripken League, co-founded the Big Train, and led the construction of Shirley Povich Field.[47]

Collegiate Summer Baseball Register ranked the Ripken League as the third and fifth best league in summer college baseball in 2018 and 2019. Big Train was ranked the nation's number six team in 2019, highest of any summer team in the country not from the Cape Cod League. In 2011, Perfect Game USA named Big Train the nation's top summer college team.[48]

After 21 seasons, 42% of Big Train players have gone on to play professional baseball with sixteen of them making it to the major leagues. After 15 seasons, 440 Ripken League alumni have been drafted by major league teams and thirteen players have signed as free agents.[49]

The league expanded to include teams throughout the greater Washington region. For the 2020 season,

Shirley Povich Field in Bethesda, Maryland, is home of the Bethesda Big Train in the Cal Ripken Collegiate Baseball League.

the Ripken League had intended to field six teams: Alexandria Aces, Bethesda Big Train, D.C. Grays, FCA Braves of Virginia, Gaithersburg Giants, and Silver Spring-Takoma Thunderbolts.[50] The 2020 Ripken League season was canceled, though, as a result of the novel coronavirus pandemic.

OTHER MARYLAND SUMMER BASEBALL LEAGUES

Along with the Ripken League, the Maryland summer college-age baseball season features two other organizational entities, a league and an association.[51] These are the Maryland Collegiate Baseball League and the Maryland State Baseball Association. They both can be associated with one man, Eddie Brooks, another AAABA Hall of Famer (1997).[52]

In 1945, a group of individuals interested in promoting amateur baseball throughout Maryland held a series of meetings that resulted in the establishment of the Maryland State Baseball Association. Edward W. "Eddie" Brooks became its first president, a job he held until his death in 1968.[53] In his honor, there have been several versions of an Eddie Brooks League, and one still exists today.

During the Seventies and Eighties, the Eddie Brooks League competition centered around Anne Arundel County with a perennial champion being Wagner's Baseball from Severna Park, as the teams fought for the privilege of representing the league at the AAABA tournament. The age caps at various points had been

18, 19, and 20.[54] In 1997, the Eddie Brooks League was reconstituted as a wooden bat league designed specifically for college freshmen and sophomores. That inaugural season saw the league with six teams from the Eastern Shore, Baltimore, Howard, and Prince George Counties, and Baltimore City.[55]

When the Maryland Collegiate Baseball League was formed in 2007, several teams from the Eddie Brooks League joined. Only the Putty Hill Panthers remain in 2019.[56] The Rockville Express is a former Ripken League team. Other teams in the league are Baltimore Chop, Baltimore Clippers, Dig In Baseball, FTB Mid-Atlantic, Koa Sports Green Wave, and Maryland Monarchs.[57]

The leagues in the Maryland State Baseball Association (MSBA) have teams that contain a mix of junior college and high school players. The association has been headed since 1968 by Charles Blackburn, who has over sixty years of experience in amateur baseball operations. He was inducted into the AAABA Hall of Fame in 2010. MSBA teams serve players 18 and under just as the Baltimore Amateur Baseball League did 100 years ago. With the Cal Ripken League featuring elite Division I players, there remains a strong need to provide player development opportunities for players 18 and under. The leagues under the MSBA are the Eddie Brooks League (reconstituted), Western Maryland League, Blue Ridge League (serving Virginia, Maryland, and Pennsylvania), and Eastern Shore League.[58]

MOVING FORWARD

The tradition of summer collegiate baseball in Maryland has been well established and has laid the groundwork for hundreds of major league and professional baseball careers. With the continuing presence of the Cal Ripken Collegiate Baseball League, the Maryland Collegiate Baseball League, and the Maryland State Baseball Association, the Chesapeake Bay State looks forward to many more years of playing its part in the development of baseball talent and showcasing this talent throughout the state. ■

Notes

1. According to the NCAA, the first baseball game between colleges was played on July 1, 1859, with Amherst beating Williams 73–32 in a game played under the Massachusetts rules (Daniel Wilco, www.NCAA.com, July 1, 2019). The NCAA was founded in 1906 to add safety and structure to intercollegiate athletics. The first College World Series (CWS) was played in 1947, eight years after the NCAA's first national basketball championship. California beat Yale by winning the first two games (17–4 and 8–7) in a best of three contest played June 27–28, 1947 (W. C. Madden and Patrick J. Stewart, *The College World Series: A Baseball History, 1947–2003, 58*, McFarland & Company, 2004).

Future president George H. W. Bush played for Yale in that series. Future American League MVP Jackie Jensen played for California.

2. AAABA website, https://aaabajohnstown.org/franchises.
3. *Baltimore Sun*, June 3, 1909, 9.
4. *Baltimore Sun*, August 4, 1909, 9.
5. *Baltimore Evening Sun*, August 21, 1930, 31, and *Baltimore Sun*, March 25, 1947, 19.
6. *Baltimore Evening Sun*, April 19, 1918, 16.
7. *Baltimore Sun*, September 2, 1929, 10.
8. *Baltimore Evening Sun*, December 24, 1936, 14
9. *Baltimore Evening Sun*, April 27, 1944, 23.
10. John Segraves, "Leone's 'Pickup' Team Ruling Riverside Roost," *Baltimore Evening Sun*, May 30, 1952, 26.
11. Robert Sommers, "Leone's, Sun Vie," *Baltimore Evening Sun*, May 27, 1953, 78.
12. *Baltimore Evening Sun*, June 22, 1953, 24.
13. J. Suter Kegg, "Tapping The Keg," *Cumberland* (MD) *Evening Times*, April 20, 1976, 8.
14. AAABA website, https://aaabajohnstown.org/hall-of-fame-class/2006.
15. While with Westport, Youse managed Al Kaline in 1950 and 1951. In one particular game, Kaline played centerfield and then pitched three innings to close out a no-hitter. *Baltimore Sun*, July 29, 1951, 31.
16. Email of January 20, 2020, to Bill Hickman from Jim Henneman, who had played under Walter Youse at Calvert High School.
17. Pat O'Malley, "Walter Youse Dead at Age 88; 'Guru of Amateur Baseball,'" *Baltimore Sun*, April 16, 2002, D1 and D4. The three minor league teams managed by Youse were Seaford (Eastern Shore League), Welch (Appalachian League), and Bluefield (Appalachian League).
18. O'Malley, "Walter Youse Dead…"
19. Bruce Adams and Bill Hickman interview with Jim Henneman and Dean Albany, January 9, 2020. Also Email of January 28, 2020 to Bruce Adams from Dean Albany.
20. Bernie Walter, baseball coach and athletic director at Arundel High school, was inducted into the American Baseball Coaches Hall of Fame and the National High School Coaches Hall of Fame in 2007, *Baltimore Sun*, April 21, 2015, B1. He was the first individual from Maryland to be inducted into the National High School Hall of Fame, which occurred in 2017.
21. AAABA website, https://aaabajohnstown.org/tournaments. Over the 46-year period of 1956–2001, Youse's teams won the AAABA title 19 times, and finished as the runner-up four times.
22. O'Malley, "Walter Youse Dead…"
23. O'Malley, "Walter Youse Dead…"
24. Email from Dean Albany, former manager of Youse's Orioles, to Bruce Adams, December 8, 2019.
25. *Salisbury* (MD) *Times*, July 18, 1967, 8, *Baltimore Evening Sun*, August 24, 1976, C 6, and *Baltimore Sun*, July 17, 1983, C 13.
26. Jim Henneman, "Reggie's Baltimore Sandlot Days Helped Pay His Big-League Ticket," *Baltimore Evening Sun*, September 6, 1985, C 1. Reggie Jackson's mother lived in Baltimore—a fact confirmed in authors' interview with Jim Henneman on January 9, 2020 and by Lou Gorman, *High And Inside: My Life In The Front Offices of Baseball*, 56, McFarland & Company, 2007.
27. Jerry Eaton, "Runs Like A HB Because He Is," *Arizona Republic*, August 7, 1965, 35.
28. Bob Ibach, "Youse Tough Man for Jackson To Convince," *Baltimore Evening Sun*, July 16, 1973, C 7.
29. Ibach, "Youse Tough Man…"
30. The years under the various franchise names were as follows: Leone's 1952–68; Leone's-Johnny's 1969–71; Johnny's 1972–91; Corrigan's 1992–99; Maryland Orioles 2000–04; Youse's Maryland Orioles 2005–08; Youse's Orioles 2009–14.
31. Other franchise managers were Dom Leone, 1952; Ray Muhl 1952-56; Bernie Walter 1966-79; Jim Foit 1980-81; Mel Montgomery, 1982–84;

and Norman Gilden 1985–91. Youse and Muhl were co-managers in 1956. Youse managed 1956–65 and again in the Nineties; held general manager position in intervening years.

32. Use of the names Maryland Orioles and Youse's Maryland Orioles may be found at *Baltimore Sun*, March 18, 2005, H4, and *Baltimore Sun*, August 14, 2005, E2.

33. The strength of the Baltimore amateur franchise over the years may be seen by the large number of major leaguers (68) developing from it. AAABA website, https://aaabajohnstown.org/franchise/baltimore.

34. Bruce Adams and Bill Hickman interview with Dean Albany and Jim Henneman, January 9, 2020.

35. Griffith League website, "History of the Clark Griffith League," https://tinyurl.com/svurngr.

36. Dave McKenna, "Cal Ripken versus Clark Griffith," *Washington City Paper*, July 9, 2010.

37. *The Washington Evening Star*, June 13, 1969, F4.

38. Frank Hughes, "Wood Bats Prove Big Hit in Clark Griffith League," *Washington Post*, June 25, 1993.

39. The AAABA was organized on Feb. 10, 1944. *Shamokin* (PA) *News-Dispatch*, February 10, 1944, 10. The AAABA's first tourney was held that September at Martin Park of the Glenn L. Martin Company in the Middle River area of Baltimore, Maryland. In the championship game, Cummins Construction of Baltimore beat the Heurich Brewers of Washington, DC. *Scrantonian Tribune* (Scranton, PA), September 17, 1944, 27.

40. AAABA website, https://aaabajohnstown.org.

41. Tom Brown was the first person to play in major league baseball and in a Super Bowl, per Mark Segraves on NBC4, February 24, 2017. AAABA website, https://aaabajohnstown.org/franchise/washington.

42. https://en.wikipedia.org/wiki/Clark_Griffith_Collegiate_Baseball_League.

43. Mark Giannotto, "Clark Griffith Collegiate Baseball League Falls on Hard Times While Counterpart Benefits," *The Washington Post*. July 30, 2010.

44. Cal Ripken Collegiate Baseball League, http://www.calripkenleague.org/view/calripkenleague/previous-champions.

45. Cal Ripken Collegiate Baseball League, http://www.calripkenleague.org/view/calripkenleague/hall-of-fame.

46. SABR members will recognize the surname Colangelo. Sal's brother, Mike, was a major league outfielder with the Angels, Padres, and A's during the 1999–2002 period.

47. For a detailed history of the Bethesda Big Train and Shirley Povich Field, see Bruce Adams, "Everything You Always Wanted to Know About the Big Train," Bethesda Big Train Baseball 2018 Souvenir Program, 6, accessible on website, http://www.bigtrain.org/history/20-questions.

48. *Collegiate Summer Baseball Register* bases its rankings on a data base of 8,000 players on the rosters of 260 teams in 32 summer leagues.

49. Statistics on Big Train players maintained by Bill Hickman. Ripken League statistics included in email of December 10, 2019 from Jason Woodward, Commissioner of Cal Ripken Collegiate Baseball League, to Bruce Adams.

50. Ripken League website, (click on "Teams"), http://www.calripkenleague.org/view/calripkenleague.

51. Historically, there have been many more alternatives than just these two. For example, the following source presented the options for summer baseball in the Washington area in 1987: David Izenson, "Summer Baseball Abounds," *Washington Post*, June 25, 1987, https://www.washingtonpost.com/archive/local/1987/06/25/summer-baseball-abounds/39db8928-d6c0-4cc2-81b3-d4596e9a2e67.

52. For decades, Eddie Brooks had been president of the Belair-Harford Road League (founded in 1929), the largest independent amateur league in the US. *Baltimore Sun*, June 28, 1948, 14. Brooks also went on to be president of the Maryland Amateur Baseball Association (the organization founded in 1936) starting in 1949 and continuing until it dissolved. Bill Hickman phone interview with Charles Blackburn, Executive Director, Maryland State Baseball Association, January 22, 2020.

53. Maryland State Baseball Association, http://www.msbabaseball.com.

54. *Baltimore Evening Sun*, August 3, 1978, E 5; Pat O'Malley, ""Wagner's, Inc., Succeeds in the Business of Sandlot Baseball, *Baltimore Sun*, June 25, 1980, 57; and Pat O'Malley, "Two Baseball Teams Combine to Make One Champion," *Anne Arundel County Sun*, July 16, 1989, 19.

55. William Haufe, "A League of Their Own," *Easton* (MD) *Star-Democrat*, May 30, 1997, 15.

56. Bill Hickman phone interview with Richard Pietryka, Commissioner, Maryland Collegiate Baseball League, December 8, 2019.

57. Maryland Collegiate Baseball League, https://www.hometeamsonline.com/teams/?u=BUCKEYE&s=baseball.

58. Bill Hickman phone interview with Charles Blackburn, Executive Director, Maryland State Baseball Association, December 13, 2019.

Howie Fox

Baltimore's Unique Oriole

Herm Krabbenhoft

I n a stunning development on September 29, 1953, the city of Baltimore went from being the home of the minor league Orioles of the International League to having the major league Orioles of the American League.[1] On that historic day, Bill Veeck, president of the St. Louis Browns, announced that "a Baltimore group headed by attorney Clarence W. Miles had purchased 79 per cent interest in the Browns." What happened to the 30 men who played at least one game with the 1953 Orioles? Where did they play in 1954? The short answer is, "Many places." The Appendix (available on the SABR website) provides pertinent information for 29 of those players. The other player, Howie Fox, is the subject of this article—he has the unique distinction of being the only man to play for both Baltimore's minor league Orioles and the major league Orioles which supplanted them.[2,3]

RESEARCH PROCEDURE

The information presented in this article was obtained from game accounts and articles provided in numerous newspapers (especially *The Baltimore Sun* and *The Sporting News*). Also utilized were various editions of the *Baseball Guide and Record Book* and the *Dope Book* (published by *The Sporting News*), Howie Fox's "Player Information Cards File" and "Player Clippings File" (National Baseball Hall of Fame Library), *The 1955 Baltimore Orioles Sketch Book*, and the Retrosheet and Baseball-Reference websites.

RESULTS AND DISCUSSION

1943–52: With the Barons, Reds, and Phillies

Howie Fox was born on March 1, 1921, and broke into organized baseball in 1943 with the Birmingham Barons, the single-A farm team of the Cincinnati Reds in the Southern Association. He turned in a 14–17 won-lost ledger with a 4.83 earned run average. In his next season, also with the Barons, Fox produced a 19–10 record and a league-leading 2.71 ERA, which earned him a late-season call-up with the Reds. He made his major league debut on September 17, 1944, in the first game of a twin bill against the Pirates in Pittsburgh.

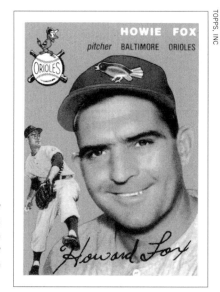

Howie Fox was the only player from the 1953 minor league Orioles to carry over to the newly relocated major league franchise in 1954.

TOPPS, INC.

Fox continued pitching for the Reds (interspersed with a couple stints with their AAA Syracuse farm team) through the 1951 season, compiling a big league W-L record of 40–63. On December 10, 1951, Fox was traded to the Philadelphia Phillies. With the Phillies in 1952, Fox produced a 2–7 W-L ledger with a 5.08 ERA. (Additional information on Fox's performance for the 1943–52 period is given in the Appendix.)

1953: Joining the IL Orioles

The Phillies opened the 1953 season in the City of Brotherly Love and split a pair of games against the New York Giants before traveling to Pittsburgh for a three-game series (April 16–18). After Philadelphia lost the first game, the next two games were rained out. Fox, whose mound performance during spring training had been deemed unimpressive, did not appear in any of the Phillies' first three games. Before the Phillies left town, Fox was notified that his contract had been sold outright to Philadelphia's AAA farm club: the Baltimore Orioles of the International League. Fox spoke out against the transaction. He stated he would not go to Baltimore and wanted to be declared a free agent or sold to a Pacific Coast League team (his home being in Coburg, Oregon). However, following a discussion of the situation with Phillies President Bob Carpenter, Fox agreed to join the Orioles at the end of the week.

Fox's first game with the Orioles was on Sunday, April 26, the lid-lifter of a twin bill against the visiting Toronto Maple Leafs. Howie started, but was knocked out of the box with one out in the second stanza. During his brief outing he gave up five runs on two hits and three bases on balls. Fortunately, the Orioles were able to eventually overcome the deficit and emerge victorious, 12–11, thereby rendering Fox's initial outing a no-decision. Perhaps contributing to Howie's dismal beginning was a pulled muscle in his side, which also delayed his next start, the first game of a double dip on May 8 in Syracuse. In spite of surrendering eight hits and issuing six walks in his six-plus innings, Fox benefitted from the home-run hitting of Jack Graham and Roy Weatherly and the last-inning relief of Ken Heintzelman to earn his first triumph, 8–6.

Fox improved to 2–0 with a relief victory on May 12, against the visiting Syracuse Chiefs, twirling six innings after replacing starter Clarence Marshall, with one man on and nobody out. Howie retired the next two batters and should have also retired the third batter, but a fielding error by shortstop Ted Kazanski prolonged the inning. A single by the Syracuse pitcher followed, driving in the run which knotted the score at 1–1. The game remained deadlocked until the bottom of the ninth when, with two down, Russell Kerns drew a walk and Joe Lonnett followed with a single. The Chiefs' skipper then ordered Damon Phillips walked intentionally to fill the bases and bring up Fox…or a pinch hitter. *The Baltimore Sun* reported that the O's manager, Don Heffner, "had a choice, and made it without hesitation. Fox took his place at the plate and dropped a clean single in center," driving in Kerns with the game-winning run.[4]

Fox provided another fireman rescue in a game two days later, also against Syracuse, taking over for Bob Greenwood in the seventh inning with the bases loaded and two outs. Howie tossed out Ben Zientara to end the inning and then proceeded to shut out the Chiefs in the eighth and ninth frames, saving the 4–0 triumph for Baltimore.

Despite pitching fairly well in his next start, on May 16, Fox absorbed his first defeat as an Oriole. After yielding a first-inning solo homer to Charley Kress, Howie pitched scoreless ball until the sixth session when he walked a pair and gave up a hit, the combination resulting in two more runs for Rochester, which completed the game's scoring. Cot Deal pitched a complete-game shutout for the Red Wings.

As the season progressed through July, Fox's mound performance was so-so. At the close of May he had fashioned a 3–1 W-L ledger. By the end of June, his record stood at 6–5; after July 8–8. Then, during the final month and a half of the regular season, Howie became the ace of the Orioles mound corps. During the month of August Howie fashioned a 5–1 record, bringing his season ledger to 13–9. He hurled three complete games, including a 2–0 whitewashing of the Maple Leafs in Toronto on August 9. Then, during the stretch drive for a playoff spot in the first two weeks of September, Howie produced two victories against one defeat. He also saved a game. Thus, at the conclusion of the regular season, Fox had compiled a 15–10 ledger. The Appendix provides a game-by-game summary of Fox's slabwork. For comparison, Table 1 presents the final full-season statistics for each of Baltimore's principal hurlers (i.e., those who pitched 45 or more innings). As can be seen, Howie topped the Baltimore mound staff in wins, innings pitched, and complete games.

The 1953 Baltimore Orioles team finished with an 82–72 (.532) record, which ranked fourth and earned them a playoff spot for the International League Championship (aka the Governor's Cup). In the first round,

Table 1. Final Regular-Season Statistics for 1953 Orioles Hurlers with 45 or More Innings Pitched[5]

Pitcher	G	GS-CG-SHO	W-L (PCT)	IP-H-HR	R-ER	BB-SO	HB-WP	ERA
Tom Herrin	40	3–1–0	8–4 (.667)	95–91–5	41–38	48–42	3–3	2.65
Ken Heintzelman *	37	9–1–1	5–4 (.556)	111–115–5	52–41	35–46	0–1	3.32
Kent Peterson *	22	7–1–0	2–5 (.286)	63–61–5	33–24	24–41	2–1	3.43
John Thompson	25	22–7–2	10–4 (.714)	154–142–16	77–65	50–68	1–2	3.80
Howie Fox	34	29–12–1	15–10 (.600)	204–193–14	95–87	76–90	3–2	3.84
Jack Sanford	32	30–11–0	14–13 (.519)	200–186–11	112–88	110–128	5–9	3.96
Ron Mrozinski *	30	7–3–0	2–5 (.286)	118–124–8	56–52	59–65	1–2	3.97
Bob Greenwood	37	20–4–3	11–12 (.478)	146–141–12	72–66	71–110	2–7	4.07
Dick Starr	37	19–7–2	11–11 (.500)	159–148–18	77–74	69–87	2	4.19

NOTES: (1) An asterisk indicates that the pitcher threw left–handed. (2) The following pitchers had less than 45 innings pitched (with their W–L record in parentheses)—Charles Bowers (1–0); Ben Flowers (3–2); Clarence Marshall (0–1); Lou Possehl (0–1); Vern Taylor (0–0).

the O's squared off against the first-place Rochester Red Wings (97–57, .630). Fox was Baltimore's starting pitcher in the opening game. He had allowed a solitary run through six frames before running into difficulty in the seventh when, after he had retired the first two batters, he gave up a single to Vern Benson and hit Charley Kress with a pitched ball. Fortunately, Kent Peterson came in to put out the fire by retiring the .346-batting Tom Burgess, thereby preserving the 2–1 Orioles lead. Unfortunately, Peterson was racked for three runs in the bottom of the eighth inning and the Flock was shackled with a 4–2 defeat.

Baltimore managed to win the next three games to take a 3–1 lead into game five. Fox started that game at home in Memorial Stadium. An O's victory would clinch the first round and promote them into the second round against the winner of the Montreal-vs.-Buffalo series. Howie pitched scoreless ball through the first three frames. The O's took a 1–0 lead in the bottom of the third when Fox singled, advanced to second on a walk to John Mayo, and scored on a single to left by Ralph (Putsy) Caballero. But in the top of the fourth inning, Rochester came right back with a pair of runs to gain the advantage. Then, in the fifth, Fox gave up a two-out solo homer to player-manager Harry Walker. Howie then pitched scoreless ball in the sixth and seventh sessions, keeping the O's in close striking distance. However, in the eighth Fox and two relievers were mauled. Wally Moon led off with a walk. Benson then scratched a bunt hit trying to sacrifice. The ball could have been handled by either Fox or first baseman Mayo, both hesitating for the other. Howie was derricked at this point and replaced by Heintzelman, who was subsequently replaced by Jack Sanford. The end result was the Red Wings tallied six runs and wound up winning the game, 9–2. Rochester would win the next two games and the series, four games to three. Baltimore's 1953 minor league season was finished. Baltimore's 1954 major league presence commenced just a week later.

1954: The "New" Orioles

Following the September 29, 1953, announcement that the St. Louis Browns were moving to Baltimore for the 1954 season, Arthur Ehlers, the general manager of the "new" Orioles, began to assemble the spring training roster. On January 16 it was reported that Ehlers "probably will take Howie Fox and Damon Phillips to the major-league Orioles spring base at Yuma, Ariz., next month."[6] And, when the "First Baltimore A.L. Roster in 50 Years" was published in the February 17, 1954, issue of *The Sporting News*, both Fox and Phillips

were on it.[7] However, before the completion of the 1954 Cactus League, the Orioles sold Phillips's contract to the Richmond Virginians.[8] When the 1954 Opening Day arrived on April 13, Howie Fox was one of 13 pitchers on the regular-season roster.[9] (The complete Opening Day roster is provided in the Appendix.) Howie's first mound appearance came on April 17 against the Tigers at Memorial Stadium, in relief of starter Joe Coleman. When he came in to pitch the ninth, "Howie [got] a rousing welcome as he made his first appearance here as a major leaguer."[10] He retired Jim Delsing on a groundout (third baseman Vern Stephens to first baseman Eddie Waitkus), walked Harvey Kuenn, and finished up by getting Ray Boone to ground into a 6–4–3 double play (Billy Hunter to Bobby Young to Waitkus).

For the remainder of the season Howie was used exclusively in relief. Overall he appeared in 38 games with a total of 73.2 innings pitched; he compiled a 1–2 record and a 2–2 SV-BSV ledger. Howie's two best stretches of relief work were as follows:

(1) The seven games from June 4 through June 19 in which he gave up one run in 11 innings

(2) The six games between June 23 and July 18 in which he pitched shutout ball for 16.1 innings

From June 4 through July 18 he was pretty much lights-out as he gave up only three earned runs in 27.1 innings, affording an ERA of 0.99 for that stretch. However, for the entire 1954 season, Fox's ERA was 3.67. For comparison, Table 2 lists the pertinent statistics for the four pitchers who were the principal relief hurlers for the 1954 Orioles. (The Appendix provides game-by-game details for Fox's 38 games.)

Howie achieved his only victory in the May 10 game against the visiting Philadelphia Athletics. The O's starting pitcher, Don Larsen, was rocked for four runs in the top of the seventh, giving the A's a 5–3 lead. Larsen was pinch-hit for in the bottom of the seventh and Fox took over the mound duties in the top of the eighth. Howie set down the three men he faced (Lou Limmer, Gus Zernial, and Bill Renna) in 1–2–3 fashion. In the top of the ninth, Howie was nicked for a run that put Philadelphia on top, 6–3. But, the Flock rallied in the bottom of the ninth, tallying four runs to win the game. Walks to Clint Courtney and Jim Fridley (batting for Fox) and a single by Bobby Young loaded the bases. Gil Coan's single batted in Courtney,

Table 2. Final Regular-Season Statistics for 1954 Orioles Hurlers Who Were Principal Relievers

Pitcher	G-GR-GF	W-L (AVE)	SV-BS (AVE)	IP-H-HR	R-ER	BB-SO	HB-WP	ERA
Bob Chakales	38–32–28	3–4 (.429)	4–0 (1.000)	57.1–45–3	18–17	25–30	0–0	2.67
Howie Fox	38–38–23	1–2 (.333)	2–2 (.500)	73.2–80–2	33–30	34–27	2–3	3.67
Marlin Stuart	22–22–19	1–2 (.333)	2–1 (.667)	38.1–46–2	23–19	15–13	2–1	4.46
Mike Blyzka	37–37–17	1–5 (.167)	1–1 (.500)	86.1–83–2	48–45	51–35	0–1	4.69

NOTES: (1) Statistics given in the "SV–BSV (AVE)" column are from the Baseball–Reference website; all other statistics are from the Retrosheet website, and were obtained by summing the numbers given in the Retrosheet Player Daily File (i.e., not from the Player Profile Page). (2) The statistics for Bob Chakales are for his relief appearances only—i.e., the numbers for his games started appearances were not included in summing the numbers given in his Retrosheet Player Daily File. For example, while with Baltimore, his overall W–L record was 3–7; in the games he started his W–L record was 0–3; therefore his W–L as a relief pitcher was 3–4. The same procedure was employed for the statistics in the other columns. (3) The following pitchers also had relief appearances (G–GR–GF): Ryne Duren (1–1–0); Jay Heard (2–2–0); Dave Koslo (3–2–1); Lou Kretlow (32–12–2); Don Larsen (29–1–1); Dick Littlefield (3–3–1); Billy O'Dell (7–5–4).

and Dick Kryhoski's double plated Fridley and Young. Sam Mele then hit a sacrifice fly to bring in Coan with the game-winning marker.

Although saves were not tracked at the time, Fox picked up his first one in the game on June 12 at Griffith Stadium against the Washington Nationals. He took over for starter Lou Kretlow in the bottom of the ninth with the O's leading, 7–3. Howie proceeded to retire the first two batters (Tom Umphlett and Ed Fitz Gerald) before walking Wayne Terwilliger. He then struck out Clyde Vollmer to end the game.

The last game that Fox pitched for the 1954 Flock was on September 25 against the White Sox; it was also the final game of the season. Chicago had a 9–0 lead when Howie took the mound to start the top of the eighth. He set the Pale Hose down in order, getting Chico Carrasquel on a popout, Nellie Fox on a flyout, and Minnie Minoso on a groundout. However, in the ninth, Fox was rocked for a pair of tallies. After he had retired the first two batters (Phil Cavarretta and Jim Rivera), Willard Marshall singled and Sherman Lollar doubled, putting runners at third and second. Joe Kirrene then hit a two-run single before Howie got Billy Pierce to ground out to end the inning.

1955: Move to the Missions

The 1954 major league Orioles (54–100) did not fare as well as the 1953 minor league Orioles (82–72). The 1954 Flock ended up in seventh place, 57 games behind the AL pennant-winning Cleveland Indians. To deal with this poor-performance issue, one major change was announced *prior to the conclusion of the 1954 season*—General Manager Ehlers and Field Manager Jimmy Dykes would be replaced by Paul Richards (who relinquished his managership of the White Sox with nine games left).[11] There were also many changes in the player roster. Howie Fox, who had played some winter ball with the Caracas Lions in the Venezuelan League after the 1954 campaign ended, signed his 1955 Orioles contract on February 8.[12] He was included in the Spring Training Roster published in the *1955 Baltimore Orioles Sketch Book*.

But in early March he was assigned to the San Antonio Missions (the O's AA farm club in the Texas League) as a pitcher-coach to help with the team's training and then later to go on San Antonio's roster as a regular hurler.[13] Even though Fox had joined the Missions, he was retained on the Baltimore roster until May 3, when he was released by the Orioles. This allowed Fox to accrue the time needed to reach ten-year status as a big leaguer.[14] In his San Antonio debut, on May 7 against Shreveport, Howie tossed a four-hitter to defeat the Sports, 6–2. For his full season with San Antonio Howie appeared in 29 games, ten of which were starting assignments. His W-L record was 3–8 (.273) and his ERA was 3.89 in 104 innings pitched. With their second-place finish, the Missions earned a spot in the playoffs. However, they were eliminated (four games to two) in the first round by Shreveport. Howie pitched in relief in three of the six games without having a decision. He gave up 2 runs (both earned) on six hits in four innings; he walked two batters and struck out one. Fox's final game was on September 11; he hurled a scoreless 8th inning in San Antonio's 11–7 setback to Shreveport in game five. As it turned out, the 1955 campaign was the final season in Howie Fox's professional baseball career. Tragically, shortly after the season ended, Howie Fox was murdered on October 9.[15]

CONCLUDING REMARKS

Altogether, in his two seasons with Baltimore, Howie Fox won 16 games and lost 12. He was the ace of the O's pitching staff in 1953, the team's last year. He was probably the second-best fireman on the Flock's relief corps in 1954 and the only man to play for both of those minor league and major league Orioles teams. ■

Acknowledgments

It is a pleasure to express my tremendous gratitude to Cassidy Lent, Research Librarian at the National Baseball Hall of Fame and Museum, for graciously providing scans of the "Player Information Cards File" and "Player Clippings File" for Howie Fox, and selected pages from *The 1955 Baltimore Orioles Sketch Book* and *The 1955 Sporting News Dope Book*. I also express my grateful thanks to Cliff Blau for his outstanding fact-checking of the information presented in this article.

Dedication

I gratefully dedicate this article to my good friend David Newman, a superb baseball researcher who has enthusiastically helped me out numerous times with special trips to the Library of Congress. THANKS so very much, Dave, for your expert collaboration. All the best to you and Carol!

Notes

1. J.G. Taylor Spink in collaboration with Paul A. Rickart, Ernest J. Lanigan, and Clifford Kachline, "The Year 1953 in Review," *Baseball Guide and Record Book 1954* (St. Louis, MO: The Sporting News, 1954), 95.
2. Hugh Trader, Jr., "Orioles Retain Pair of Vets, Sell 14 From Team's International Roster," *The Sporting News*, January 27, 1954, 16.
3. While Howie Fox is unique in being the only player from the 1953 *minor* league Baltimore Orioles to play with the *major* league Orioles in 1954, there were five other players who had played with the minor league Orioles *prior* to 1953 and subsequently played with the major league Orioles in 1954 or later: Bob Kuzava, Joe Frazier, Bobby Avila, Bobby Young, and Jim Dyck. The Appendix provides the pertinent information for each of these players.
4. C.M. Gibbs, "Pitcher Wins Contest With Two Men Out—Singles To Score Kearns; Gains Victory in Relief Role," *Baltimore Sun*, May 13, 1953, 21.
5. Statistics compiled by Al Munro, Elias Baseball Bureau, from *Baseball Guide and Record Book 1954*, 214.
6. Louis M. Hatter, "Richmond Nine Eyes Ex-Birds," *Baltimore Sun*, January 16, 1954, 11.
7. Herb Heft, "Orioles Weak in Pitching? Not in Numbers at Least," *The Sporting News*, February 17, 1954, 16.
8. "Deals of the Week," The Sporting News, April 7, 1954, 28.
9. "Orioles Roster and Playing Records," *The* (Baltimore) *Evening Sun*, April 15, 1954, 58.
10. Ned Burks, "Orioles Bow to Tigers, 1–0," *Baltimore Sun*, April 18, 1954, 29.
11. Ned Burks, "Richards Accepts 3-Year Contract With Orioles," *Baltimore Sun*, September 15, 1954, 17.
12. Bob Maisel, "11 Players Remain Out of Bird Fold…Howie Fox Signs Oriole Contract," *Baltimore Sun*, February 8, 1955, 19.
13. "Fox Sent to San Antonio," *The Evening Sun*, March 2, 1955, 50. See also related items in *Baltimore Sun*, March 3, 1955, 21 and *The Evening Sun*, March 29, 1955, 29.
14. Jesse A. Linthicum, "Bird Seed," *The Sporting News*, March 9, 1955, 24. See also related items in *The Sporting News*, May 18, 1955, 32, 34.
15. "Howie Fox, Former Oriole, Stabbed to Death in Texas," *Baltimore Sun*, October 10, 1955, 1.

Appendices

https://sabr.org/journal/article/appendix-1-howie-fox-baltimores-unique-oriole

A-1. Where the 1953 Baltimore Orioles Played in 1954; The Men Who Participated in the 1953 Playoffs.

A-2. Where the 1953 Baltimore Orioles Played in 1954; The Men Who Did Not Participate in the 1953 Playoffs.

B. Paths Followed by the Men Who Played for the Baltimore Orioles in Both the Minor and Major Leagues.

C. Brief Summary of Howie Fox's Professional Baseball Career.

D. Howie Fox's Game-By-Game Pitching Record with the 1953 Baltimore Orioles.

E. Opening Day Player Roster for the 1954 Baltimore Orioles.

F. Howie Fox's Game-By-Game Pitching Record with the 1954 Baltimore Orioles.

Dick Armstrong

Orioles PR Pioneer and His "Mr. Oriole"

Bob Golon

Major league public relations (PR) practices evolved slowly during the first half of the twentieth century. In the early days, front offices had only a few employees, more resembling mom and pop businesses than the major corporations they are today. Teams today have entire departments devoted to public relations, community outreach, and media, but in the early part of last century, local newspaper writers often functioned as non-salaried ambassadors for the clubs, actively involved in both promoting and defending the game to the public.[1] The effects of the 1930s depression and World War II forced the clubs to reevaluate their PR efforts in attracting fans back into ballparks. During the 1940s, clubs began using professional advertising agencies to this end, then gradually established in-house PR representatives to serve as a direct link between the clubs, the press, and the fans. By 1951, 14 of the 16 major league clubs had PR directors.[2]

Baltimore native Richard Stoll (Dick) Armstrong became the first PR director of Connie Mack's Philadelphia A's in 1950. The Princeton-educated 25-year-old attracted Mack's attention while spending the 1947–49 seasons in the A's minor league organization, first as a player and then as business manager of the Portsmouth (Ohio) A's of the Ohio-Indiana League. A's farm director Art Ehlers spotted business sense and leadership qualities in the young Armstrong, and in 1949 encouraged him to submit a proposal for the newly-established position of A's public relations director. Armstrong got the job based on his vision for a golden jubilee celebration of Connie Mack's 50 years with the A's in 1950.[3] J.G. Taylor Spink of *The Sporting News* referred to Armstrong as "a young man with ideas."[4] He became known for his innovative promotions for the otherwise downtrodden A's. Armstrong left the A's in 1953 to accept a position as copy and plans director for the W. Wallace Orr advertising agency in Philadelphia. Even though he left the game, he never strayed far from it and continued assisting the A's as their account manager with the Orr Agency.[5]

In late 1953, the majority owners of the St. Louis Browns sold the American League club to a Maryland group led by attorney Clarence W. Miles. The triple-A Orioles were a successful minor league club, and their strong attendance convinced American League owners to award Miles the AL franchise in Baltimore for the 1954 season. Miles brought in Art Ehlers from the A's as general manager, and Ehlers immediately knew he wanted Dick Armstrong as his PR director.[6] Dick embraced the challenge of selling major league baseball to his hometown, and brought with him the same out-of-the-box creativity from his days in Philadelphia.

There was much to be done, including the design of promotional materials, ticket plans, and advertising strategies with the local media. Armstrong realized he needed a likable symbol to be used as a logo on team promotional materials. With the help of *Baltimore Sun* cartoonist Jim Hartzell, the original "Mr. Oriole" was born. "I was looking for a jaunty but likable bird, one with plenty of personality…and his perky bird face was quickly popularized," Armstrong recalled.[7] After Mr. Oriole appeared on the cover of the 1954 Orioles Yearbook, Armstrong took his smiling bird to a whole new level as baseball's first stylized, in-stadium performing mascot— a forerunner of the mascots that became popular in major and minor league stadiums from the 1960s until today.

Armstrong wondered "if it would be possible to create a costume that would replicate the expression and appearance of Mr. Oriole so that a three-dimensional version of the bird could cavort on the field and in the stands during the games."[8] His long-time friend Johnny Myers knew a designer who used the cartoon Mr. Oriole as a model to produce an excellent costume likeness of the bird, complete with feathered wing stripes. Myers also happened to be an accomplished trumpet player with a natural stage presence, and Armstrong convinced his friend to dress in the suit and take his act to the ballpark. "When the strikingly colorful bird made his first public appearance at Memorial Stadium following a proper introduction over the public address system, the fans went wild," explained Armstrong, "but the piece de resistance was when he whipped out from beneath one of his feathered wings a trumpet, which he could play through his beak…the effect was sensational! We had the only trumpet-playing bird in captivity!"[9]

Around 2013, Armstrong contacted the Orioles office to inquire if they knew of the whereabouts of the Mr. Oriole costume. "Apparently, the costume disappeared along with many other invaluable materials… when the Birds moved to Camden Yards," Armstrong recalled. "The person I talked with had never heard of Mr. Oriole. 'Our mascot is The Bird,' he declared, 'He was hatched in 1979.'"[10] Armstrong explained to the person that The Bird had a predecessor who was hatched in 1954. The Mascot Hall of Fame in Whiting, Indiana, included The Oriole Bird in its Class of 2020 in June, and they have updated the historical record concerning his origins. "In the case of the Oriole Bird," explains museum executive director Orestes Hernandez, "we recently discovered that he was introduced as the mascot of the franchise earlier than first thought. Previously it was thought Mr. Met was the first to have been introduced. The Bird has Mr. Met beat by a long shot!"[11]

While concerned with entertainment and promotions for short-term fan appeal, Armstrong understood that the long-term viability of the Orioles franchise depended on a thorough knowledge of the fan base. Having studied scientific polling techniques at Princeton University, Armstrong knew research was a necessity.[12] He had also worked for pollster George Gallup in 1948, polling presidential preferences in the New York area.[13] Armstrong embarked on what was believed to be the first fan survey ever taken at the major league level utilizing scientific polling methods in 1954.[14] Conducted at games during July and August, 2,500 questionnaires containing 19 questions were distributed; 2,400 were returned. Surveys were handed out to fans upon arrival at the park, and collected by the third inning, before the score of the game could influence fan responses.[15] The results revealed some surprises about the average fan in the ballpark, chief among them that 26.1 per cent of attendees came from out-of-town (as opposed to five per cent forecasted prior to the season) and these fans contributed at least an additional $5.5 million to Baltimore's economy in 1954.[16]

The findings and techniques of the survey were published throughout major league baseball and resulted in Armstrong receiving queries from a national audience.[17] In *The Sporting News*, cartoonist Walt Munson devoted a multi-column spread to the survey results, and the paper opined in its editorial column

OPENING-YEAR OFFICIAL SOUVENIR SKETCHBOOK

The original Mr. Oriole logo was drawn by Jim Hartzell of the Baltimore Sun. Dick Armstrong then created the major leagues' first performing mascot via a costume based on Hartzell's drawing.

that the "latest evidence of the Orioles' wide-awake approach is the poll conducted by Publicist Dick Armstrong...the comprehensive nature of his questionnaire and the useful information by it seldom have been matched by similar endeavors."[18] Dick Armstrong established himself as a rising star in major league administration and his future in PR seemed secure.

But in 1955 Armstrong heard a different calling. During spring training at Daytona Beach that year, Armstrong received a personal calling to the ministry, which he described as his "Damascus Road Experience."[19] He left the Orioles at the end of the 1955 season to study at the Princeton Theological Seminary. Armstrong spent the next 60-plus years, until his death in early 2019, as a pastor, educator, author, and missionary in the Presbyterian Church. He was also one of the founding members of the Fellowship of Christian Athletes.[20]

Dick Armstrong never forgot his Baltimore roots, and was a life-long devotee of the Orioles. On August 8, 2014, the Orioles celebrated their 60th anniversary in Baltimore at Camden Yards, and Armstrong was invited to throw the first pitch as the only surviving member of the 1954 Orioles front office. Dick was proud to say, "I somehow managed to get the ball over the plate."[21] ■

Notes

1. William B. Anderson, "Crafting the National Pastime's Image: The History of Major League Baseball Public Relations," *Journalism and Communication Monographs* 5, no. 1 (2003) 12.
2. Anderson, "Crafting the National Pastime's Image..."
3. Dick Armstrong, telephone conversation with Bob Golon, November 16, 2018.
4. J.G. Taylor Spink, "He's Giving Young Ideas to Athletics," *The Sporting News*, October 1950, article accessed from the Armstrong Collection, National Baseball Hall of Fame Library, Cooperstown, NY. BA MS 110, October 1, 2018.
5. Richard Stoll Armstrong, *A Sense of Being Called* (Eugene, OR: Cascade Books, 2011), 7.
6. Armstrong, *A Sense of Being Called*, 8.
7. Richard Stoll Armstrong, *Minding What Matters* (blog), "Mr. Met Was Not the First M.L Mascot!" May 4, 2012. Accessed at http://rsarm.blogspot.com.
8. Armstrong, *Minding What Matters*.
9. Armstrong, *Minding What Matters*.
10. Armstrong, *Minding What Matters*.
11. Mail from Orestes Hernandez, Executive Director of the Mascot Hall of Fame, Whiting, IN. January 27, 2020.
12. "BalKmore Polls Its Fans, Finds Only 65 Per Cent of Them Root for Orioles," *Washington Post*, January 6, 1955.
13. Herb Heft, "Armstrong Worked on 1948 Presidential Poll by Gallup," *The Sporting News*, January 12, 1955.
14. "Baltimore Polls Its Fans..." *Washington Post*,.
15. Richard Stoll Armstrong, *Baltimore Baseball Club Survey, 1954*, (in-house publication) January 1955.
16. Heft, "Armstrong Worked on 1948 Presidential Poll by Gallup."
17. Armstrong Collection, National Baseball Hall of Fame Library, Cooperstown, NY. BA MS 110, Box 4 Folder 3.
18. "Games $ Value to Community Shown," *The Sporting News*, January 19, 1955.
19. Armstrong, *A Sense of Being Called*, 19.
20. Armstrong, *A Sense of Being Called*, 80.
21. Richard Stoll Armstrong, *Minding What Matters* (blog), "A First and Last Pitch," May 2014. Accessed at http://rsarm.blogspot.com.

The Final Flight of Tom Gastall

Cort Vitty

The 1955 crop of baseball "bonus babies" included Massachusetts native Tom Gastall, born on June 13, 1932, in Fall River, to Thomas and Concetta Gastall. (A "bonus baby" rule was first implemented by the major leagues in 1947, intended to restrict the inflated offers made by wealthy club owners seeking to monopolize the best young talent.[1] Stipulated in the rule implemented in 1953 was the requirement that prospects signing a contract exceeding $4,000 remain on the major-league roster, rather than honing their skills at the minor-league level, for two years.) Young Tom developed into an exceptional all-around athlete while attending Durfee High School in Fall River, class of 1951.

Tom next attended Boston University, where the 6-foot-2, 187-pounder was a multisport star, including starting at quarterback on the football team. In a grim coincidence, Gastall took over signal-calling duties following the graduation of Harry Agganis, who, like Gastall, was a prized baseball prospect who would meet an early end.[2]

Despite the potential of a promising gridiron career, Gastall chose to sign a baseball contract following graduation. At the time, he was considered "the finest catching prospect since Mickey Cochrane in the greater Boston Area."[3] The Baltimore Orioles ownership group exhibited a firm commitment toward improving the performance of the club by signing Gastall to a $40,000 contract.

The right-handed hitter reported to Orioles spring training in Scottsdale, Arizona, in 1955. Gastall immediately struck teammates as a nice, kind-hearted guy. This view apparently stemmed from an incident early in spring training. Gastall found a stray dog wandering around the team's training facility—or the pooch located Tom. Gastall and the pup became inseparable; his new canine companion followed him everywhere. The tuckered-out pup routinely napped in the pocket of Tom's catcher's mitt.[4]

During the 1955 season, Gastall saw action in 20 major-league games. He essentially served as the team's fourth-string catcher, slotted behind Hal Smith, Gus Triandos and the competent Les Moss. Facing big-league pitching, Gastall recorded three singles and a double in 27 at-bats, compiling a batting mark of .148/.233/.185.

Gastall used $2,000 of his bonus money to become the proud owner of a second-hand Ercoupe small aircraft. He housed the plane at Harbor Field, a small airport just east of Baltimore City. Soon after Gastall made the purchase, a fellow pilot recognized the plane as an aircraft previously involved in an accident.[5]

In the 1955–56 offseason, Gastall devoted a good deal of his time to taking practice flights; his student license qualified him to fly solo only in a small aircraft. Gastall diligently worked toward logging sufficient flying hours to become a full-fledged pilot.

On September 19, 1956, the Orioles returned home from a road trip and manager Paul Richards announced that there would be a workout the next day, an open date on the schedule. The day dawned bright and sunny, but gusty winds began swirling around the field at noontime. The rapidly changing weather conditions prompted Richards to cancel the afternoon practice.

Suddenly presented with an unexpected free afternoon, Gastall considered taking a flight and logging some flying hours. Gastall had feared that Richards might try to stop him from flying, but numerous teammates knew of his hobby. Upon hearing Gastall's plan for the afternoon, teammate Willy Miranda minced no words: "The wind will blow that bucket of bolts all over the place."[6] Gastall shrugged and issued his standard reply to such comments, saying that flying was safer than driving.[7] Gastall's mentor and friend, first-string catcher Triandos, also attempted to dissuade him from flying.

Gastall arrived at Harbor Field at around 4:50 PM to prepare for takeoff. About 90 minutes into the flight, he issued a distress message via radio: "I'm going down into the water."[8] It was his only transmission.

A rescue force of 21 planes and nine boats was quickly deployed. Despite this intensive effort, no remains were recovered.

BALTIMORE ORIOLES

Tom Gastall was only 24 when his flight met its tragic end.

The next night, as teammates prepared for Baltimore's game against the Washington Nationals, the clubhouse went silent following an announcement about Gastall's crash. The Orioles gathered around his locker, devoting a moment of silent prayer in acknowledgment of his apparent passing. Uniform number 10 was still hanging next to his catcher's gear.

During the search, a set of seat cushions washed ashore near Riviera Beach, and Tom's wife, Rosemary, was contacted at the couple's home. She arrived on the scene to examine the debris and sadly verified the gear as belonging to Tom.[9]

Finally, on the morning of September 25, a body washed ashore onto Riviera Beach. A personalized Boston University ring bearing the inscription "TEG 1955" confirmed it as Tom Gastall's body. Upon hearing the news, road roommate Billy Gardner said, "It's the saddest story there is, a good guy dying like that with his whole life ahead of him."[10]

Tom Gastall saw action in 52 games over two major-league seasons, with 15 hits in 83 at-bats; he registered six bases-on-balls while striking out 13 times. His lifetime batting average was .181, with an on-base average of .242 and a slugging average of .217. He was only 24 when he died. There's no telling what the future may have brought.

Funeral services were held on September 29, 1956, at St. Patrick's Catholic Church in Fall River. Survivors included Rosemary and their 15-month-old son.

In his *Baltimore Sun* column, sports editor Bob Maisel wrote: "The home runs and no-hit games eventually fade, but the sight of other players casting sidelong glances at a locker they knew would never be used again is something that can't be forgotten."[11] ■

Notes

1. Paul Dickson, *The Baseball Dictionary*, Third Edition (New York: Norton & Company, 2011), 125.
2. Agganis was a first baseman who turned down a big contract from the Cleveland Browns to sign with the Boston Red Sox, for whom he played in 1954 and '55. He died of a pulmonary embolism at the age of 26 on June 27, 1955. Mark Brown and Mark Armour, "Harry Agganis," SABR Biography Project, https://sabr.org/bioproj/person/69d56ecd.
3. "Tom Gastall, Orioles Player; Missing After Flight Over Harbor," *Baltimore Sun*, September 21, 1956.
4. Bob Maisel, "Morning After," *Baltimore Sun*, January 15, 1961.
5. Maisel.
6. Maisel.
7. Maisel.
8. *Baltimore Sun*, September 21, 1956.
9. "Tom Gastall's Body Found at Riviera Beach," *Baltimore Sun*, September 26, 1956.
10. Bob Maisel, "Gloom Fills Bird Players," *Baltimore Sun*, September 23, 1956.
11. Maisel.

The 1958 Midsummer Classic

July 8, 1958: American League 4, National League 3, at Memorial Stadium, Baltimore

Jimmy Keenan

Major league baseball held its 25th annual All-Star Game at Memorial Stadium in Baltimore on July 8, 1958. The game was broadcast nationally on NBC Radio and TV. Ernie Harwell and Bob Neal were the radio announcers while Mel Allen and Al Helfer handled the television broadcast. MLB had recently signed a five-year contract with NBC worth an estimated $3.25 million per year for exclusive rights to the All-Star Game and World Series. A portion of the gate receipts and NBC revenue from the game would go directly to the Players Pension Fund.

The Cincinnati Reds had monopolized the voting in 1957 thanks to blatant ballot-box stuffing by their fans. At that point, Commissioner Ford Frick stepped in. To keep the selections balanced, Frick dropped two Cincinnati players, replacing them with Willie Mays and Henry Aaron. Stan Musial was also added (though the eventual tally would show he received sufficient votes to be named to the roster regardless).

A new format was developed for 1958 to avoid geographic bias. The players, coaches, and managers would select eight starting position players from their respective leagues. In order to circumvent any favoritism, no one could choose a player from his own team. Baltimore fans were elated when Gus Triandos of the Orioles edged out Yankees backstop Yogi Berra as the American League's starting catcher.

The managers from the previous year's World Series would pilot the All-Star squads in addition to selecting the remaining 17 players, including their starting pitchers. Each starting player except the pitchers was required to play three innings unless he was injured.

The Emerson Hotel served as the headquarters for the American League contingent as well as the radio and press corps. Commissioner Frick and his staff were quartered at the Sheraton-Belvedere, while the National League entourage stayed at the Lord Baltimore. The pre-game festivities included a parade that featured players from both leagues riding in open convertibles from downtown Baltimore to Memorial Stadium on 33rd Street.

It was a humid day with temperatures hovering around 90 degrees as the first of the 48,829 fans passed through the turnstiles at the ballpark. The attendance for the game was the second largest in Baltimore baseball history. The highest total had been on October 9, 1944, when the International League Orioles drew 52,833 in Game Four of the Junior World Series against Louisville. The huge crowd in 1944 had served notice to the baseball world that Baltimore was ready to support a major-league team.

Coming into the 1958 All-Star Game, the American League held a 14–10 edge over the senior circuit. Milwaukee Braves manager Fred Haney was at the helm of the Nationals while Yankees skipper Casey Stengel led the Americans. Haney chose the mainstay of his staff, Warren Spahn, as his starter. Stengel, showing

Gus Triandos was the starting catcher in the 1958 All-Star game, one of only two hometown Orioles to make the AL squad.

a similar sentiment, gave the starting nod to Yankee Bob Turley.

Both starting pitchers had uncommon deliveries. Spahn, a master of changing speeds, employed an elongated leg kick, his knee rising almost up to his shoulder. During his follow-through, his glove deceptively passed by his face as he delivered the baseball.

Turley had no discernible windup. It was strictly rear back and fire. With a variety of pitches in his arsenal, it was his blazing fastball that earned him the nickname "Bullet Bob." Turley lived in the Baltimore suburb of Lutherville. Pitching for the Orioles in 1954, he'd won the inaugural home opener at Memorial Stadium.

Baltimore's ballpark had its own unique dimensions. The distance down each foul line was 309 feet. Short by most standards, the degree of difficulty was heightened by a 14-foot wall that started at each outfield corner. The imposing barrier angled out to 360 feet, where it met a seven-foot-high chain-link fence that ringed the perimeter of the outfield. The deepest part of the park was 410 feet in center. Additional seating was added for the game alongside each dugout, which necessitated moving the bullpens from foul territory to behind the outfield fence.

After Vice President Richard Nixon tossed the ceremonial first ball, Mays stepped to the plate. Haney mixed things up by putting Mays, who had been hitting third for San Francisco, in the leadoff spot. The move paid off when the Giants star smacked Turley's first pitch off the third-base bag. The ball caromed high in the air, and by the time it landed in Frank Malzone's glove, Mays was past the bag at first. Bob Skinner followed with a fly out to right.

The next batter was Stan Musial, playing in his 15th All-Star Game. With the count 3–1, Musial stroked a single to right field. Mays, running on the pitch, made it all the way to third. The hit was the 17th of Musial's All-Star career. Aaron then lofted a sacrifice fly to deep left center that plated Mays. Turley plunked Ernie Banks in the back with a curveball. After Frank Thomas walked to load the bases, Stengel came out to the mound for a conference. With Bill Mazeroski at the plate, Turley's first toss to the Pittsburgh second baseman eluded the glove of Triandos, sending Musial home with the second run of the game. Mazeroski drove the next pitch into left field. Bob Cerv, playing with a broken toe, lost his balance as he ran in for the ball, but he somehow managed to make the shoestring grab for the final out.

Leading off the Americans' half of the first, Nellie Fox reached on a throwing error by shortstop Banks

Billy O'Dell, the second Oriole on the All-Star roster, finished the game by setting down all nine men he faced. He garnered the Hearst Newspaper Award for his performance.

and went to third on a single by Mickey Mantle. The next man, Jackie Jensen, leading both leagues with 24 home runs, grounded into a double play, with Fox scoring. Cerv singled but Bill Skowron flied out to end the frame.

Del Crandall was retired starting off the top of the second. Spahn was able to work Turley for a walk before being erased on a Mays fielder's choice. With Skinner at-bat, Mays took off for second. Triandos's peg got past Luis Aparicio, allowing Mays to advance to third. Skinner proceeded to knock Turley out of the box with an RBI single. Stengel replaced Turley with Cleveland Indians pitcher Ray Narleski, who checked the threat by retiring Musial on an infield popup.

With one down in the bottom of the second, Triandos drove a base hit up the middle. Aparicio hit into a fielder's choice, forcing Triandos. Narleski came through with a safety, putting two men on base. After a Fox RBI single, Mantle flied out, halting the rally.

For the next few frames, both pitchers held their opponents scoreless. Bob Friend replaced Spahn in the bottom of the fourth.

Mickey Vernon, pinch-hitting for Narleski, opened the fifth with a single. Fox followed suit with Mantle drawing a walk to load the bases. Vernon scored on a

Jensen groundout. After Cerv was walked intentionally, Skowron bounced into an inning-ending double play.

Early Wynn came in for Narleski in the sixth, retiring the side in order.

Malzone started off the bottom of the stanza with a single. A crescendo of boos rose from the stands as Stengel sent in Berra to pinch-hit for Triandos. Berra's infield popout elicited a chorus of sarcastic hurrahs from the Baltimore crowd. Stengel told a reporter after the game, "I have been hissed all my life. You can't be in this business a long time and have all the cheers."[1]

The next man up was Ted Williams, pinch-hitting for Aparicio. He proceeded to bounce a chopper to the left side that Thomas mishandled. With runners now on first and second, Gil McDougald, batting for Wynn, lofted a single into short left center that scored Malzone. With the score 4–3 in favor of the Americans, Haney pulled Friend, replacing him with Larry Jackson. Fox grounded into a double play to end the inning.

In the seventh, Stengel brought in 25-year-old Orioles southpaw Billy O'Dell from the bullpen. O'Dell, the first "Bonus Baby" signed by Baltimore in 1954, retired the next nine batters in order on 27 pitches, sealing the win for the American League.[2] Turk Farrell of the Phillies pitched the last two innings for the Nationals, striking out four batters, including Williams. Baltimore native Al Kaline replaced Williams in left field in the top of the ninth.

In what was the first All-Star Game without an extra-base hit, there were three outstanding defensive plays, two by Cerv, the other by Williams. In addition to the Mazeroski grab, Cerv slammed into the left-field wall hauling in a Del Crandall drive in the sixth. An inning later, Williams made a leaping catch, robbing pinch-hitter Johnny Logan.

When asked about his game-winning bloop hit after the game, McDougald, who was in the midst of an 0-for-18 slump, replied, "I'm not ashamed of it. The way I have been hitting lately, I'll take anything."[3]

Stengel congratulated his players in the clubhouse: "I want to thank all you men for a splendid job. But most of all I want to shake the hand of this young fella right out here from the Orioles. He made all those National Leaguers look the same size didn't he?"[4]

O'Dell, who received the Hearst Newspaper Award for his outstanding performance, told reporters, "The only pitches I used were my slider and fastball. When my control is good I know I'll do all right. I had only one worry all the time I was out there and his name was Stan Musial. It seemed all downhill once I got past him in the eighth inning. I know doggone well that all of those National League hitters are tough or else they wouldn't be there. As far as I was concerned, though, Musial was the fellow that could hurt me the most."[5] ■

Author's Notes

- In 1933, Baltimore native Babe Ruth hit the first home run in the inaugural All-Star Game, leading the American League to a 4–2 victory.
- Baltimorean Eddie Rommel, a former major-league pitcher, started out the 1958 All-Star Game as the home plate umpire. Rommel had served in the same capacity for Baltimore's home opener in 1954. In the spirit of fairness to All-Star competition, Rommel, an American League ump, switched places with third-base umpire Jocko Conlon of the National League in the middle of the fourth inning. While a member of the Philadelphia Athletics, Rommel pitched batting practice at the first All-Star Game in 1933.

Sources

Baseball-Almanac.com
Baseball-Reference.com
Baltimore Sun
Boston Journal
Genealogy Bank
Knoxville News Sentinel
Richmond Times Dispatch
The Sporting News

Notes

1. "Stengel Lauds His Relievers, O'Dell Mostly," *Richmond Daily Dispatch*, July 9, 1958.
2. "Billy O'Dell," BR Bullpen, https://www.baseball-reference.com/bullpen/Billy_O'Dell, accessed March 28, 2020. O'Dell signed with the Orioles for a reported $12,500 on June 8, 1954.
3. "All-Star Twinklers," *The Sporting News*, July 16, 1958.
4. "'Give It All You Got,' Stengel Told O'Dell So Baltimore Lefty Retired Nine in Row," *Milwaukee Journal*, July 9, 1958.
5. Billy O'Dell, "Stan Musial Was My Only Worry in All-Star Game," *Knoxville News-Sentinel*, July 9, 1958.

Stu Miller

The (Almost) Lost Oriole

Wayne M. Towers, PhD

Although best remembered for a windswept balk during the July 11, 1961, All-Star Game in San Francisco, Stuart Leonard "Stu" Miller put together a notable relief career with 153 career saves, 1952–68. He pitched primarily with the New York/San Francisco Giants (47 saves, 1957–62) and, perhaps surprisingly to some, with the Baltimore Orioles (99 saves, 1963–67).[1]

After a humble beginning with the St. Louis Cardinals and Philadelphia Phillies, Miller joined the Giants in New York, then traveled with them to San Francisco where his ill-fated balk took place at San Francisco's Candlestick Park.[2]

Candlestick Park was the home of the San Francisco Giants from 1960 to 1999. It was named for its location at San Francisco Bay's Candlestick Point, which was named in turn for a shorebird called the candlestick bird (*Numenius americanus*; status: *threatened*[4]), a long-legged, long-billed curlew about a foot tall. Considered a delicacy, the birds had been hunted out of the area, but the wind that remained took revenge on the human occupants. According to the National Weather Service, winds there could reach 62 miles-per-hour and shift 180 degrees during the times most games were typically played.[5] Winds during game times were described as "cold," "howling and swirling," and "gale force" and with terms like "small craft warning," "wind pixies," and "devils at play."[6] One promotion awarded hardy fans a medallion called the "Croix de Candlestick" which proclaimed "Veni, Vidi, Vixi"(I came, I saw, I survived).[7]

"The Stick" aka "Windlestick" lived up to its wind-tunnel reputation that All-Star day. Miller was noted for his slight frame.[8] Officially, he was listed at 5-foot-11 and 165 pounds, but observers have estimated him to be anywhere from 5-foot-8, 150 up to 5-foot-11½ and 175.[9] He was thrown off balance after coming to the set position by a gust of wind. Despite a reputation for a deceptive pitching motion with a last-second head fake, he was called for a balk.[10] In the hyperbole that followed, Miller was compared to windblown leaves, Dorothy and Toto in *The Wizard of Oz*, and

later television's *The Flying Nun* (seriously[11]). Miller disliked the exaggerations. "The papers made it sound like I was pinned against the center-field fence," he recalled.[12] "You'd think I'd been blown into the Bay."[13]

The less-remembered part of Miller's career would come with the Baltimore Orioles. Hall of Famer Hoyt Wilhelm's mid-career stay with the Orioles (40 saves, 1958–62) had cemented the bullpen in the Baltimore psyche at a time when bullpen work was viewed as a demotion.[14] As manager Paul Richards was said to have pointed out, "Anyone can start a game but it's important who finishes it!"[15] Miller replaced Wilhelm's (in)famous knuckleball with a variety of off-speed pitches described as somewhere between slow/slower/slowest and slow/slower/reverse.[16] According to *The Great American Baseball Card Flipping, Trading and Bubble Gum Book*, "You had time for a coke and sandwich while waiting for his fastball to arrive."[17] His pitches were labeled change/change-up/change-up curve and a change-up off of a change-up, described as "moth and butterfly," "banana ball and custard pie," having "died from malnutrition," "couldn't break a pane of glass" nor a "wet paper sack."[18]

During the 1960s, Miller's Orioles performance, 99 saves between 1963 and 1967, was comparable to Wilhelm's successes with the Chicago White Sox (99 saves 1963–1968). Miller helped Baltimore to the pennant in 1966 with a team-leading 18 saves and nine bullpen wins.[19] But he was upstaged in the 1966 World Series by the bravura performance of Myron "Moe" Drabowsky aka Miroslav Drabowski.[20]

Known as a journeyman with control issues (1162 career strikeouts against 702 career walks), Drabowsky was more famous for pranks including snakes, hot-foots, firecrackers, phone calls, greased toilet seats, sneezing powder, goldfish in water coolers, and a towed airplane banner.[21] Drabowsky also held the dubious distinctions of surrendering Stan Musial's 3,000th hit and losing Early Wynn's 300th win. Suddenly, he became a World Series legend. He relieved in the third inning of the first game, pitched 6⅔ innings of one-hit, shutout ball, and struck out eleven,

NATIONAL BASEBALL HALL OF FAME AND LIBRARY, COOPERSTOWN, NY

Often remembered for a windswept balk as a San Francisco Giant in a 1961 All-Star Game, Miller was a key contributor to the 1963–67 Orioles.

including six in a row. Perhaps humbly, Drabowsky stated "It's about time I got in the books for something except the wrong end of the record."[22] His triumph was the only relief appearance in the entire Series for the Orioles, who swept the remaining three contests with complete-game shutouts.[23] Afterwards, Drabowsky remained in Baltimore before finishing his career with three different teams.

Miller stayed one more year in Baltimore, then finished his career with the Atlanta Braves, but not before a final indignity in Baltimore. On April 30, 1967, lefty Steve Barber carried a no-hitter into the ninth inning. That inning Barber walked the first two batters, retired two batters, then uncorked a score-tying wild pitch. After walking a third batter, he left with an unenviable line of 10 walks, two hit batsmen, the aforementioned wild pitch, and a fielding error, but no hits.[24] Miller entered the game and induced a surefire rally-ending ground ball, only to have an infielder drop the force-out for an error, allowing the winning run to score. Miller recorded the inning-ending out, but ended up with the dubious honor of sharing (with Barber) the second no-hitter loss in MLB history.[25]

In the end, Miller's positive Baltimore legacy was being the Orioles team career saves leader with 99 until he was supplanted by lefty Felix Anthony "Tippy" Martinez, who earned 105 saves with Baltimore between 1976 and 1986.[26]

Even given the hard luck of the 1961 All-Star balk, the 1966 World Series absence, and the 1967 no-hitter loss, characterizing Stu Miller as a kind of Joe Btfsplk—cartoonist Al Capp's comic character

dogged by perpetual misfortune—would be a mistake. Overall, Miller's record was far from undistinguished. His 153 career saves compare favorably with contemporaries Don McMahon (152) and Ted Abernathy (148), the first reliever to earn over 30 saves in a season. He also compared favorably with Hoyt Wilhelm himself in the 1960s (153 saves, 1960–69). The key difference in Wilhelm's career total is that he added saves in the 1950s (58) and 1970s (17).[27]

In terms of career contemporaries, Miller, McMahon, Abernathy and 1960s-Wilhelm were on a tier just below the most successful relievers in the 1960s like Roy Face (191 career saves, 1953–69), lefty Ron Perranoski (178 career saves, 1961–73), and Lindy McDaniel (174 career saves, 1955–75). Taken together, this half dozen or so represented a relief pitching elite prior to the 1973 advent of the designated hitter.[28]

Although Miller tends to be remembered for the early part of his career with San Francisco rather than the latter years with Baltimore, during which he recorded 99 of 153 career saves, his selections to both the Giants Wall of Fame and the Orioles Hall of Fame preserve the memory of his achievements (and disappointments) for fans who sport the black and orange of the Orioles and Giants. Perhaps the sixtieth anniversary of his infamous All-Star balk (July 11, 2021) or the fifty-fifth anniversary of his lost no-hitter (April 30, 2022) could serve to revive his fame among fans who wear the colors of other teams. As he once reflected: "I guess that's better than 'Stu Who?' I'd rather be remembered for something."[29] ∎

Additional Source

All career statistics from Baseball-Reference.com.

Notes

1. Ron Firmite, "Gone with the wind?," *Sports Illustrated*, September 01, 1986, Accessed January 14, 2019, https://www.si.com/vault/1986/09/01/113879/gonewith-the-wind-the-giants-want-out-of-blustery-candlestick-park-and-one-of-these-daysthey-just-might-get-their-wish; John Thorn, *The Relief Pitcher: Baseball's New Hero* (New York: E.P. Dutton, 1979), 145.

2. Jim Brooks, "Did Stu Miller Really Get Blown Off the Mound at Candlestick Park?" KQED News, January 8, 2016., Accessed November 24, 2019, https://www.kqed.org/news/10400321/did-stu-miller-really-get-blown-off-themound-at-candlestick-park.

3. Alan Taylor, "The Lights Go Out on Candlestick Park," *The Atlantic*, June 11, 2015, Accessed November 24, 2019, https://www.theatlantic.com/photo/2015/06/thelights-go-out-on-candlestick-park/395633.

4. "Candlestick Bird: Numenius americanus," Project Noah, Accessed January 26, 2020, https://www.projectnoah.org/spo2ngs/2088457561; "Long-billed Curlew: Numenius americanus," International Union for Conservation of Nature (IUCN) Red List, Downloaded January 26, 2020, https://www.iucnredlist.org/species/22693195/93390204#taxonomy.

5. Firmite, "Gone with the wind?"

6. Mark Byrnes, "Goodbye, Candlestick Park (Finally)," CityLab, Accessed November 24, 2019, https://www.citylab.com/design/2015/02/

goodbye-finallycandlestick-park/385232/; "Candlestick Park/3Com Park Historical Analysis," *Baseball Almanac*; Brooks, "Did Stu Miller Really Get Blown Off the Mound at Candlestick Park?;" Firmite, "Gone with the wind?"

7. Byrnes, "Goodbye, Candlestick Park (Finally)."

8. Brooks, "Did Stu Miller Really Get Blown Off the Mound at Candlestick Park?;" Firmite, "Gone with the wind?"

9. "Stu Miller," Baseball-Reference.com, Warren Corbett, "Stu Miller," SABR BioProject, Accessed July 4, 2019, https://sabr.org/bioproj/person/f1cee86c.

10. Corbett, "Stu Miller."

11. "The Flying Nun," FETV:real family entertainment, Accessed January 20, 2020, https://fetv.tv/show/the-flying-nun.

12. "1961," Franchise Timeline, MLB.com.

13. Firmite, "Gone with the wind?"

14. Bob Cairns, *Pen Men: Stories Told by the Men Who Brought the Game Relief* (New York: St. Martin's Press, 1992), 249.

15. Cairns, Pen Men, 141. Thorn, *The Relief Pitcher*, 145.

16. James and Neyer, T*he Neyer/James Guide to Pitching: An Historical Comparison of Pitching, Pitchers, and Pitches*, 310. Thorn, *The Relief Pitcher*, 146; Corbett, "Stu Miller."

17. Brendon C. Boyd and Fred C. Harris, *The Great American Baseball Card Flipping, Trading, and Bubble Gum Book* (Boston: Little, Brown and Company, 1973), 59.

18. *The Neyer/James Guide to Pitching*, 309–10; Cairns, *Pen Men*, 119; Corbett, "Stu Miller," Thorn, *The Relief Pitcher*, Tex Maule, 146; "The Young Pitchers Take Command," *Sports Illustrated*, June 26, 1961, Accessed January 14, 2020, https://www.si.com/vault/1961/06/26/581768/the-young-pitchers-take-command.

19. Tex Maule, "The Young Pitchers Take Command," Childs Walker and Mike Klingman, "Remembering 1966: The Orioles' World Series that began with a remarkable run," *Baltimore Sun*, April 1, 2016, Accessed July 2, 2019, https://www.baltimoresun.com/sports/orioles/bs-sp-orioles-1966-anniversary-20160402-story.html.

20. R.J. Lesch, "Moe Drabowsky", SABR BioProject, Accessed November 24, 2019, https://sabr.org/bioproj/person/51ef7eab; Roger Angell, *The Summer Game* (New York: Popular Library, 1962–72), 158.

21. Richard Goldstein, "Moe Drabowsky, Pitcher and Accomplished Prankster, Dies at 70", *The New York Times*, June 13, 2006, Accessed January 10, 2020, https://www.nytimes.com/2006/06/13/ sports/13drabowsky.html. Edward Kiersh, *Where Have You Gone Vince DiMaggio?* (New York: Bantam Books, 1983), 19. Lesch, "Moe Drabowsky;" Bill Ordine, "O's Series Hero was prankster, too," *Baltimore Sun*, June 11, 2006,

Accessed January 13, 2020, https://www.baltimoresun.com/ sports/bal-sp.drabowsky11jun11-story.html. Walker and Klingman, "Remembering 1966: The Orioles' World Series that began with a remarkable run." Snake pranks included wearing them, mailing to ex-teammates, and hiding them in teammate's lockers, personal items, and apparel, as well as in a bread basket at a banquet. Hotfoot pranks were played on players and coaches, Commissioner Bowie Kuhn, and sportswriter Hal Bock twice on the same road trip. Firecrackers turned up on benches, in restroom stalls, and once in the teepee of the Atlanta Braves mascot, Chief Noc-A-Homa. Prank calls included ordering takeout from a Hong Kong restaurant and impersonating rival manager Alvin Dark on a bullpen telephone and owner Charles O. Finley during a contract dispute. Before the first game of the 1969 World Series, an airplane flew over Baltimore's Memorial Stadium towing a banner warning to beware of him, even though he was playing for neither team.

22. Lesch, "Moe Drabowsky."

23. Angell, *The Summer Game*, 156, 163; Corbett, "*Stu Miller*;" Lesch, "*Moe Drabowsky.*"

24. Jimmy Keenan, "April 30, 1967: Steve Barber and Stu Miller combine for nohitter in a loss," Accessed January 10, 2020, SABR GameLog, https://sabr.org/gamesproj/game/april-30-1967-steve-barber-and-stu-miller-combine-no-hitter-loss; Thorn, *The Relief Pitcher*, 147.

25. The first was Ken Johnson on April 23, 1964.

26. Martinez, in turn, was succeeded by Gregg Olson (217 career saves: 1988–2001) with 160 saves for the 1988–93 Orioles, a team record that stood through the 2019 season. "Tippy Martinez," Baseball-Reference, Accessed July 3, 2019, https://www.baseball-reference.com/players/m/martiti01.shtml; "Baltimore Orioles Top 10 Career Pitching Leaders," Baseball-Reference.

27. Wilhelm had no saves in 1959 when he was used primarily as a starting pitcher. "Hoyt Wilhelm," Baseball-Reference.com.

28. Next tiers for pre-DH are primarily 1960s relievers with 100 or more career saves: Jack Aker (124 career saves 1964–74), Dick Radatz (120 career saves, 1962–69); then Ron Kline (108 career saves, 1952–70) and Wayne Granger (108 career saves, 1968–76). The DH rule may have contributed to the first reliever generation with 300 (or more) career saves, pitching mainly during the Seventies and into the Eighties, including the following: Hall of Famers Rollie Fingers (341 saves, 1968–85); Rich Gossage (310 career saves, 1972–94) and Bruce Sutter (300 saves, 1977–88).

29. Brooks, "Did Stu Miller Really Get Blown Off the Mound at Candlestick Park?"

Dick Hall's Baltimore Legacy

Thomas E. Van Hyning

Dick Hall's trade to the Baltimore Orioles—with Dick Williams—on April 12, 1961, for Jerry Walker and Chuck Essegian, was influenced by Charles Finley's resolve not to trade with the Yankees, a team he despised. Finley once pointed a school bus in the direction of New York and burned it to symbolize the end of the special "Kansas City-New York Yankees relationship."[1] Lee MacPhail, Baltimore's General Manager (GM), earned his 1939 degree from Swarthmore, Hall's alma mater. "Dick Hall was a [1952] Swarthmore graduate, so you might say I was prejudiced," affirmed MacPhail, who had high hopes for Hall.[2]

Hall was 8-13, 4.05 ERA, 1.212 walks plus hits per innings pitched (WHIP) with the 1960 A's. He transitioned from a starter to an excellent reliever. His pinpoint control was despite a "herky-jerky motion" that made him look like "a drunken giraffe on roller skates."[3] *Baltimore Sun* sportswriter Mike Klingaman noted the 6'6" Hall had a "lofty IQ, low ERA, could compute batting averages in his head; most of those who faced him watched their numbers fall."[4] Hall started 13 games in 1961, relieved 16 times, and went 7-5 with a 3.09 ERA. His 122.1 innings included 92 strikeouts–30 walks.

TRANSITION TO THE ORIOLES BULLPEN, 1962–66

From 1962–66, Hall walked 1.3 batters/nine innings with a strikeout-walk ratio of 4.6, MLB-best for relievers with 150-plus innings. Hall's five-year WHIP was 0.9721.[5] His 1962 WHIP was a team-best 1.0225. He was 6-6, 2.28 ERA—102 hits allowed in 118.1 innings, 71 strikeouts, and 19 walks. Hall's move to the bullpen was good for his career.[6] In 1963, he permitted 91 hits and 16 walks in 111.2 innings, for a 0.9582 WHIP, saved 12, split 10 decisions with a 2.98 ERA, and had a 4.63 strikeout-walk ratio (74/16). From July 24 to August 17, 1963, he retired 28 straight hitters in five games. "That was my first perfect game," Hall said. "I never had one before and this one took 25 days."[7]

On July 24, Hall relieved Dave McNally in the third after Don Zimmer's run-scoring hit, finished the game, and retired the last four Senators. On August 4 at Yankee Stadium, Hall retired eight straight to preserve Steve Barber's victory. On August 9, he set down nine Senators, and on August 15, retired four straight Twins at Minnesota. Two days later, he pitched the ninth in a 6–1 victory at Kansas City. Ed Charles struck out; Norm Siebern popped to third; Doc Edwards skied to left. Seven strikeouts, three saves, and one win comprised this streak. Albie Pearson (Angels) ended it with a sixth-inning single in Baltimore on August 21.

Hall dominated in 1964: 9-1, 1.85 ERA, nine saves, 0.8441 WHIP; 87.2 innings/58 hits allowed; he fanned 52 and walked 16. He caught the eye of Yogi Berra, 1964 Yankee manager. "I know he's been good against us for a couple of years," said Berra. "But I don't know why? The ball sure looks good to hit, but we don't hit it."[8] Berra recalled Hall retiring three straight Yankees on three pitches, after singles by Bobby Richardson and Mickey Mantle.[9] Hall was a 1963–64 "Yankee Killer" with 22 innings, two runs allowed, 4-1 record, and four saves!

Hall's 1965 ledger was 11-8, 3.07 ERA, 12 saves, 84 hits allowed in 93.2 innings, 79 strikeouts, 11 walks, and 1.0142 WHIP. Hall, age 35 by season's end, was the youngest of the bullpen quartet of Stu Miller (37), Don Larsen (36), and Harvey Haddix (39). Haddix said

Three weeks after pitching in Game Four of the 1969 World Series, Dick Hall passed the three-day-long CPA exam with flying colors.

Hall's pitching "improved dramatically versus 1959 with Pittsburgh."[10]

Baltimore's 1966 spring training began in Miami, Florida, February 22. On March 7, Dick Brown, Hall's 1963–65 road roommate, was diagnosed with a brain tumor and never played again. Andy Etchebarren became the primary catcher.[11] Baltimore clinched their first AL pennant since moving from St. Louis in Kansas City, September 22. Hall's 1.0152 WHIP was from 59 hits and eight walks permitted in 66 innings. He was shut down due to right elbow tendinitis, with a 6–2 record and 3.95 ERA, but traveled with Baltimore to Los Angeles for the first two World Series games.

"By the Fall of 1966, I took additional [accounting] classes at Johns Hopkins University," said Hall. "The professor said [October 5 or 6], 'One of our students is in Los Angeles and we're canceling class!'"[12] Hall's winning share of $11,683.04 was over half of his $21,750 regular season salary.

PHILADELPHIA DETOUR: 1967–68

Hall's 1:00 AM off-season phone call from GM Harry Dalton, on December 16, 1966, informed him of his trade to Philadelphia for a player to be named later. Hall told the Philadelphia press it wasn't much of a shock.[13] "Phils were looking for pitching," he said. "Player to be named was John Miller, sent to Philadelphia December 15, 1967!"[14] Hall lasted in Philly through the 1968 season and was then released.

RENEWED SUCCESS: BALTIMORE, 1969–71

Hall called Dalton pre-spring training 1969 and was told: "Come down; we'll give you a shot."[15] Earl Weaver had become Orioles manager after Dalton fired Hank Bauer during the 1968 All-Star break. Hall impressed Weaver with 11 scoreless innings, motivating Weaver to state, "The way he has looked, Hall could pick up the phone right now and get five jobs."[16] Hall liked Weaver's style.

"Weaver would not bring in a closer to start an inning…save rules were different," said Hall. "You could get a save with more than a three-run lead."[17] Hall's pitching style suited Weaver just fine. "I bent over like a sidearm pitcher, but my release point was on or near the ear," said Hall. "Threw overhand from the side. Ball came out from my uniform…arms and legs, sneaky riding fastball."[18]

In 1969, Hall went 5–2, 1.92 ERA, with six saves, 0.8832 WHIP, 65.2 innings, 31 strikeouts, nine walks, and 49 hits allowed. Baltimore (109–53) swept Minnesota in the ALCS. "Our [October 4] game on TV came first [before Mets-Braves]," said Hall.

I came in the 12th with bases loaded and got two quick strikes on Cárdenas; threw a slider in the dirt—swung and missed; committed himself a split second too soon—turned just before I released the ball…Roseboro flied to left, on an outside fastball.[19]

Baltimore won, 3–2, on a walk-off bunt by Paul Blair. Twins pitcher Ron Perranoski called it "a perfect bunt."[20] Billy Martin, Twins manager, told a sportswriter, "There's no way to beat a perfect bunt."[21] Baltimore won games two and three. "It was the only time I've ever seen a team give up," said Hall. "Carew trotted after a ball [game three] and it's over."[22]

Hall recalled the 10-inning Game Four of the 1969 World Series. Earl Weaver was ejected for arguing balls and strikes in the third. "It was a sunny day in Shea," remembered Hall. "Buford is looking into the sun [in the 10th] and there's a huge, black background due to the stands. Buford could not pick up the ball hit by [Jerry] Grote. Belanger almost caught it." Grote's bloop double put him at second. Gil Hodges summoned Rod Gaspar to pinch-run. Coach Billy Hunter had Hall walk Al Weis intentionally. Pete Richert faced J.C. Martin, who bunted. Hall indicated: "Martin is running in fair territory; ball ricochets off his shoulder and Gaspar scores."[23] Hall got the loss. He took the CPA three-day exam—three weeks later—and tied for second of 200 candidates who sat for it![24]

In 1970, Baltimore won 108 games, swept Minnesota in the ALCS, and bested Cincinnati in the World Series. Hall won 10 of 15 decisions. His 61.1 innings led Orioles relievers. Hall's WHIP was 0.9293. He fanned 30 walked six, allowed 51 hits—and posted a 3.08 ERA. Ted Williams, Washington Senators manager, compared Hall's 1970 pitching to 1960 when he faced Hall. "His control is sharper," said Williams. "You can't wait around for him to walk you. You'd better go up there swinging."[25]

Hall won Game One of the ALCS, October 3, with 4.2 scoreless innings of relief; he faced 14 batters, gave up a hit to Tony Oliva, and fanned three. He induced Danny Thompson to hit into a 4-6-3 double-play, after relieving Miguel Cuéllar, whose grand slam in the fourth preceded Hall's sixth-inning single and run, in a 10–6 win. "Hall was a great teammate and we conversed in Spanish," recalled Cuéllar. "His wife is from Mazatlán, Mexico, where he played winter ball."[26]

In Game Two of the 1970 World Series, October 11, Hall preserved a 6–5 win. Tony Pérez grounded out, with two on, before Johnny Bench, Lee May, and Hal McRae were retired in the eighth and Tommy Helms,

Bernie Carbo, and Jimmy Stewart retired in the ninth. Tony Pérez opined, "He's got that funny motion. He throws a change-up or a palm ball. I don't know what it is. Oh, that pitch he gave to me was a good one to hit."[27] Johnny Bench added, "I tried to go right on him, then I changed my swing and I got all screwed up."[28] Brooks Robinson ensured Hall translated Spanish-speaking interviews with Cuéllar and Marcelino López.[29]

Hall—6-6, 4.98 ERA, one save—threw the only wild pitch (WP) of his MLB career, August 20, 1971. Minnesota's George Mitterwald doubled in the ninth and advanced to third on the WP. Hall turned 41 on September 27. The next oldest Orioles were Orlando Peña (37) and Frank Robinson (36). Baltimore (101–57) swept Oakland, managed by Dick Williams, in the ALCS.

Hall pitched the ninth in Game Two of the 1971 World Series on October 11. The Orioles were up, 11–3, when Weaver told Hall, "We got a big lead. I need Palmer later in the Series."[30] Al Oliver singled to right; Bob Robertson popped to 2B; Manny Sanguillen grounded into a forceout and Milt May, hitting for Jackie Hernández, grounded to Boog Powell, who flipped it to Hall. "I put the ball in my back pocket—saved it—[was] the last pitch I ever threw in a regular season or World Series game," said Hall. "It's in a plastic case…[I] have shown it to my grandson."[31]

Sadaharu Oh hit the last home run Hall gave up, in Kokura, an ancient castle town, during the Orioles post-1971 World Series tour of Japan. Baltimore went 12–2–4. "After the last game, I [knew I] wasn't coming back in 1972…arm trouble," said Hall, who pitched three innings against the Yomiuri Giants."[32]

Hall threw batting practice for the 1972 Orioles, at Memorial Stadium. Baltimore's pro soccer team played Santos, Brazil's powerhouse club, one day, when Hall met superstar Pelé. "He [Pelé]] spoke English, Spanish and Portuguese," said Hall. "We spoke in Spanish. Pelé knew about Orlando Peña—both were married to sisters from Guadalajara, Mexico!"[33]

BALTIMORE, SWARTHMORE, AND MLB RECOGNITION

In 1989, Hall was inducted into the Baltimore Orioles Hall of Fame. Swarthmore College inducted Hall into their Athletics Hall of Fame in 2012. That same year, Paul Hartzell met Hall at the Orioles Hall of Fame Ceremony. "I admired you when I was a young man, and thought of you as a real 'professional' when I met you in person," stated Hartzell.[34]

In 2017, Fox Sports named Hall one of Baltimore's four all-time relievers on their All-Time 25-man Orioles roster, with Gregg Olson, Tippy Martínez, and Zach Britton.[35] In nine Baltimore seasons, Hall was 65–40 (.619) with a 2.89 ERA, 60 saves, 770 IP, 499 strikeouts, 126 walks (46 intentional), and 1.0052 WHIP. When asked about his fondest memory as an Oriole, Hall said, "Four World Series, that's pretty good."[36]

Hall's 1.1019 career MLB WHIP tied Rube Waddell for 25th, all-time, 1,000 plus career innings, behind #24 Juan Marichal's 1.1012. Two relievers made the top 10: Mariano Rivera—1.0003 (third) and Trevor Hoffman—1.0584 (10th). Hall outpaced #29 Sandy Koufax's 1.1061 and many other Cooperstown inductees. ∎

Acknowledgments
Thanks to Dick Hall, Harvey Haddix, Lee MacPhail, Miguel Cuéllar, and Paul Hartzell.

Sources
Internet Resources
https://www.baseball-reference.com/players/h/halldi01.shtml.
https://www.baseball-reference.com/register/player.fcgi?id=hall--004ric.

Magazine and SABR Articles
Robert Creamer, "The Invisible Man on the Mound," *Sports Illustrated*, (June 24, 1963). Accessed at https://www.si.com/vault/1963/06/24/594274/the-invisible-man-on-the-mound.
Stew Thornley, "October 3, 1970: Slam, errors give Orioles playoff opener," SABR Games Project. Accessed at https://sabr.org/gamesproj/game/october-3-1970-slam-errors-give-orioles-playoff-opener.

Notes
1. G. Michael Green and Roger D. Launius, *Charlie Finley: The Outrageous Story of Baseball's Super Showman* (New York: Bloomsbury Publishing, 2010), 44. Finley also approved the January 24, 1961 trade: Whitey Herzog, and Russ Snyder went to Baltimore for Bob Boyd, Al Pilarcik, Jim Archer, Wayne Causey, and Clint Courtney.
2. Lee MacPhail, *My Nine Innings: An Autobiography of 50 Years in Baseball* (Westport, CT: Meckler Books, 1989), 69. MacPhail was a high school and Swarthmore College classmate of Paula Swarthe Van Hyning, the author's mother. The author corresponded with MacPhail in 2011 on various topics.
3. Mike Klingaman, "Catching Up With ex-Oriole Dick Hall," *Baltimore Sun*, May 26, 2009. Located at: https://www.baltimoresun.com/bs-mtblog-2009-05-catching_up_with_dick_hall-story.html. Accessed May 2, 2019.
4. Mike Klingaman, "Catching Up" *Baltimore Sun*, May 26, 2009.
5. Fox Sports, "Baltimore Orioles All-Time 25-Man Roster," June 30, 2017 blog. https://www.foxsports.com/mlb/story/baltimore-orioles-all-time-25-man-roster-120516. Accessed April 25, 2019.
6. Dick Hall, telephone interview, April 30, 2019.
7. Doug Brown, "'Perfect Game' by Reliever Hall; Retired 28 in Row over 25 Days," *The Sporting News*, August 31, 1963, 10.
8. Doug Brown, "Hitters Flunk in Facing Scholar Hall: Oriole Bull-Pen Ace Looks Awkward, Has Jerky Style," *The Sporting News*, July 25, 1964.
9. Nelson 'Chip' Greene, Dick Hall SABR bio. https://sabr.org/bioproj/person/0cfab8b4. Accessed April 10, 2019.
10. Harvey Haddix, telephone interview, April 14, 1992.
11. Ben Klein, Andy Etchebarren SABR bio. https://sabr.org/bioproj/person/6746ad5c. Accessed January 2, 2020.
12. Dick Hall, telephone interview, May 3, 2019.
13. 'Chip' Greene, Dick Hall SABR bio.
14. Dick Hall, telephone interview, May 3, 2019.
15. Dick Hall, telephone interview, May 3, 2019.
16. Doug Brown, "Dick Hall Tireless and Oriole Retread," *The Sporting News*, April 19, 1969, 4.

17. Dick Hall, telephone interview, May 3, 2019.
18. Dick Hall, telephone interview, May 3, 2019.
19. Dick Hall, telephone interview, May 3, 2019.
20. Jimmy Keenan, "October 4, 1969: Orioles win first-ever ALCS game," SABR Games Project. https://sabr.org/gamesproj/game/october-4-1969-orioles-win-first-ever-alcs-game. Accessed May 3, 2019.
21. Jimmy Keenan, "October 4, 1969" SABR Games Project.
22. Dick Hall, telephone interview, May 3, 2019.
23. Dick Hall, telephone interview, May 3, 2019.
24. 'Chip' Greene, Dick Hall SABR bio. Hall prepared tax returns for Latin American teammates as far back as 1959, including Ed Bauta and Carlos Bernier, Salt Lake City teammates, per Bauta's 2018 SABR bio by Van Hyning. https://sabr.org/bioproj/person/b078dcf3. Accessed December 24, 2019.
25. Ed Rumill, "The pitching machine: Hall has 'built-in file on every hitter,'" *Christian Science Monitor*, June 25, 1970.
26. Miguel Cuéllar, in-person interview, Chain of Lakes Park, Winter Haven, Florida, March 1992. Hall's nickname in Mexico was "Siete Leguas," Francisco "Pancho" Villa's favorite horse. Hall got this nickname by the way he galloped around the bases. He first pitched professionally in Mexico, 1954–55 winter season. See Bernabé López Padilla, "Dick Hall: Siete Leguas," August 24, 2015 blog. http://beisbolredes.blogspot.com/2015/08/dick-hall-siete-leguas.html. Accessed April 24, 2019.
27. 'Chip' Greene, Dick Hall SABR bio.
28. 'Chip' Greene, Dick Hall SABR bio.
29. Dick Hall, telephone interview, April 30, 2019.
30. Dick Hall, telephone interview, May 3, 2019.
31. Dick Hall, telephone interview, May 3, 2019. Roberto Clemente, MVP of the 1971 World Series, was the first player in a NL or AL uniform to hit a home run off Hall, in a 1955 spring training Pittsburgh intersquad game, at Fort Myers, Florida.
32. Dick Hall, telephone interview, May 3, 2019. Hall visited with his brother-in-law, a Pan Am pilot, who stayed at the same hotel in Japan.
33. Dick Hall, telephone interview, May 3, 2019.
34. Paul Hartzell, e-mail to Thomas E. Van Hyning, May 10, 2019. Hartzell grew up in Bloomsburg, Pennsylvania, a three-hour drive from Baltimore. He pitched for the 1980 Orioles and 1973 Johnny's amateur team in Baltimore. Rich Dauer, Mike Mussina, and Walter Youse (posthumously) were inducted at the 2012 Orioles Hall of Fame Ceremony. Jim Gentile and Stu Miller were inducted with Hall—1989.
35. Fox Sports, "Baltimore Orioles All-Time 25-Man Roster," June 30, 2017 blog. By "All-Time" they mean 1954 through 2016, only considering the current Orioles franchise.
36. Pete Korzel, "Reliever Hall was a constant of early O's world series squads," May 11, 2012 blog. https://www.masnsports.com/orioles-buzz/2012/05/. Accessed January 5, 2020.

The 1966 Orioles
More than Frank Robinson

David W. Smith

The 1966 season was the culmination of several good seasons for the Orioles, a pattern that began with the 1960 team and the famous "Kiddie Corps" that made an unexpected great run at the AL pennant. From 1961 through 1965, they finished 3rd, 7th, 4th, 3rd, and 3rd—a solid run after the first dismal seasons following the 1954 transfer from their previous reality as the St. Louis Browns. During this six-year stretch they won over 90 games 3 times and 89 on another occasion for a total of 538 wins and a winning average of .558. Only the White Sox and Yankees had higher winning averages over that period. In addition to the surprising second-place finish in 1960, they were only two games out (but in third place) in 1964, a pennant race that was very close all season.

The player who probably comes to mind first in discussions of the 1966 Orioles is Frank Robinson. He was acquired from Cincinnati in December 1965 for Milt Pappas and two others. Despite Reds owner Bill DeWitt describing him as "not a young 30," Robinson had an exceptional first year in the American League, winning the 1966 Triple Crown (.316, 49 home runs, 122 RBIs), the first to complete the feat since Mickey Mantle in 1956. At season's end he was voted the Most Valuable Player in the American League, the first—and still the only—player to win the MVP in both leagues. He would also be named the Most Valuable Player in the 1966 World Series.[1] But it takes a complete roster to have the success that the 1966 Orioles did, and the other 33 Birds were much more than mere bit players. This article will discuss many players' contributions and the collective accomplishments of the team.

The team was largely built from within, augmented by a few key acquisitions over several years. Eighteen members of the 1966 team started their major-league careers with Baltimore, including Steve Barber, Sam Bowens, Wally Bunker, Andy Etchebarren, Davey Johnson, Dave McNally, Jim Palmer, Boog Powell, Brooks Robinson, and Eddie Watt. Other stalwarts arrived in Charm City from other teams 1961–63: Luis Aparicio from the White Sox in a 1963 trade; Paul Blair from the Mets in the 1962 first-year player draft, Curt Blefary from the Yankees as a 1963 first-year waiver choice, and Stu Miller and Russ Snyder in trades with the Giants (1962) and Athletics (1961).

There were minimal changes to the team from 1965 to 1966 with only two significant modifications. In addition to the advent of Frank Robinson, 20-year old Jim Palmer became a regular part of the rotation with 30 starts after six in his rookie season the year before, taking up most of the work done in 1965 by the departed Pappas. Very few other players who had significant playing time in 1965 left after that season, all veterans: outfielder Jackie Brandt, first baseman Norm Siebern, and pitcher Robin Roberts.

Upon becoming a regular in 1960, Brooks Robinson was the first major Orioles fan favorite, and is arguably the greatest third baseman of all time.[2] He played over 140 games at third base for each of the next 16 years, winning the Gold Glove all 16 seasons. He was on the AL All-Star team 15 of those years, winning the AL Most Valuable Player award in 1964, the All-Star game MVP in 1966, and the World Series MVP in 1970 when he dazzled the nation with his extraordinary fielding (ask Lee May!), batting .429 with two doubles and two home runs among his nine hits. In his first World Series at bat in 1966, in the first inning of Game One in Los Angeles he homered off Don Drysdale of the Dodgers. The Orioles scored three times and set a definitive tone for the dramatic four-game sweep. He was the anchor of the franchise before Frank Robinson arrived and after Frank departed.

Boog Powell was the second home-grown player to become a fixture for the team. Signed when he was 17, Boog progressed quickly through the Orioles minor league system, becoming the team's regular left fielder in 1962 at the age of 20. Although he is best remembered as a first baseman, in his first three seasons after his 1961 cup of coffee, Powell appeared in 356 games in left field and only 29 at first. The presence of Frank Robinson stabilized the outfield composition, enabling Boog's permanent move to first base in 1966.[3] This was a significant step for the Orioles as they established their core lineup for years to come. Powell's 34

Before Luis Aparicio came to the Orioles, the shortstop position had been split between Jerry Adair and Ron Hansen.

home runs in 1966 were third in the AL, trailing only Frank Robinson's 49 and the 39 mashed by Harmon Killebrew of the Twins.

Luis Aparicio became the regular shortstop immediately upon his arrival in Baltimore in 1963, playing over 140 games there each season through 1965. The win-win trade which brought him from Chicago involved six players, with Aparicio and fellow future Hall-of Famer Hoyt Wilhelm the marquee names.[4] Before he took over the position, time at shortstop had been split between serviceable infielders Jerry Adair and Ron Hansen. With Brooks Robinson to Aparicio's right, the Orioles had a Hall-of-Fame left side of the infield from 1963 through 1967 as Luis won a pair of Gold Gloves along with Brooks. He also provided most of the speed for the Orioles, with over 50% of the team's stolen bases 1963–65 (123 of 242), including 40 of the team's 97 in 1963 when he made the AL All-Star team. His 57 steals in 1964 are still the single season record for the current Orioles.

Davey Johnson played briefly for the Orioles in the early part of 1965 before returning to the minors for more seasoning. Upon his return in 1966, he became the regular second baseman for seven seasons, playing in two All-Star games and winning three Gold Gloves. With Powell and Johnson in place, the Baltimore infield was anchored for many years. Johnson has the interesting distinction of being the last man to have a base hit against Sandy Koufax, collecting a single in

the sixth inning of Game Two of the 1966 World Series. Following his playing career, Johnson became a very successful major league manager, compiling a winning average of .562 while at the helm of five different teams, including a two-year stretch with the Orioles in 1996 and 1997, when he guided them to second and first place finishes, the latter earning him the first of his two Manager of the Year awards.

As mentioned above, the arrival of Frank Robinson stabilized the outfield with Robinson playing 151 games and three others, Paul Blair, Curt Blefary (AL rookie of the year in 1965) and Russ Snyder each playing over 100 games. Blefary (23 home runs) and Snyder (batting average .306) made significant offensive contributions as well. Sam Bowens appeared in 68 games, playing all three outfield positions.

The Orioles were a very stable team in terms of starting lineups with only 44 different lineups of 8 position players. (By comparison, the average for the 1966 AL was 66 different "Starting 8's"—the most being 87 by the White Sox.) Seven Orioles each started more than 100 games at the same position: Luis Aparicio, Curt Blefary, Andy Etchebarren, Davey Johnson, Boog Powell, Brooks Robinson, and Frank Robinson. The only other AL team that had seven men start 100 games each in one spot was the Red Sox. The team with the fewest was the Yankees, who had only two. Frank Robinson's arrival stabilized positions throughout the field. Not only did he start 132 games in right field (19 in left), but the other outfield positions were much less variable, with the most dramatic change being the Boog Powell move as mentioned above.

After two brief stints in 1962 and 1965, Andy Etchebarren became the Orioles regular catcher in 1966, starting 118 games. His offensive production was modest, but he did hit 11 home runs with 50 RBIs. On the defensive side, he was effective at throwing out would-be base stealers, doing so at a 39% rate both for 1966 and for his career. He played for the Orioles through mid-1975 when he was sold to the Angels. During those years, 1967 was the only other time that he caught 100 games in a single season. After his playing career ended, Etchebarren was a coach for the Angels, Brewers, and Orioles.

The pitching for the 1966 team was good, but not spectacular, finishing fourth in ERA with a team value of 3.32; the league average was 3.44. Manager Hank Bauer used 11 different starting pitchers, with two having 30 or more starts, two others with more than 20 and two with more than 10. These six men had 138 starts in the Orioles' 160 games with 20 of their 23 complete games. That complete game total was next

Fan favorite Brooks Robinson won the Gold Glove 16 seasons in a row, was on the AL All-Star team 15 of those years, and won AL MVP in 1964, All-Star game MVP in 1966, and World Series MVP in 1970.

to last in the league, surpassing only the Kansas City Athletics. Their great pitching strength was the bullpen. The starters had a collective ERA of 3.50, but relievers combined for 2.98, a close third to Minnesota (2.93) and Chicago (2.55). Stu Miller led the way with an ERA of 2.25 in 51 appearances. Eddie Fisher relieved in 44 games with an ERA of 2.64. The other two main figures from the bullpen were Moe Drabowsky (41 relief games with 2.71 ERA, plus three starts) and Eddie Watt (30 relief appearances with 3.56 ERA, and 13 starts).

The starters were a combined 58–47 while the bullpen compiled a record of 39–16 with 51 saves. This is somewhat startling given the tremendous and highly visible accomplishments of the starters in the World Series in which they had three consecutive complete game shutouts in games two through four. Jim Palmer led the starters with 15 wins, Dave McNally had 13, Steve Barber 10, and Wally Bunker 10. The Orioles had 14 different pitchers with at least one win, showing a very diverse and balanced staff working under the tutelage of pitching coach Harry Brecheen.

The offense led the way for the 1966 Orioles as shown by WAR (Wins Above Replacement). The team led the AL with 13.6 WAR, well ahead of the Twins with 8.3. Within that 13.6 WAR, the Baltimore lineup accumulated 11.5, easily leading the AL over next-best Detroit (6.4) and trailing only the Pirates (15.2). Baltimore pitchers had a collective WAR of 2.1, fourth in the AL and well behind the major league-leading Dodgers (14.6). The offense of the Orioles was outstanding in

every way, leading the AL in runs scored, batting average, on-base average and slugging average. They were the only AL team to lead in all these categories between 1954 (Yankees) and 1975 (Red Sox). Their 179 home runs were second to Detroit by four.

This production translated to success throughout the season, as they were in first place for 130 of 170 days. Their low point came on May 28 when they trailed Cleveland by 4.5 games. They then won 12 of their next 16, moving back into first place on June 7 and not relinquishing the top spot for the rest of the year, eventually winning by nine games over the Twins.

Overall, the 1966 Orioles were a young team. Five of their nine Opening Day starters were under 25 and only Aparicio and Frank Robinson were older than 29, at 31 and 30, respectively. This youth likely contributed to their very low number of injuries during that championship season, without any long stints on the disabled list—although pitchers Barber, Bunker, and Palmer did miss a few starts due to arm problems.

No discussion of the 1966 Orioles would be complete without mentioning the manager, Hank Bauer. Hank had a solid career with the Yankees, appearing in nine World Series in his 11 full years with the Bombers. He was widely regarded as tough as nails, based in part on his record as a Marine in WWII, during which he won two Bronze Stars and two Purple Hearts. It is perhaps surprising that someone with such a rugged background was not an unfeeling tyrant with his players. He was relaxed with his young team and they respected him for it. Bauer praised Frank Robinson for having a positive effect on the "young players just by talking to them…"

Even as Frank Robinson was exciting Baltimore fans and becoming hugely popular, he and his family had some rough times off the field as they encountered the starkly segregated housing market in Baltimore. He had not been active in civil rights issues before this, but became more outspoken when the Orioles did not support his efforts to overcome the bigotry of the city's real estate business.[5] This was a turbulent time in American society as the Civil Rights Act (1964) and Voting Rights Act (1965) were still new and both engendered stiff opposition. The Vietnam War was also escalating rapidly with the authorized troop level in the Southeast Asian conflict rising to just under 400,000 in 1966.

The 1966 season was also a significant transitional year for baseball as the institution underwent profound changes at the same time as the social upheaval in the country at large. The two most dominant teams since the end of World War II were the Yankees and the

Dodgers. The Yankees' incredible run of 15 pennants in 18 seasons ended in 1964 and they hit rock bottom in 1966, finishing last, and they languished for most of the next decade. The gap left by the Yankees was filled by several teams, but the most successful was the Orioles, who won over 100 games in three straight seasons (1969–71).[6]

In retrospect it is clear that the Orioles had been building and improving for several years, positioning them ideally to fill the vacuum left by the Yankees. The addition of Frank Robinson was the deciding action that put them over the top to become champions, but it was not a one-man effort; the rest of the team was much more than a supporting cast. The team had four men elected to the Hall of Fame: Brooks and Frank Robinson, Palmer, and Aparicio. Their unexpected World Series sweep of the Dodgers in four games showed how solid they were. It was the most dominating World Series performance in history: The Dodgers scored a total of two runs in the four games and none at all in the last 33 innings, as they were shut out the last three games. The 1966 Orioles had established themselves dramatically for all the baseball world to see. ■

Sources

The SABR biographies of Frank Robinson (by Maxwell Kates) and Hank Bauer (by Warren Corbett) were extremely valuable.
The WAR values are from Baseball-Reference.com.
All other statistical data are from Retrosheet (https://www.retrosheet.org).

Notes

1. Frank Robinson was also rookie of the year in 1956. He became manager of four different teams including the Orioles and won the 1989 Manager of the Year Award for leading the Birds to an exciting second-place finish, an unexpected comeback from the 1988 season in which the team began the season 0–21. As a player-manager of the Indians in 1975, he became the first African-American to hold a major-league managerial post.
2. Brooks Robinson was elected to the Hall of Fame in 1983, his first year of eligibility.
3. Jim Gentile had been firmly entrenched at first base 1960–63 after arriving from Los Angeles. Gentile was traded after the 1963 season to Kansas City for Norm Siebern who was the regular first baseman for the Orioles in 1964 (149 games). The 1965 season began with Siebern at first until mid-June when Powell moved in from the outfield. Boog would play much more at first than the outfield for the rest of the year.
4. Aparicio was elected to the Hall of Fame in 1984.
5. "Frank Robinson," Black History in America website. Accessed July 6, 2020: http://www.myblackhistory.net/Frank_Robinson.htm.
6. In the NL, a similar pattern occurred with the Dodgers. Although they won the 1966 NL pennant, it was the end of the Brooklyn influence, as only Koufax, Drysdale, Jim Gilliam, and John Roseboro remained from their East coast incarnation. They were a weak team for nearly a decade after.

The Trade that Ignited Two (!) Dynasties

William Schneider

"Bad trades are a part of baseball; I mean who can forget
Frank Robinson for Milt Pappas for gosh sakes."
– Annie, *Bull Durham*

Outside of the 1919 sale of Babe Ruth to the Yankees, baseball trades do not often occupy a persistent niche in pop culture. As the *Bull Durham* quotation indicates, the December 1965 trade of Frank Robinson from the Reds to the Orioles is a notable exception.

Annie doesn't have the details quite right, though. In actuality, the Reds traded 30-year-old All-Star outfielder Frank Robinson to the Orioles on December 9, 1965, for a package of players that included 26-year-old starting pitcher Milt Pappas, 29-year-old reliever Jack Baldschun, and 22-year-old outfield prospect Dick Simpson. The trade has gone down in baseball lore as a lopsided deal that gave rise to the strong Orioles team of the late sixties and early seventies while condemning the Reds to second division status. Many articles and books have attempted to dissect the trade, and it frequently makes lists of the worst trades in baseball history.[1]

On the surface, the facts seem indisputable. In Robinson, the Orioles acquired a Hall of Fame outfielder in the late prime of his career. He not only won the Triple Crown in his first year in Baltimore (1966), but also was arguably the most important player on Orioles teams that won two World Series and four American League pennants across six seasons. In return, the Reds acquired a good, not great, starting pitcher (Pappas), a washed-up reliever who never contributed (Baldschun), and a prospect who failed to make a major-league impact (Simpson).

However, as is often the case, there is more to the story. The "obvious" evaluation of this trade might not be the most accurate one. This article will explore an alternative viewpoint, that this trade was much closer to a "Win-Win" than is commonly perceived. In fact, the Big Red Machine might never have existed without it.

THE REDS' PERSPECTIVE

Frank Robinson had played for the Reds at an elite level since entering the league in 1956. During his ten seasons (1956–65), he had accumulated 64 WAR and consistently ranked as one of the best players in the major leagues. In 1965, he delivered a slash line of .296/.386/.540, with 33 home runs, and 113 runs batted in. These numbers were very strong, but at least in terms of conventional stats were down from his 1962 peak of .342/.421/.624, 39 homers, and 136 RBIs.

All was not well in Reds country, though. The 1965 Reds had finished 4th in the NL standings, as their strong offense (825 runs, most in the NL) was offset by weak defense (704 runs allowed, fourth worst in the NL). Since appearing in the 1961 World Series, the Reds had won 98, 86, 92, and 89 games, but had yet to claim another NL pennant. The 1965 team had finished a distant eight games behind the National League champion Dodgers.

Moreover, the relationship between Reds owner/GM Bill DeWitt, a portion of the Reds fan base, and Frank Robinson was rocky. Frank had been arrested for possessing a firearm without a permit in Florida during Spring Training in 1961, and DeWitt had elected to let Robinson spend a night in jail without attempting to intervene. Robinson was commonly thought to resent this.[2] Additionally, Robinson and the perennially cash-strapped DeWitt had annual salary squabbles for several years. Robinson had even threatened to retire in September 1963 until he received a substantial raise. Reds fans were frustrated at the team's lack of competitiveness in 1965, and Robinson drew a great deal of their ire. Reds manager Dick Sisler had taken the unusual step of imploring fans to cease booing the outfielder at Crosley Field in August of 1965.

Bill DeWitt, under pressure to improve team pitching and in possession of a valuable asset he thought was in decline, proceeded to offer Robinson in trade to several teams. When the Orioles obtained pitcher Baldschun and outfielder Simpson in separate deals and included them with Pappas in their offer, the Reds agreed to the trade.

DeWitt had already been unsuccessful at acquiring Baldschun from the Phillies, and he liked Simpson for his speed and potential. He viewed Pappas as the incoming ace of the Reds staff, and furthermore emphasized his desire to maximize the return for Robinson while he still could. In fact, in a trade defense that is often misquoted, DeWitt described Robinson as "not a young 30,"[3] and stated, "We'd rather trade a player a year too soon than a year late."[4]

THE ORIOLES' PERSPECTIVE

The Baltimore Orioles of the mid-1960s were a team on the rise. They had won 97 games in 1964 and 94 games in 1965, although they finished third in the American League standings both years. Those Orioles teams were pretty well balanced, having finished fourth in the majors both years in runs allowed and ninth (1964) and twelfth (1965) in runs scored. Nonetheless, Orioles General Manager Lee MacPhail thought they needed a change to break through.

In fact, per Orioles' Farm Director Harry Dalton, the Orioles were specifically seeking an upgrade to their outfield. After the acquisition of Robinson, Dalton commented, "Oh boy, cannons at the corners!"[5] With Robinson in right field, Curt Blefary in left, Brooks Robinson at third, and Boog Powell transitioning from left field to first base, the Orioles did indeed feature strong production at each of these positions.

Frank Robinson came to the Orioles in the late prime of his career and immediately won the Triple Crown in his first year in Baltimore (1966).

Pappas had been the Orioles' best starter in 1965, and the All-Star had pitched over 200 effective innings six out of seven seasons since assuming a full-time role in 1959. Nonetheless, a dearth of effective pitching was not really a concern for the Orioles. All six of the pitchers who had made 15 or more starts in 1965 had an ERA better than the league average, 19-year old Jim Palmer had thrown 92 effective innings, and Tom Phoebus, Jim Hardin, and Eddie Watt were in the Orioles' minor league pipeline. The team certainly felt that they had a pitching surplus to leverage, particularly if the payoff was someone of Robinson's stature.

As for Baldschun and Simpson, neither had actually appeared in a game as part of the Orioles organization. Both were acquired in December 1965 deals prior to their inclusion in the Robinson trade.

THE RESULTS

From the Orioles' perspective, the trade bore immediate fruit. Robinson came out of the gate exceptionally well in 1966, hitting for a slash line of .463/.585/.976 in April. He finished the year with 49 home runs, 122 runs, 122 runs batted in, and a batting average of .316, winning the American League's first Triple Crown since 1956 (Mickey Mantle).

From a team perspective, the Orioles were also very successful. The team went 11–1 in April, on their way to a 97–63 overall record. They beat the Twins by nine games for the American League pennant, then proceeded to sweep the Dodgers for the first World Series title in franchise history. Robinson capped his dominant season by winning the American League Most Valuable Player award, and was named the World Series MVP as well.

The significance of Robinson's arrival in Baltimore went beyond his stellar on-the-field contributions. Robinson's competitive nature and leadership abilities also helped spur a normally solid team to greatness. Jim Palmer, then just starting his second big league season, noted that the Orioles prior to 1966 had always hoped to win, but, "After [Frank Robinson] got there, we expected to win."[6] Outfielder Paul Blair echoed this sentiment: "We were good before—had great defense, good pitching, decent hitting—but Frank was the key. Not only did he play great, he showed us how to be all business and get the job done."[7]

What did Robinson do for an encore? He continued to slug, and made the All-Star team four of the next five seasons. Although he never won another Most Valuable Player Award, he finished third in the voting in 1969 and 1971 and garnered votes each year except for 1968.

Robinson was arguably the most important player on the Orioles teams that won two World Series and four American League pennants.

The Orioles as a franchise, after a brief decline in 1967, also continued their strong run. After finishing sixth in the American League standings in 1967, the Orioles climbed to second in 1968, then concluded Frank Robinson's tenure with the team with three straight 100-win seasons, three straight American League pennants, and another World Series championship in 1970 (ironically defeating the Reds).

Meanwhile, in Cincinnati the results of the trade were not as promising. Pappas struggled out of the gate in 1966, and had a mediocre first season with the Reds (12–11 record, 4.29 ERA, allowed more hits than innings pitched, ERA+ of only 92). Jack Baldschun was a disaster as a reliever, delivering a 5.49 ERA in 57 innings. Prospect Dick Simpson was similarly disappointing, as he contributed a slash line of .238/.333/.405 in 99 plate appearances.

The Reds' fortunes, as might be expected after swapping their best player for middling contributors, collapsed. Cincinnati had been in the thick of the pennant race in 1964, won 89 games in 1965 (fourth place), and in 1966 could only manage 76 wins and a seventh-place finish. The Reds' traditionally strong offense dropped off considerably, and the pitching did not substantially improve, despite trading Robinson for pitching help.

Fan and pundit reactions were mixed immediately after the trade, but the criticism mounted throughout the season as Robinson continued to produce and the Reds continued to struggle. Reds fans did not accept the team's declining fortunes, and Bill DeWitt took the brunt of their ire. DeWitt experienced the ignominy of being hung in effigy in downtown Cincinnati in June, his earlier good work in shepherding the Reds to the 1961 National League pennant seemingly forgotten.[8]

DeWitt was embattled on another front as well, as the Reds were in discussions with the city of Cincinnati

for a new stadium to replace Crosley Field. DeWitt believed the Reds should move out of downtown Cincinnati to a suburban location, and as a result was unwilling to commit to an extended lease in a downtown location. When National League president Warren Giles said he would block any move out of the city, DeWitt was left with few viable alternatives.[9] He sold the team to a group of local businessmen on December 5, 1966, only four days shy of a year after the trade that ultimately defined his legacy.

Milt Pappas would enjoy a strong year for the Reds in 1967, going 16–13 with a 3.35 ERA in 217 innings. But he struggled in 1968, and he was traded to the Atlanta Braves in June after delivering a 5.60 ERA in 15 games for the Reds. Jack Baldschun only appeared in nine games in 1967 and spent the rest of his time with the Reds in the minors until his 1969 release. Dick Simpson played in only 44 games and batted .259/.339/.370 in 62 plate appearances in 1967, and then was traded to the St. Louis Cardinals in the offseason.

Most conventional analyses of the "Frank Robinson trade" end here, as Robinson continued to play well for the Orioles, while the Reds had parted ways with all of the players they had acquired. Using WAR, here is how the trade stacked up:

Table 1. WAR Comparison for Directly Traded Players

Season	Orioles WAR	Reds WAR
1966	Robinson 7.7	Pappas 2.4
1967	Robinson 5.4	Pappas 3.6
1968	Robinson 3.7	
1969	Robinson 7.5	
1970	Robinson 4.8	
1971	Robinson 3.3	
	Orioles Total 32.4	**Reds Total 6.0**

NOTE: Baldschun and Simpson failed to contribute positive WAR to the Reds.

On the surface, this seems a convincing win for the Orioles. But although the Reds released Baldschun, Pappas and Simpson would eventually be traded for other players. A comprehensive review of the total impact of the Reds-Orioles trade not only needs to consider the contributions the players made directly to their respective teams, but also the contributions made by players that were acquired in exchange for them. Here's where the story gets more interesting.

Milt Pappas was traded to the Atlanta Braves on June 11, 1968, along with pitcher Ted Davidson and infielder Bob Johnson, for pitcher Clay Carroll, pitcher Tony Cloninger, and shortstop Woody Woodward. At the time of the trade, Davidson was a 28-year-old with

THE SECOND FRANK ROBINSON TRADE

Another bad Frank Robinson trade? The sidebar practically writes itself. On December 6, 1971, the Orioles traded Frank Robinson and reliever Pete Richert to the Los Angeles Dodgers for a package of young players including pitcher Doyle Alexander, pitcher Bob O'Brien, catcher Sergio Robles, and outfielder Royle Stillman. Here's the positive bWAR earned by the players in the trade (regardless of team) until the end of Robinson's playing career in 1976:

Los Angeles Dodgers Received		Baltimore Orioles Received	
Frank Robinson	11.2	Doyle Alexander	3.7
Pete Richert	2.4	Bob O'Brien	0
Sergio Robles			0
Royle Stillman			.2
Dodgers Total	**13.6**	**Orioles Total**	**3.9**

Despite Robinson's advanced age (he was 36 at the time of the trade), this appears to be a second trade that confirms the idea that you will not get value when trading Robinson. However, just like the 1965 Reds-Orioles trade, there is more to the story.

On June 15, 1976, the Orioles traded Doyle Alexander, Jimmy Freeman, Elrod Hendricks, Ken Holtzman, and Grant Jackson to the New York Yankees for catcher Rick Dempsey and four pitchers: Tippy Martinez, Rudy May, Scott McGregor, and Dave Pagan. The headline players were Alexander (coming off a 2.1 WAR season in 1975) and Holtzman (5–4 with a 2.86 ERA at trade time), while Hendricks (aged 35) was nearing the end of his career, Freeman was a non-prospect by that point, and Jackson would be left unprotected in the 1976 expansion draft.

In return, the Orioles received quite a haul. Dempsey, Martinez, and McGregor would all be important players in the Orioles next run of greatness (1977 to 1983), with each playing for the team through at least 1986. May kicked in 2.2 WAR 1976–77, while Pagan failed to develop and was left unprotected in the expansion draft. Dempsey, Martinez, McGregor, and May contributed 53.8 WAR to the Orioles in total.

The Alexander trade, which was only possible because Alexander had come for Robinson, was one of the best trades in Orioles history. Unlike Bill DeWitt in 1965, Orioles general manager Frank Cashen successfully executed Branch Rickey's "better to trade them a year early than a year late" dictum.

a 6.23 ERA and Johnson was a 32-year-old with only 17 plate appearances. It is clear the Braves were trading for Pappas.

Dick Simpson was traded to the St. Louis Cardinals on January 11, 1968, for outfielder Alex Johnson. Johnson would play two years for the Reds before he was traded in turn, along with utility man Chico Ruiz, to the California Angels for pitchers Pedro Borbon, Jim McGlothlin, and Vern Geishert.

The sum contributions of all the players acquired by the Reds need to be contrasted with Robinson's value to the Orioles to evaluate the total on-field impact of the Robinson trade.

I chose to use Baseball-Reference.com's Wins Above Replacement (WAR) to measure value, and I have further chosen to utilize only positive WAR and ignore negative WAR. My logic is this: the purpose of a trade is to provide assets to the team. Suboptimal deployment of those assets (such as continuing to start a below-replacement level pitcher every five days) are not necessarily reflective of the trade. I also restricted the analysis to the years 1966–71 when Robinson played for the Orioles. Going beyond that point gets increasingly complicated due to the number of players involved.

Here is how the trade stacks up considering all assets acquired by the Reds through 1971:

Table 2. WAR Comparison for All Acquired Assets

Season	Orioles WAR		Reds WAR		
1966	Robinson	7.7	2.4	Pappas	2.4
1967	Robinson	5.4	3.6	Pappas	3.6
1968	Robinson	3.7	6.2	Carroll	3.1
				A. Johnson	3.1
1969	Robinson	7.5	5.1	Carroll	1.2
				Woodward	0.5
				A. Johnson	3.4
1970	Robinson	4.8	7.8	Carroll	2.0
				Cloninger	1.8
				Woodward	0.5
				McGlothlin	3.5
1971	Robinson	3.3	3.9	Carroll	1.7
				Cloninger	0.4
				Woodward	0.4
				McGlothlin	1.4
Total:	**Orioles 31.4**		**Reds 29.0**		

NOTES: Baldschun and Simpson failed to contribute positive WAR to the Reds and Pappas didn't in 1968; Carroll played for the Reds through 1975, Borbon through 1979.

When seen through this lens, the trade was not nearly the disaster for the Reds it has widely been assumed to be. In fact, the trade was arguably a significant enabler to the launching of the "Big Red Machine" Reds team of 1970–76.

There is one more very significant consideration when evaluating this trade. The architect of the Reds of 1970–76 was legendary general manager Bob Howsam. He masterminded the 1972 trade that brought Joe Morgan to the Reds, hired Sparky Anderson, traded for George Foster, drafted Ken Griffey Sr., and made many other roster moves that were essential to creating one of baseball's all-time best teams.

If the Robinson trade had not occurred, it is likely that Bill DeWitt would have remained in charge of the Reds, Howsam would have gone elsewhere, and baseball history might have been very different. Despite his accomplishments prior to the Robinson trade, there is nothing in DeWitt's resume to indicate that he had the acumen to forge the Reds into the perennial championship-winning force they would become.

The acquisition of Frank Robinson spurred the start of the Orioles dominance. There is no doubt that with the benefit of hindsight the Orioles would make the trade again and the Reds would not. However, that 1965 trade of Frank Robinson for Milt Pappas, Jack Baldschun, and Dick Simpson ignited the great Reds team, as well. ■

Notes

1. "For those reasons, and they are good reasons, many people in Cincinnati will always view the Robinson trade as the worst trade ever made by the Reds." Doug Decatur, *Traded: Inside the Most Lopsided Trades in Baseball History* (ACTA Sports, 2009).

2. "Two thoughts stayed with him (Robinson). He didn't know he needed a permit for the gun, but he should have known; and if Gabe Paul had still been the General Manager he would not have had to spend the night in jail." John C. Skipper, *Frank Robinson* (McFarland and Company, 2015).

3. Rob Neyer, *Rob Neyer's Book of Baseball Blunders* (Simon and Schuster, Inc., 2006).

4. Robert H. Boyle, "Cincinnati's Brain Picker," *Sports Illustrated* Jun 13, 1966.

5. G. Richard McKelvey, *The MacPhails: Baseball's First Family of the Front Office* (McFarland & Co., 2000).

6. John Eisenberg, *From 33rd Street to Camden Yards: An Oral History of the Baltimore Orioles* (Contemporary Books, 2001).

7. Eisenberg, *From 33rd Street to Camden Yards*.

8. "Fans Hang DeWitt Effigy in Downtown Cincinnati," *The Sporting News*, July 2, 1966.

9. Mark J. Schmetzer, *Before the Machine* (Cleristy Press, 2011).

The Baltimore Orioles' 1971 Japan Trip

Steven M. Glassman

On January 1, 1971, the chairman of the board of the Baltimore Orioles, Jerold C. Hoffberger, with the approval of Commissioner of Baseball Bowie Kuhn, accepted an invitation from *Yomiuri Shimbum* President Mitsuo Mutai to play an 18-game, 25-day schedule versus Japanese Central and Pacific League teams in October 1971.

Ten games would be versus the team owned by the *Yomiuri Shimbum* newspaper, the Giants, then reigning champions of the Nippon Series (Japan's equivalent of the World Series, a postseason interleague championship). The Giants had just won their sixth straight championship, defeating the Lotte Orions in five games. Other teams participating were the Chunichi Dragons, Hankyu Braves, Hiroshima Carp, Nankai Hawks, and Nishitetsu Lions. The Orioles would travel to the following cities and locales: Fukuoka, Hiroshima, Kita Koriyama, Kyoto, Kyushu, Matsuyama, Nagoya, Niigata, Nishinomiya, Sendai, Osaka, Tokyo, and Toyama.

The first game was scheduled for October 23. According to the *Baltimore Sun*, "Sixty members of the Oriole organization have been invited to make the trip, including the wives of the players and front office executives. All expenses of the tour will be defrayed by the *Yomiuri Shimbum*."[1]

"We are extremely honored to invite the champion baseball team of the United States," said Mutai in making the announcement. "We look forward to having all of their great stars playing here in Japan."[2] Of course, at the time of the tour's announcement, the 1971 season was yet to be played.

The Orioles finished the 1971 season with a 101–61 record, won their third consecutive American League East title, and fourth pennant in six seasons. However, they lost their second World Series in three years when the Pirates won in seven games.[3] The host Giants continued to dominate the Central League, finishing with a 70–52–8 mark and winning the club's seventh straight Nippon Series title in five games versus the Pacific League Champions Hankyu Braves.

The 73-member official travel party included the following: "[Commissioner] Kuhn, AL President Joe Cronin, Hoffberger, and Orioles' Executive Vice President Frank Cashen, Umpire Jim Honochick, Manager Earl Weaver, two coaches, 24 Orioles players, Trainer Ralph Salvon, five additional Orioles' officials, Major League Public Relations Director Joe Reichler, two newspapermen (Ken Nigro of the *Baltimore Sun* and Al Cartwright of the *Wilmington News Journal*), and many wives."[4] The 24 players were as follows: pitchers Mike

The Baltimore Orioles visited the Hiroshima Peace Memorial as part of their tour of Japan.

Cuellar, Pat Dobson, Tom Dukes, Dick Hall, Grant Jackson, Dave McNally, Jim Palmer, Pete Richert, and Eddie Watt; catchers Clay Dalrymple, Andy Etchebarren, and Elrod Hendricks; infielders Mark Belanger, Jerry DaVanon, Dave Johnson, Boog Powell, Brooks Robinson, and Chico Salmon; outfielders Paul Blair, Don Buford, Curt Motton, Merv Rettenmund, Frank Robinson, and Tom Shopay.[5] The travel party flew on a Japan Airlines DC-8 from Friendship Airport and arrived in Tokyo on October 21.

GAME 1: Giants at Korakuen Stadium in Tokyo (October 23)
The Orioles won the first game in front of 30,000 attendees. Japanese baseball officials, Kuhn, and Hoffberger spoke before the contest. In the second inning, Brooks Robinson opened the scoring with a home run and the remaining four runs in the inning came from four Giant errors. Palmer pitched the first six innings, allowing three runs on home runs by Shozo Doi and Koji Ano. Dukes threw the last three innings, allowing one run in the seventh, and got credit for the save. Buford got three hits and Blair and Powell (who also homered) contributed two apiece.

GAME 2: Giants at Korakuen Stadium in Tokyo (October 24)
Frank Robinson and Hendricks hit third-inning home runs off Tsuneo Horiuchi which gave the Orioles a 3–0 lead. Cuellar started the game and got credit for the win in the 8–2 victory in front of 49,000.

The Orioles-Giants game in Sapporo on October 26 was postponed due to rain and was rescheduled to be played in Tokyo on November 18. McNally, the scheduled starter, was scratched for the October 27 game due to left elbow soreness and Dobson would start in his place. "McNally's arm started hurting again the last two times he pitched in the World Series," said manager Earl Weaver.[6]

GAME 3: Giants at Miyagi Stadium in Sendai (October 27)
Pitching on the all-dirt infield of Miyagi Stadium, Dobson allowed one run, three hits, and struck out eight in the complete game effort as the Orioles won, 10–1, in front 25,000. The Orioles offense was led by Belanger (two triples and four RBIs), Blair (two singles and a double), and Buford (second consecutive game with a home run).

GAME 4: Giants in Koriyama (October 28)
It looked like the Giants might get the first hometown win of the tour, when the Giants scored three runs off the starter Palmer in the first four innings. Jackson, Hall, and Richert blanked the Giants for the rest of the game, but Giants starter Horiuchi held the Orioles to only two runs. He also got the first two outs in the top of the ninth with a 3–2 lead. However, Etchebarren tied the game with a home run. The game finished 3–3 after 10 innings.

GAME 5: Giants/Nankai Hawks at Koshien Stadium (October 31)
This game was originally scheduled for October 30 and was to be aired on ABC's *Wide World of Sports*, but was delayed a day by rain. The opponent that day would be the Nankai Hawks, except the Orioles actually faced a combined squad. In all the games against teams other than the Giants, some Giants players—especially legendary Giants slugger Sadaharu Oh—were placed into the host team's lineup. The move bolstered both the lineups of the teams and the publicity efforts of Yomiuri. The Giants wore their own uniforms and each team was managed by the host team's manager.[7]

Cuellar threw a complete game, allowing one first-inning run, five singles, and struck out 12 in a 4–1 win in front of 55,000. "I had good control," he said later, "and my fast ball was jumping."[8] The Orioles scored their runs on an error, Powell single, Frank Robinson double, and a Blair home run. Dalrymple "was given permission to return home to Philadelphia to visit his wife, who [was] critically ill."[9]

GAME 6: Giants/Nankai Hawks in Osaka (November 1)
McNally's tour debut was his first start since October 16—Game Six of the World Series versus the Pirates. His elbow had kept him sidelined.[10] He allowed four singles in seven innings and combined with Richert and Watt for the five-hit shutout. Brooks Robinson and Johnson hit back-to-back home runs in the fifth for the game's only runs in a 2–0 win.

GAME 7: Giants in Toyama (November 2)
Dobson became the first American pitcher on the Japan Tour to no-hit an opponent. He struck out seven, walked three, and threw 115 pitches. The 18,000 in attendance gave him a standing ovation after he got Isao Shibata to ground out to Powell to complete the no-hitter. "It's funny but I had a bad cold and didn't get much sleep the night before," Dobson said later. "I've also had some tendonitis of the shoulder and I didn't think I had a thing warming up.[11] I didn't pitch any differently than during the season (when he won 20 games)," the *Sun* reported him as saying. "But I did have a good fast ball today and I really don't think the Japanese can handle a good fast one."[12] Powell's fourth-inning, two-run home run off Horiuchi accounted for

Promotional poster touting the Orioles' tour of Japan.

the game's only runs. This game was also broadcast on WFBR-AM (1300) radio in Maryland.

GAME 8: Japan All-Stars in Tokyo (November 3)
Palmer pitched a complete game in the 7–0 win, allowing three singles, five walks, and striking out 10 in front of a crowd of 45,000. Brooks Robinson and Hendricks contributed home runs. Palmer struck out Shigeo Nagashima and got Sadaharu Oh to pop out to Powell after allowing two baserunners to reach with one out. In the ninth, "Blair's long running catch of slugger Koichi Tabuchi's drive preserved the shutout."[13] Palmer said, "I probably had one of the better games of the year…I had a good fast ball and curves to go with it."[14]

GAME 9: Giants in Niigata (November 5)
This was one of the more competitive contests of the tour. The Orioles' scoreless pitching streak ended in the second inning when the Giants took the lead with two runs on a Tamito Suetsugu double and Ano's bunt off Cuellar. They added another run in the third, but Buford's three-run home run in the fifth gave the Orioles a 4–3 lead. The Giants tied the game in the eighth off Dukes when Suetsugu doubled and Ano singled. Richert replaced Dukes and retired his first hitter, but

his throwing error to second allowed the tying run to score. The game ended as a 4–4 tie.

GAME 10: Giants in Tokyo at Korakuen Stadium (November 6)
The Giants' bats finally woke up on their home grounds. The teams put on a hitting display for the crowd of 20,000, combining for 18 runs on 29 hits (including eight home runs). Jackson started in place of McNally. The Giants led, 5–0, after six innings. The Orioles tied the game in the seventh on RBI singles by Buford and Salmon and a three-run Belanger home run. The Giants retook the lead in the seventh and Powell's three-run home run gave the Orioles an 8–6 lead in the eighth. The Giants tied the game again in the eighth. Blair's home run in the 10th gave the Orioles a 9–8 lead. However, Shibata's two-out, two-strike home run off Dukes tied the game for the third and final time. "I might have had it on a clear day," said the 5-foot-9 Shopay. "But it was so dark I had trouble following the ball."[15] The game ended in a 9–9, 10-inning tie due to rain and darkness.

GAME 11: Giants in Tokyo (November 7)
The Orioles scored five runs in the first on a three-run home run by Frank Robinson and solo home runs by Brooks Robinson and Etchebarren, en route to a 7–0 win in five rain-shortened innings. Dobson pitched the complete game, allowing two hits.

GAME 12: Giants/Hankyu Braves in Kyoto (November 9)
The Orioles lost their first game of the tour, 8–2. The Giants/Braves hit three home runs off of losing pitcher Palmer in four innings. Although the Orioles tied the game at one in the second, on consecutive Brooks Robinson and Johnson doubles, the Giants/Braves scored six straight runs over the next four innings. Altogether the Giants/Braves hit four home runs led by legendary Japanese slugger Oh (plus Nagashima, Tokaji Nagaike, and Yutaka Fukumoto). Powell hit a home run in the sixth. Hisashi Yamada pitched a complete game, allowing seven hits. Richert took a ground ball to the face and left the game with a bruised right eye.

GAME 13: Giants/Hiroshima Carp in Hiroshima (November 10)
The Orioles visited the Hiroshima Peace Memorial Museum before playing the Giants/Carp. The museum displayed pictures and artifacts from when Hiroshima was hit with an atomic bomb on August 6, 1945. "Something like this doesn't give you much of a stomach to play baseball," said utility infielder Jerry DaVanon.[16] Buford broke a scoreless tie in the fifth with a two-run home run. He also scored another run and stole a pair

of bases. Powell contributed an eighth-inning RBI. Cuellar allowed two runs in 8⅓ innings. Dukes got a game-ending ground ball double play, and the Orioles won, 4–2.

GAME 14: Giants in Matsuyama (November 11)

Paul Blair was the difference-maker in this game. Jackson and Horiuchi matched zeros for the first nine innings. Watt relieved in the tenth and got defensive help when Koji Ano's potential game-winning home run was taken away by Blair. Hendricks's RBI double in the 11th broke the scoreless tie and Blair scored on a Horiuchi wild pitch.

GAME 15: Giants/Nishitetsu Lions in Fukuoka (November 13)

The Orioles led, 8–4, on solo home runs by Hendricks and Frank Robinson and a two-run contribution by Belanger. However, Yukinobu Kuroe hit a three-run home run versus Dukes in the fifth and the Giants/ Lions tied the game in the eighth. Hendricks's RBI single, his fourth hit of the game, in the tenth gave the Orioles the lead. However, Oh's two-run home run tied the game and the contest was called a tie after the inning was over. Both teams combined for six home runs in front of 24,000.

GAME 16: Giants at Kitakyushu (November 14)

The Giants scored four in the third and led 5–0. However, the Orioles scored three in the fourth and Frank Robinson's home run tied the game in the fifth. Etchebarren's two-run home run gave the Orioles a lead in the sixth. The Giants tied the game again in the seventh. Palmer allowed seven runs in seven innings on five hits and nine walks. The Orioles also committed four errors. Buford scored the go-ahead run in the ninth on a Shopay sacrifice fly, and the Orioles eked out a 7–5 win.

GAME 17: Giants/Chunichi Dragons at Nagoya (November 16)

The Giants/Dragons opened the scoring on a Brooks Robinson fielding error in the second that led to two runs. They scored four runs on six straight hits and opened up a 7–1 lead in the sixth off Jackson. Jackson allowed seven runs on six hits in 5⅔ innings. Instead of using one of the Orioles' relief pitchers, Weaver called on infielder DaVanon to pitch.[17] "Our other pitchers are all tired," he explained. "If it was a close game I wouldn't have used him."[18] He allowed a two-run home run to Tatsuhiko Kimata in the seventh after an Oh walk. All told DaVanon allowed two runs on three hits in 2⅓ innings. Mitsuo Inaba and Hisatoshi Ito combined to allow four Oriole hits. Powell's fourth-inning home run was the Orioles' only run of the game.

The Japanese media, including the tour's sponsor *Yomiuri Shimbum*, criticized Weaver for using a position player instead of one of his pitchers in the 9–1 loss. Weaver stood by his decision. "'We're out of gas,' added Weaver who always has had a reputation of hating to lose anytime, anywhere. 'I'm sorry the Japanese feel the way they do but there is nothing we can do about it. If they don't like it…well, they can lump it.'"[19]

The final game of the Tour was postponed due to rain on November 18 and rescheduled for November 20.

GAME 18: Giants in Tokyo (November 20)

Dukes and Hall combined on a four-hit 5–0 shutout in the final game of the Tour in front of 17,880. Johnson hit a two-run home run and Hendricks finished off the scoring with a solo home run in the ninth.

———

The Orioles finished 12–2–4 on the Japan Tour, traveling over 20,000 miles during the 18-game, 31-day schedule in 14 different cities. They traveled by airplane, bus, ferry, hydrofoil, and train. Approximately 450,000 spectators attended the games, an average of 25,000 per game.

Hendricks led Orioles hitters with a .400 batting average (16-for-40). Powell batted .397 (23-for-58) and led the squad with six home runs and 14 RBIs. Shopay was the team's other hitter over .300 with a .375 batting average (6-for-16). Brooks Robinson's five home runs were second to Powell. Buford and Frank Robinson were second to Powell with 11 RBIs each.

Cuellar shared the wins lead with Dobson, going 3–0 each. Cuellar also paced the Orioles in innings pitched (31⅔) and ERA (2.27) and did not allow a home run. Palmer went 2–1 in five starts, including a shutout. McNally won his only start. Altogether, the Orioles' four 1971 20-game winners went 9–1.

Meanwhile, Suetsugu led the Giants with a .319 batting average (15-for-47). Nagashima batted .268 (16-for-62) with a team-leading eight RBIs. Oh batted 0.111 (six-for-54), but three of his hits were home runs. Horiuchi appeared in six games, throwing 47 innings, allowing 44 hits, striking out 27, and compiling a 3.64 ERA.

Ultimately, the Orioles played 213 games in 260 days between March 6 and November 20, 1971. "The Orioles created a very good impression," *The Sporting News* reported a Yomiuri executive as saying. "They played seriously…to win and that's one of the reasons so many people came out."[21] The Orioles for their part were pleased with the trip, too. "They treated us like kings, and the way things were organized couldn't have been better, even though they kept us pretty busy," McNally told the *Baltimore Sun*. "You can't be treated any nicer than they treated us. But as great as it was, it's always great to get home.'"[22]

The Orioles would return to Japan in 1984, playing from October 27 through November 14, compiling an 8–5–1 record. ■

Acknowledgments

Thank you to SABR members Yoshihiro Koda, Inohiza Takeyuki, and Robert Fitts for research assistance.

Notes

1. "Orioles to Tour Japan in Fall," *Baltimore Sun*, January 1, 1971.
2. "Orioles to Tour Japan in Fall."
3. Including the 1971 Orioles, none of the other major league teams who traveled to Japan won the World Series the season they were invited. The 1968 St. Louis Cardinals (lost in seven to the Tigers) and 1955 New York Yankees (lost in seven to the Dodgers) came the closest.
4. Bob Brown, Phil Itzoe, and Fran Moulden, eds. *1972 Baltimore Orioles Media Guide*: 25. Public Relations Director Bob Brown, Promotions Director Walter Freeman, and Director of Scouting Walter Shannon were three of the five Orioles' staffers who went on the trip. It is not known who the other two were.
5. We do not know the names of the two coaches who were part of the official travel party. Pitching coach George Bamberger was at home for the remaining eight Orioles postseason games and the Japan tour due to a heart attack, per Joe Elliot, "Orioles' Bamberger at home, feels 'perfect'," *Baltimore Sun*, October 26, 1971.
6. Ken Nigro, "Birds get rain, even in Japan," *Baltimore Sun*, October 27, 1971.
7. Yoshihiro Koda, email correspondence, July 14, 2020.
8. Ken Nigro, "Orioles' Cuellar throttles Japan All-Stars, 4–1," *Baltimore Sun*, November 1, 1971.
9. Ken Nigro, "Orioles' Cuellar throttles Japan All-Stars, 4–1."
10. McNally spent 27 days on the disabled list in 1971 due to his elbow. This was also his only appearance in Japan.
11. Ken Nigro, "'Not so hot' Dobson no-hit Giants as Orioles win, 2–0," *Baltimore Sun*, November 3, 1971.
12. Ken Nigro, "'Not so hot' Dobson no-hit Giants as Orioles win, 2–0."
13. "Palmer Three Hitter Beats Japan All-Stars," *Cumberland News*, November 4, 1971.
14. "Palmer Three Hitter Beats Japan All-Stars."
15. Ken Nigro, "Orioles settle for Tie," *Baltimore Sun*, November 7, 1971.
16. Ken Nigro, "Birds sobered by visit to Hiroshima Museum," *Baltimore Sun*, November 11, 1971.
17. This was DaVanon's pitching debut. He never pitched in the major leagues.
18. Ken Nigro, "Orioles lose 9–1, near end of sojourn," *Baltimore Sun*, November 17, 1971.
19. Ken Nigro, "Japanese rip use of DaVanon," *Baltimore Sun*, November 18, 1971.
20. Lou Hatter, "After 8½ long months, the Birds are finished," *Baltimore Sun*, November 23, 1971. The breakdown is as follows: 27 Spring Training, 158 regular season, three American League Championship Series, seven World Series, and 18 Japan Tour games.
21. Ken Nigro, "Japanese Caliber Better in Orioles' Estimation," *The Sporting News*, December 25, 1971: 31–32.
22. Lou Hatter, "After 8½ long months, the Birds are finished."
23. Bob Brown, Rick Vaughn, Dr. Charles Steinberg, and Helen Conklin, eds. *Orioles Media Guide '85*: 44–46.

Dave McNally and Peter Seitz at the Intersection of Baseball Labor History

Ed Edmonds

On September 26, 1962, Dave McNally took the mound for the first time as a Baltimore Orioles starter in game one of a doubleheader at Memorial Stadium. The lefty, who spent most of the year pitching for the Elmira Pioneers, hurled the first of his 33 career shutouts. McNally's two-hit, three-walk effort produced the first of his 184 career wins. McNally undoubtedly did not realize that evening that he would personally be at the forefront of a baseball labor movement over the next thirteen years that would radically change baseball's reserve system and salary structure. During those years, McNally would first battle with Orioles general managers Harry Dalton and Frank Cashen over his annual salary; second, agree in 1974 to be one of 29 players who were the first to use a union-negotiated system of salary arbitration hearings; third, demand a trade after the 1974 season for a needed "change of scenery" and not sign a contract with his new team; and, fourth, with fellow pitcher Andy Messersmith, force an arbitration panel decision over the reach of the reserve system.[1]

The arbitrator in McNally's 1974 salary arbitration in New York City was, like the pitcher, a veteran at his craft. Peter Seitz's labor resume was impressive. He served in the mid-1960s as a member of the American Arbitration Association's labor-management panel that analyzed New York City's collective-bargaining procedures. The panel's recommendations established the city's Office of Collective Bargaining and produced a foundational labor law scheme. Seitz also served on the National Wage Stabilization Board, as counsel and assistant to the director of the Federal Mediation and Conciliation Service, and director of industrial relations for the Defense Department.[2] By 1974, Seitz was already the principal arbitrator for disputes between the National Basketball Association and the National Basketball Players Association.[3] He would succeed Gabriel Alexander that year as the third permanent arbitrator for major league baseball and the Major League Baseball Players Association.[4] Seitz delivered a major decision in an arbitration grievance that declared Jim Hunter a free agent because of a breach of contract by Oakland Athletics owner Charles Finley.[5] McNally probably knew little about Peter Seitz when Seitz decided the hurler's salary dispute with the Orioles in McNally's favor. Although McNally was a critical backup plan behind the December 1975 grievance in front of John Gaherin, Marvin Miller, and Seitz, McNally was back home in Billings, Montana, and never appeared before the panel.[6] However, Dave McNally and Peter Seitz are forever linked in baseball's critical decision that altered the reserve system and established the foundation for baseball's free agency system.

This article will focus on McNally's labor conflicts with Orioles management and his salary arbitration hearing. Although much has been written about Seitz's McNally-Messersmith decision, Dave McNally rarely discussed it. The article will finish with a few of McNally's reported comments on that decision.

SALARY DISPUTES 1969–73

After McNally's single game appearance in 1962, the left-hander joined a starting staff the following year that included future Hall of Famer Robin Roberts and veterans Milt Pappas and Steve Barber. By 1965, McNally had moved from the fifth starter to the middle of the rotation and pushed his salary from $12,000 to $17,000.[7] The following year, he was at the top of the rotation and won the decisive fourth game in the World Series sweep over the Los Angeles Dodgers. The effort pushed McNally's salary to $24,000. When Baltimore dropped to a sixth-place finish in 1967—in part due to McNally's sore elbow as well as injuries to Barber, Wally Bunker, and Jim Palmer—Dalton initially reduced McNally's salary by $4,000 with a stipulation that it would return to the same $24,000 as the previous year if the pitcher was on the Active List for the first thirty days of the season.[8] Dalton's decision would establish an atmosphere of conflict between McNally and the front office for the remainder of the pitcher's Oriole career.

McNally had a breakout 1968 season when he posted the first of his four consecutive 20-win seasons by winning 22 of 32 decisions with a 1.95 ERA and a fifth-place finish in the MVP voting. However, baseball's offseason was highlighted by labor strife and it impacted McNally's salary negotiations. *Baltimore Sun* writer Lou Hatter wrote that "McNally and [Tom] Phoebus, especially the former, will remain Baltimore-based holdouts for two reasons. Not only are both upholding the Players Association posture against the owners; neither has been satisfied by three 1969 salary offers from Oriole personnel director Harry Dalton."[9] McNally asserted that "'the owners' arbitration refusal is a good point in our favor as far as outside people are concerned. I think they (the owners) must be afraid of something.'"[10] McNally did not sign his new deal until February 28, holding out for nine days. McNally was described by *Sun* writer Jim Elliot as "extremely satisfied" with his resulting salary increase to $51,000.[11]

McNally's negotiations with Dalton were even more protracted in 1970, when McNally missed two and a half weeks in a holdout resolved on March 5 when he signed for $65,000.[12] The pitcher remarked after signing the new deal that he "didn't come to Florida to become a holdout. …Considering my performance the last two years, I proposed what I considered to be a fair figure. I was trying to sign. [Orioles management] were being difficult about it."[13]

The 1971 Orioles lost the World Series in seven games to the Pittsburgh Pirates, but McNally won 21 of his 26 regular season decisions, and he was joined by Mike Cueller, Pat Dobson, and Jim Palmer as 20-game winners. McNally managed to wrangle a $20,000 raise for the season by signing on February 24 after missing one week of spring training. Jim Elliot reported that McNally was "'very close' to the $100,000

he was seeking," but, in reality, he was well short of the mark. The writer reported that a smiling McNally noted that "I'm not supposed to give out any figures, but I got very close to what I wanted."[14]

After posting his fourth straight 20-win season in 1971, McNally finally broke through the $100,000 barrier, but it did not come without the usual struggle with the front office. In becoming the first American League pitcher to exceed the magical figure, McNally and his agent waited until February 27 to finally work out a $20,000 raise over his 1971 salary.[15] A few days after signing the deal, McNally argued. "It sounds funny for me to say this, but I don't think I should have to fight to have gotten what I did. Look at it this way: My record the past four years was better than Seaver's and Jenkins', wasn't it?"[16] McNally was referencing his understanding that Tom Seaver and Ferguson Jenkins were two of the four National League pitchers making over $100,000. Bob Gibson and Juan Marichal were also supposedly above the $100,000 mark.[17]

The 1972 Orioles dropped to 80–74, and McNally posted the fewest wins of the Birds' top four starters despite a solid 2.95 ERA. McNally missed only the beginning of Orioles spring training before signing for the same $105,000 for 1973.[18] He posted a 17–17 record in 1973, but, again, McNally was not pleased with management's contract offer of the same $105,000 for the 1974 season, so he decided to join the first class of players to use the recently negotiated salary arbitration process to determine his compensation for the upcoming season. Years later manager Earl Weaver reflected on McNally, stating that the pitcher was "a great competitor, a gentleman…I will say this, though, when it came down to contract dealings, he was mercenary. He was as tough as any player I have ever seen. Every spring, [general manager] Harry Dalton would start out with a dollar offer, and McNally would stay away [from camp] until Dalton got all the way up to the figure Dave wanted. It was simple, really. Unless he got what he wanted, he would not play."[19]

THE SALARY ARBITRATION HEARING

McNally and agent Ed Keating joined with Cleveland attorney Bill Carpenter of International Management Company to fashion their arbitration case. After a hearing in New York, Peter Seitz ruled in their favor.[20] Seitz heard five cases in the initial year of salary arbitration, the most of any arbitrator.[21] He also found in favor of Bill Sudakis while ruling against Paul Blair, Tim Foli, and Gene Michael.[22]

McNally's arbitration hearing was held on Thursday, February 21, 1974, in a New York City hotel.[23] Prior to

After suffering a sore elbow in 1967, Dave McNally won 22 games in 1968, the first of his four consecutive 20-win seasons.

the hearing, McNally presented his thoughts to *Sun* reporter Cameron Snyder. After recounting his earlier disputes with management over salary offers, he said, "You can go back [to previous years of negotiations] where you thought you were not treated right and that also has to be considered by the arbitrator. We think we have a good case."[24] McNally researched his 1973 pitching record and Bill Carpenter "put them together in written form."[25] *Sun* writer Ken Nigro observed that the pair "obviously based their case mostly on the fact the Birds were shut out six times while McNally was on the mound. They lost three of the games by 1–0 scores, two by 2–0 and another by 3–0."[26] A split of those six starts would have improved McNally's record from 17–17 to 20–14, a fifth 20-win season. Although McNally felt that the hearing was a "helluva experience" where "I learned a lot," he felt that Frank Cashen breached some confidences, noting that "I don't mind Frank... saying anything about my ability or his personal opinion of me. ...He is entitled to that. But there were some things said during the hearing that I don't think should have been said. That's all I want to say about it."[27] He was obviously pleased with Seitz's favorable decision because "we were $10,000 apart... And if it wasn't for arbitration, we probably still would have been $10,000 apart when I finally signed."[28]

The hearing lasted over three and one-half hours, "from 10 AM until about 1:40 PM"[29] As McNally told the *Sun*'s Nigro:

> We presented our case then they presented theirs. After that both sides add any additional information. The arbitrator asked very few questions. In fact, I would say he was 90 per cent a listener. He seemed to know about baseball, but it was tough to tell what he was listening to and what he wasn't. ...It was much more formal than I thought it would be. ... I had talked to Dick Moss [counsel for the Players' Association] and he told me it would be a very informal hearing with a relaxed atmosphere. But it was more like a regular court trial. ...Was I nervous? I sure was.[30]

The length of the hearing was "because everything was detailed."[31] Cashen came well prepared for the hearing, and presented a written summation with 22 points supporting their position.[32]

Peter Seitz was also the arbitrator for teammate Paul Blair, who felt that it was unfortunate that they shared the same decision maker, saying, "The one thing I didn't like was that the same arbitrator heard my case and Dave's and I don't think that helped."[33]

MARVIN MILLER ON 1974 SALARY ARBITRATION

Marvin Miller generally felt comfortable about the arbitration decisions, but one aspect bothered him about the decision-making process of the arbitrators. "It might be unfair for me to say this…but I was struck by the general inclination of the arbitrators to split their cases. Maybe it was pure coincidence. I don't know," he told Jerome Holtzman of *The Sporting News*. According to Miller, every arbitrator who presided at two hearings split his decision, 1–1. Those who had three cases voted 2–1 and the one who heard five voted 3–2. There was only one exception. One arbitrator heard four cases, all involving Oakland players, and voted 3–1 in favor of the players.[34]

PETER SEITZ ON ARBITRATION

Peter Seitz, in reflecting on what he preferred to call "High-Low Arbitration," wrote a short piece for *The Arbitration Journal* with the hope "that the desperate thirst for information may be slaked by a few observations of a participant."[35] Claiming that "the writer can testify only as to the five hearings at which he presided," Seitz argued that "it seemed to him that the clubs, on the whole (with exceptions), were better prepared and made a more professional presentation than the players."[36] Pushing his observations further, Seitz stated that "the hearings were noteworthy in the respect that the hearings at which I presided were inundated by a torrent of statistical data."[37] Seitz next presented a hypothetical illustration with an explicit statement in a footnote that it should not be taken as an actual example of one of the presentations that he heard. However, his example did track closely the facts in the McNally case: "For example; if a club asserts that in the past year, the earned run average of batters against a pitcher increased significantly and his win-lose figure was less impressive than in previous years. Accordingly, no increase in pay was offered by the club. The pitcher, however, argues, with a wealth of figures, that in the games he lost, the margin of defeat was mostly by one or two runs; and in most of those games, his team hit well below its season's batting average."[38] McNally's hearing was the only one of Seitz's five to involve a pitcher, and McNally's primary arguments were close decisions and weak offensive support. Furthermore, McNally's 1973 salary of $105,000 matched the Orioles offer.

MCNALLY-MESSERSMITH ARBITRATION

After the 1974 season, McNally requested a trade, and he was sent to Montreal.[39] When negotiations with the Expos broke down, Montreal renewed McNally's salary for the 1975 season with a small increase. McNally played part of the season without signing that deal, and he agreed to remain unsigned after retiring on June 9. McNally agreed to join Andy Messersmith on the historic grievance that determined that both players were now free agents and no longer bound by the reserve system. Later in the year the Expos tried to negotiate a deal, but McNally, despite no future plans to return to the game, refused to sign. "To this day, I have tremendous respect for Dave," says Wally Bunker, "because he turned down significant money in his pocket for a cause that helped a lot of other future players."[40]

Peter Seitz once again was pivotal as the lead arbitrator on the three-person panel including Marvin Miller and John Gaherin. Much has been written about the historically important McNally-Messersmith decision and Seitz's written opinion. However, McNally rarely spoke about it. In a 1986 article by John Eisenberg, he noted that "eleven years later, McNally does not consider himself a revolutionary." McNally argued, "I do not look back at [the case] with pride, or anything like that. …Maybe I would feel differently about it if I had testified. But I did not. I never left Billings. The only part I played was a name on a suit. My name was involved. But not me."[41] ■

Notes

1. Ian MacDonald, "Expos' Trade For Fryman May Be Calm Before Storm," *Montreal Gazette*, December 5, 1974.
2. For the assertion that Peter Seitz was the arbitrator, the author relies primarily on a document listing all arbitrators from 1974 through 2008. Salary Arbitration Results by Season, 1998–2008, MLBPA and STATS, Inc., 22. The information that Seitz heard McNally's case was verified via telephone call on February 28, 2020. The information on Seitz's labor background was taken from Damon Stetson, "Peter Seitz, 78, The Arbitrator in Baseball Free-Agent Case," *The New York Times*, October 19, 1983.
3. Stetson, "Peter Seitz."
4. Robert F. Burk, *More Than a Game: Players, Owners, & American Baseball Since 1921* (Chapel Hill: University of North Carolina Press, 2001), 197; Charles Korr provides some commentary on MLBPA's Dick Moss offering Peter Seitz the position as permanent arbitrator. Charles P. Korr, *The End of Baseball As We Knew It: The Players Union, 1961–81* (Urbana: University of Illinois Press, 2002), 141–42. Alexander's resignation is discussed by Marvin Miller in his autobiography. Marvin Miller, *A Whole Different Ball Game: The Sport and Business of Baseball* (New York, Carol Publishing Group, 1991), 246.
5. Jerome Holtzman provided a detailed discussion of the Hunter decision in the *Official Baseball Guide*. Jerome Holtzman, *Official Baseball Guide for 1975*, 284–300 (St. Louis: The Sporting News, 1975), 284–300; Korr, *The End of Baseball*, 142–46.
6. John Eisenberg, "McNally Shook Baseball's Foundation, But He Has Solid One Now in Montana," *Baltimore Sun*, July 17, 1986.

7. The salary information in this article is based upon McNally's contract card held by the Giamatti Research Center at the National Baseball Hall of Fame and Museum.
8. McNally's contract card.
9. Lou Hatter, "Four Orioles Prepare to Sit Tight," *Baltimore Sun*, February 19, 1969.
10. Hatter, "Four Orioles."
11. Jim Elliot, "Powell and Phoebus Remain Bird Holdouts," *Baltimore Sun*, March 1, 1969.
12. McNally's contract card. The figure was also reported "as an estimated $65,000 contract, after setting an $80,000 price which would have doubled his 1969 income." Lou Hatter, "Dave McNally's Late Start Puts Guess In His Condition," *Baltimore Sun*, March 19, 1970.
13. Lou Hatter, "Dave McNally's Late Start;"Dave McNally Inks Early Bird Contract," *Casper Star Tribune*, February 26, 1974.
14. Jim Elliot, "McNally, Cueller In Line," *Baltimore Sun*, February 25, 1971.
15. Edwin Pope, "$100,000-a-Year Club Now Includes 23 Major Leaguers," *The Sporting News*, April 8, 1972 (McNally "was the first American League pitcher to receive a contract worth $100,000 when he signed with the Orioles prior to the 1972 season.")
16. Milton Richman, "Big Money O's," *Tampa Times*, March 4, 1972.
17. Richman, "Big Money O's."
18. McNally's Contract Card. Elliot lists Denny McLain as the first $100,000 American League pitcher based on the final year of his three-year contract. Baseball-Reference.com has a note to such effect by his 1971 Washington Senators salary entry, but does not list him at $100,000 in any main column. Jim Elliot, "McNally Signs, Looks for Comeback Season," *Baltimore Sun*, March 5, 1973.
19. John Eisenberg, "McNally Shook Baseball's Foundation, But He has Solid One Now in Montana," *Baltimore Sun*, July 17, 1986.
20. Gary Long, "O's McNally Already 1–0 In $ League," *Miami Herald*, February 27, 1974 ("Peter Sykes (sic) of the American Arbitration Association apparently believed him."); Ken Nigro, McNally Is Bitter Despite Salary Win, *Baltimore Sun*, February 27, 1974; Cameron C. Snyder, "3 Oriole Stars Take Salaries to Arbitration," *Baltimore Sun*, February 12, 1974.
21. "Salary Arbitration Results by Season."
22. "Salary Arbitration Results by Season."
23. Snyder, "3 Oriole Stars."
24. Snyder, "3 Oriole Stars."
25. Nigro, "McNally Is Bitter."
26. Nigro, "McNally Is Bitter."
27. Nigro, "McNally Is Bitter."
28. Nigro, "McNally Is Bitter."
29. Nigro, "McNally Is Bitter."
30. Nigro, "McNally Is Bitter."
31. Long, "O's McNally Already 1–0"
32. Nigro, "McNally Is Bitter."
33. Nigro, "McNally Is Bitter."
34. Jerome Holtzman, "Arbitration a Success, Players and Owners Agree," *The Sporting News*, March 16, 1974, 53.
35. Peter Seitz, "Footnotes to Baseball Salary Arbitration," *The Arbitration Journal* (1974) 29:98.
36. Seitz, "Footnotes," 99.
37. Seitz, "Footnotes," 100.
38. Seitz, "Footnotes," 100.
39. MacDonald, "Expos' Trade For Fryman."
40. Eisenberg, "McNally Shook Baseball's Foundation."
41. Eisenberg, "McNally Shook Baseball's Foundation."

Black Cats, Blue Suits, and Orange Socks

How Earl Weaver's Orioles Thrived on Superstition

Dan VanDeMortel

Meooowwwwww, avoid black cats! Don't step on the base lines! Don your rally cap! Grab your magic seat and jewelry!

Superstition has been a part of baseball since the game's earliest days. Almost anything and anyone have been fair game to promote personal and team good fortune: pre-game meal rituals, lucky clothes and equipment, mascots, dwarves, albinos, hunchbacks, peculiar avoidances, cherished habits, spiritual Hail Marys, even voodoo.

It's impossible to quantify baseball's all-time most superstitious team, but Earl Weaver's Baltimore Orioles during his 17-year managerial career (1968–82, 1985–86) would be a good candidate for the title. Plus, modern research indicates it may even have contributed to the team's success.

From afar, a Weaver clubhouse seems an improbable place for superstition. Outwardly, the 5-foot-7 combative field general came across as a no-nonsense fire plug, more likely to argue with players and umpires than touch wood. Weaver was a highly rational baseball man who relied on statistical research, platoons, walks, and the three-run home run in a time when analytics was confined to a few "traditional" statisticians, computer nerds, and a young Bill James toiling in the wilderness.[1] Weaver's intense focus yielded impeccable results: a .583 winning percentage, four American League pennants, and a 1970 World Series championship. The team obviously bought into Weaver's approach. But underneath that rational veneer lay enough superstitious behavior to fill 12 or 14 (not "13," please) psychology notebooks.

Let's start with the boss. Weaver was a two-pack-a-day cigarette smoker who lit up proudly and often in the dugout, sometimes while televised, rationalizing his addiction through his insistence that the opposition scored every time he failed to smoke between innings.[2] In the Memorial Stadium dugout, he rested his foot against a "good-luck" pole and ordered anyone nearby to stay away. When the Orioles were winning, he avoided looking at a clock. He used the same red pen until the team lost, then switched to another color in hopes one would propel new success. According to Orioles' public address announcer Rex Barney, Weaver would even become violent if his pen ran out of ink during a winning streak.[3] And during some hot streaks that occurred while Weaver was "on vacation"—serving suspensions for unpleasant interactions with umpires—upon his reinstatement he would either refuse to sit on the Orioles' bench or simply let a coach manage until the winning stopped.

Under Weaver's penchant for good luck charms and fortune-inducing habits, his ballplayers followed suit, often surpassing the master with their individual and collective oddities. During one successful 1974 stretch, slick-fielding shortstop Mark Belanger traced an "S" route on and off the field each inning, faithfully circling outside the third-base coach's box, then veering between the coach's rectangle and bag en route to his position, then reversing course for the Orioles' turn at bat. That same year, pitching ace Jim Palmer made sure to sit in his "defensive seat" on top of the back rest to the left of pitching coach George Bamberger and next to the bat rack when the Orioles were on offense. Bamberger, meanwhile, during a stretch of six consecutive

Earl Weaver was known for his combative nature with umpires, once being tossed twice in one day during a 1976 doubleheader.

victories and 10 out of 11, hit the bench three times with a bat during each inning. And when a rally was needed, infielder Enos Cabell batted the water cooler repeatedly, sometimes assisted by outfielder Al "The Bumblebee" Bumbry and infielder Tim Nordbrook. Weaver, favoring superstition over discipline, made no effort to interfere, observing, "It's noisy, but we like it."[4]

Pitcher Pat Dobson's 1971 behavior was equally strange. While readying for his June 8 start, he discovered his socks were missing from his locker. Noticing that pitcher Mike Cuellar's locker contained an extra pair of orange socks, Dobson nabbed them and pulled them on while immersed in a 45-minute discussion with Baltimore *News-American* writer Chan Keith. Once their topics and his feet were covered, Dobson went on to beat the Twins, 8–2. During his next start, he became involved in another long chat with Keith "about the price of automobiles, the headaches of sports writing, [an] athlete's responsibilities to the public," and, perhaps, baseball.[5] This time, Dobson was clubbed, 7–3, by the White Sox. Talking with Keith, obviously, was not the good luck charm, right? Wrong. The problem, Dobson deduced, was that he had not worn Cuellar's "magic" socks. For his next several starts, Dobson wore the same pair of Cuellar's socks and sought out Keith for his conversational "fix," even waiting once until the last minute in Oakland when Keith's arrival was delayed. As the wins mounted on the way to 20 victories, Dobson quipped Keith would receive one percent of any offseason salary increase: just a bit short of Keith's jocular counterproposal of 20 percent.

A black cat probably did not cross Dobson's path during this successful stretch, but one did encounter outfielder Rich Coggins during winter ball in Puerto Rico. One season while Coggins was mired in a slump and personal problems, a black cat walked in front of his car several days in a row. "Before that, I was never superstitious about black cats. Then I started entertaining that superstition and letting it bother me," Coggins admitted.[6] Later while Coggins was arriving at a Burger King, a black cat came to rest in front of his car. Exiting the car and slowly approaching the cat, Coggins asked, "Why are you on me?" The cat stayed put and stared at him. Coggins spoke to it some more, then walked away, as did the cat. "I realized as I talked to it both good and evil are around and that you have to deal with them. It became a challenge to overcome my problems rather than sulking. Now I understand black cats," Coggins concluded.[7]

Coggins's *el gato negro*, however, would have needed a Gatorade bucket of catnip to imagine the Orioles

Miguel Angel "Mike" Cuellar won 20 games four times for the Orioles. Perhaps all his superstitions worked.

most superstitious player of all time, perhaps baseball's, too: Mike Cuellar. The Cuban screwball-tossing lefty's oddball rituals and quirks earned him the nickname "Crazy Horse" for good reason. No black cats were involved, but his "action verb" theatrical resume was and is legendary, confusing, and amusing, including:

- Flying in a blue suit while wearing a special gold-chain medallion.

- Believing in the spirit of his magic baseball cap, which he wore when he pitched. Once while on the road in Milwaukee, he insisted the Orioles fly the forgotten cap to him. Noticing upon arrival that it was only his practice hat, Cuellar refused to pitch.

- Eating Chinese food the night before he pitched.

- Taking batting practice on start days, even after the designated hitter rule took effect.

- Smoking a cigarette per inning in the runway off the dugout or in the same seat on start days.

- Sitting on the "lucky" end of the training table before taking the field, receiving an arm massage with his medallion safely draped around his neck.

- Allowing only select catchers and coaches to receive his warm-up pitches and simulate a batter.[8] Never finishing warm up tosses until the opposing starter completed his.

- Insisting that upon completing warm-ups the ball be thrown to a specifically designated person in the dugout (usually Jim Palmer, though an alternate receiver could be designated).[9]

- Observing a strict mound entrance behavior code. Waiting for his teammates, including his gear-donning regular catcher, to take the field while requiring one of them to place the ball on the mound (do not toss it to him!). Hopping carefully over the top dugout step, walking purposefully, avoiding contact with the baseline, proceeding to the front of the mound, waiting for someone to kick the resin bag to the back of it, then ascending at an angle from which the batter could not see his face.

- Departing the mound per a similar code: Retracing his path to the dugout, avoiding the baseline, and making a precise number of steps to the water cooler.

- Retrieving his glove if an inning ended while at bat or on the bases. Always carrying his glove to the mound and never allowing anyone to hand it to him.

Whew. Wait, there's more. In 1972 Indians outfielder Alex Johnson tried to disrupt this rhythm by carrying his third inning-ending caught ball to the infield, timing his arrival with Cuellar's. When Johnson tossed the ball to him, Cuellar ducked and the ball rolled free. Subsequently, the bat boy, first baseman Boog Powell, and the umpire all unsuccessfully attempted to throw the ball to a dodging Cuellar. Only after second baseman Bobby Grich rolled it to the mound did Cuellar finally pick it up. Just to turn the screw a little tighter, Johnson tried the same trick in the fourth. Cuellar, however, would not take the bait, waiting in the dugout for Johnson to flip the ball to Powell, who then rolled it to the mound. With order restored, Cuellar then followed his usual mound entrance checklist.[10]

Amidst this surreal team pursuit of favorable intervention, Jim Palmer asked, "We all know that superstitions aren't winning ballgames for us. But who wants to find out?" Well, some researchers do, and it turns out Palmer is wrong on superstition's ability to influence events.[11]

University of San Francisco anthropology professor George Gmelch has been studying baseball superstition for decades. Considering the game's three essential activities of pitching, hitting, and fielding, he's found that chance plays an important role in the first two. In particular, the pitcher is the player least able to control events, given his reliance upon his own skill plus the abilities of his teammates, the skill or ineptitude of the opposition, and luck. Hitting likewise offers uncertainty due to its low success rate and chance's role in sometimes determining whether a batted ball will be caught or just barely elude an outstretched glove.

Gmelch has identified three types of magical behavior players use to combat these uncertainties. The most common one is to develop and adhere to a regularly followed daily routine, bringing comfort, order, and concentration into a world which offers challenge and randomness. Some players extend this further by engaging in rituals—such as Orioles players banging on objects—to bring luck to their side. These rituals grow out of successful performances, the repetition of which is used to gain control over future uncertainties. Second, some players adopt taboos, mostly idiosyncratic behavior—such as avoiding stepping on foul lines—that is used to avoid bad luck. Lastly, players resort to fetishes such as special clothing, coins, jewelry, gloves, and the like that coincide with lucky streaks or provide some sort of supernatural ability to create them. Individually or collectively, these behaviors combine to give players confidence and a dose of security.[12]

Other experts concur. Vrije Universiteit (VU) Amsterdam professor Dr. Paul van Lange finds that these practices help people including athletes cope with unknown outcomes, especially individuals who perceive and externalize events as subject to chance and unpredictability and in situations where the stakes are high and the opponent is formidable.[13] And in a 2010 breakthrough study, University of Cologne (Germany) researchers' experiments found that belief in luck can improve performance at a skilled activity when luck-enhancing superstitions produce psychological benefits that translate to better performance on the field.[14]

These findings illuminate a "crazy" player such as Cuellar, who, like many Latin players of his generation, was often ignored by sportswriters or quoted in "pidgin English." Cuellar was a private person, a man who was uncomfortable talking about personal matters and who had not seen his parents for many years after leaving Cuba to play baseball in the US. Who wouldn't turn to superstition if given that same kind of precarious psychological, emotional, and geographical lifeline? As for other players with more average, untroubled backgrounds, they faced and still face prospective slumps, doubts, demotions, trades, salary negotiations, fan abuse, press attacks, and injuries on a daily basis. Nowadays, they face social media dissection, too. When dealt that hand, the line between superstitious belief and desired salvation is thin, indeed. ■

Acknowledgments

A knock on wood goes out toward Professor George Gmelch and Ken Manyin for their assistance with this article.

Notes

1. Umpires ejected Weaver 97 times, placing him fourth on the all-time list.
2. Weaver's nickname for Orioles relief pitcher Don Stanhouse was "Full Pack." Weaver claimed he went through a full pack of cigarettes while Stanhouse pitched. See "Don Stanhouse," Baseball-Reference.com, https://www.baseball-reference.com/bullpen/Don_Stanhouse.
3. Ira Berkow, "Players; Weaver Keeps Whirring," *The New York Times*, September 23, 1982.
4. Lou Hatter, "Birds Beat Water Cooler, Bench As Well As Foes," *Baltimore Sun*, October 1, 1974.
5. Lou Hatter, "Dobson Adheres To Pat Pattern," *Baltimore Sun*, August 2, 1971.
6. Phil Hersch, "Will The 'Twin' Image Hurt Al Bumbry and Rich Coggins?," *Baltimore Sun*, October 7, 1973.
7. As for the cat, it likely sauntered away to a nearby food bowl to ponder cosmology, followed by a nap. If Coggins knew the background behind black cats and luck, he might have held a more nuanced view of his furry visitor. Throughout history and in some countries black cats have sometimes been a sign of good luck or fortune. But, in the Middle Ages, they became linked with witches, which led to their origin of distrust in America where they became associated with the Devil and witchcraft. Supposedly, having one cross your path means you have been noticed by the Devil. All a bit humorous until you consider that black cats are adopted at shelters less than other cats, partly because of negative superstitious beliefs.
8. Dobson and Palmer also adhered to this ritual.
9. Hatter, "Birds Beat Water Cooler, Bench As Well As Foes."
10. Johnson was a talented but troubled player. Although his interaction with Cuellar was in jest, he suffered from mental health issues that contributed to a career of tempestuous relationships with opponents, teammates, coaches, management, and sportswriters.
11. Hatter, "Birds Beat Water Cooler, Bench As Well As Foes."
12. George Gmelch, "Baseball Magic," *Human Nature*, Vol. 1, No. 8, 1978, https://meissinger.com/uploads/3/4/9/1/34919185/gmelch_baseball_magic.pdf; Gmelch, George, *Inside Pitch* (Washington: Smithsonian Institution Press, 2001), 133–43; George Gmelch, email, February 24, 2020.
13. Paul Van Lange, "The Psychological Benefits of Superstitious Rituals In Top Sport: A Study Among Sportspersons," *Journal of Applied Social Psychology* (Hoboken: Blackwell Publishing, Inc., 2006), 2532–53.
14. Stuart Vyse, *Believing In Magic: The Psychology of Superstition* (New York: Oxford University Press, 2014), xi, 232–33.

Steve Stone's Cy Young Season

Joseph Wancho

The 1978 Baltimore Orioles already had a stable full of thoroughbreds as far as their starting pitching corps was concerned. Jim Palmer (21–12, 2.46 ERA) led a talented group of pitchers who could stack up against any club in the major leagues. Mike Flanagan (19–15, 4.03 ERA), Dennis Martinez (16–11, 3.52 ERA) and Scott McGregor (15–13, 3.32 ERA) filled out the rest of manager Earl Weaver's rotation.

But on November 29, 1978, the Birds added another hurler to their pitching staff. Steve Stone signed a four-year deal worth a reported $800,000.[1] The 1979 season would be Stone's ninth in the big leagues. The right-handed pitcher from Kent State University had garnered a career 67–72 record in the previous eight. Stone was a veteran arm who could offer a viable option for Weaver should the opportunity present itself. "There's a chance we might go with five starters instead of four next year," said Weaver. "At least, we now have that choice, and there's nothing wrong with having a little depth."[2]

Stone had broken into the big leagues in 1971 with San Francisco. He split the season between the Giants and AAA Phoenix of the Pacific Coast League. It was the only time in his career that he had been part of a playoff team. The Giants won the National League West with a 90–72 record, but they were eliminated by Pittsburgh in the NLCS. Stone did not see any playing time in the NLCS.

The only other time Stone was on a competitive team was in 1977 when he was a starter for the Chicago White Sox, going 15–12 with a 4.51 ERA.[3] Dubbed the "South Side Hitmen" for their offensive prowess, Chicago finished third in the AL West with a 90–72 record.

The Orioles won the American League East in 1979. Surprisingly, they accomplished this feat with Palmer being hurt for most of the season. The Orioles' ace battled a sore arm, making two trips to the disabled list. But Flanagan (23–9, 3.08 ERA) took the lead of the staff and was rewarded with a Cy Young Award.

For Stone, the 1979 season had its ups and downs. He would win three games in a row, lose four straight,

and then win three more. But the losses mounted and the opposition was smacking home runs at a high rate (Stone surrendered 26 home runs through August). "I was our only weakness," said Stone."Everybody else was having a renaissance year. Every time I picked up a newspaper, I read that I should be banished to the bullpen. There were some unpleasant noises whenever my name was announced. The fans booed the hell out of me and that was not a pleasant experience. I wasn't pleased with what was going on."[4]

Stone ended the season on a positive note. In the last thirteen games he started, Stone won five. He posted an 11–7 record and a 3.77 ERA.

The Orioles ousted California in four games of the ALCS, but Stone did not pitch in the series. He made his lone appearance of the World Series in Game Four at Three Rivers Stadium. In two innings, Stone surrendered two runs. The Orioles blew their three games to one lead, losing to Pittsburgh in seven games.

In 1980, Palmer bounced back, but Martinez went down. The Orioles' right-hander complained of a sore shoulder and was placed on the 21-day disabled list. His stint on the DL ended up lasting much longer. "I'm concerned," said Baltimore pitching coach Ray Miller, "because Dennis never complained about his arm before."[5]

Weaver's comment about needing depth came true two years in a row. The reigning pennant winners in the AL now turned to Stone to pick up the slack.

"Last year I was trying to prove that I was worth what they paid me and do it all in a month," said Stone. "The harder I threw, the worse I got. This year I feel confident."[6]

Stone went 2–2 in April and opened May with a start at home against Minnesota. Rob Wilfong and Glenn Adams each connected for a solo home run, and Stone was relieved after 4⅔ innings. Stone walked four, struck out two and surrendered three earned runs as he picked up his third loss on the year.

It would be a long time before another "L" would be affixed next to Stone's name on a scorecard or in a box score. Stone won his next four games; the fourth of which was an eight-inning, three-hit, six-strikeout effort against the Tigers that the Orioles would win, 5–3. Ken Singleton's two-run home run in the bottom of the eighth inning broke the 3–3 tie to deliver the win. "I had never beaten this club before," said Stone. "They just seem to hit everything I throw. This time, I didn't use as many breaking balls. I stuck with fast balls and hard sliders and forgot what happened before."[7]

Following three no-decisions, Stone won 10 straight games from June 12 to July 26. Among these wins was a season-high 11-strikeout effort in a victory over California on June 17.

In the midst of his winning streak, Stone was selected as the American League starter of the 1980 All-Star Game at Dodger Stadium. "I thought one day I might get a chance to play in an All-Star Game," said Stone. "It's a tremendous thrill making it, but starting is something I couldn't hope for in my wildest dreams. I thought Steve Carlton would start for the National League and then everyone would have said Steve Carlton against Steve Who?"[8]

Stone (12–3, 3.10 ERA) continued with his hot hand, pitching three scoreless innings, mowing down nine straight batters and whiffing three. (But the NL won the game, 4–2.)

In spite of the success that Stone was having on the mound, the Orioles were scuffling in the middle of the AL East standings. Baltimore (42–36) was in fourth place and trailed New York (51–27) by nine games. In addition to Stone, McGregor (8–4), Palmer (8–5) and Flanagan (8–7) were all pitching well at the break.

Stone's winning streak was snapped on July 31 at Texas. He gave up six runs (three earned), and he was lifted after three innings as the Rangers won, 7–4. Stone then won five straight.

On August 19 at Anaheim, Stone won his 20th game of the season. For the first seven innings, he had a 5-0 lead and was throwing a no-hitter at the Angels. With one down in the bottom of the eighth inning, Stone walked two batters, gave up two singles, and the Angels scored two runs. The score was 5–2 when Weaver relieved Stone and Tippy Martinez finished the game for his ninth save. "I'm not a shutout pitcher," said Stone. "The secret to my success has been great defense and our ability to score runs. I was thinking about the no-hitter from the second inning on, but I'm not disappointed that I didn't get it. I feel terrific about getting 20."[9]

Stone became the 22nd pitcher in Orioles history to win 20 games.[10] The Orioles' pitching performance prompted teammate Ken Singleton to say, "We have

Cy Young in Mike Flanagan, we have Cy Old in Jim Palmer, Cy Present in Steve Stone and Cy Future in Scott McGregor."[11]

Although Stone may have been acting coy by crediting his teammates for his achievement, there was another source for his sudden success. He gave much of the credit to Miller. "Ray got me to take less time between pitches," said Stone. "I think when you take longer, maybe you're not confident and certainly it's tough on the fielders behind you. Certainly, it's helped me tremendously.

"Ray told me to get out of the habit of trying to throw all four pitches in the early innings. He told me to take two pitches and establish them early. Then, I go to the others when I need them later in the game."

Stone was not the only one surging in the Charm City. The Orioles posted a 21–8 record in August while the Yankees went 15–14. As the calendar flipped to September, the Orioles (76–52) drew to within 1½ games of division leader New York (78–51).

The Orioles stayed hot in September with a 21–9 record. But the Yankees rebounded from a mediocre August by going 21–7 in September, and as a result, put the division title in their back pocket. Baltimore (100–62) finished in second place, three games behind New York (103–59).

After signing with the fully-stocked Orioles in 1978, Steve Stone proved the adage "you can never have too much pitching," winning 20 games and the Cy Young award.

Stone went 4–2 in September to complete his season with a record of 25–7 and a 3.23 ERA. Through the 2019 season, Stone's 25 victories still stands as the high-water mark in Orioles history since relocating from St. Louis in 1953.

Oakland's Mike Norris was Stone's toughest competition for Cy Young honors in 1980. Table 1, below, is a comparison of statistics between Stone and Norris.

With the exception of the number of wins and losses, Norris led Stone in all of the other categories and the two hurlers tied in shutouts. But when the voting was tabulated, Norris had been narrowly defeated. The voting results for the top three finishers are shown in Table 2, below.

Stone and Norris tied for first and third place votes, but Norris received three fewer second place votes, causing him to fall nine points short.

"I've been written off a lot because I am not 6 foot 5 and 220 pounds, because I'm not durable or strong or heavy enough," said Stone. "There were always a lot of things other people were telling me I couldn't do. I preferred to concentrate on what I could do."[13]

Said Baltimore general manager Hank Peters, "There was a world of difference in the kind of pitching Steve had to do, in the heat of a pennant race and Norris, who performed without the pressure."[14]

Norris, as expected, had a different point of view. "The Cy Young is an individual pitching award," said Norris. "It does not mean completing only nine of your starts and getting 18 wins from the bullpen and infield defense. If my stats this year didn't prove it, then I still have a succession of years to prove it."[15]

Stone retired after the 1981 season, after experiencing pain in his right elbow. He retired with a career record of 107–93, and a 3.97 ERA in 11 MLB seasons. ∎

Notes

1. Ken Nigro, "Free-agent Stone signs with Birds," *Baltimore Sun*, November 30, 1978: D5.
2. Nigro, "Free-agent Stone signs with Birds" D5.
3. Stone's other memorable 1977 achievement was serving up Duane Kuiper's only home run in the major leagues on August 29 at Cleveland Stadium.
4. Ken Nigro, "Over 30s Find Good Life: Year of Stone in Baltimore," *The Sporting News*, August 23, 1980: 3.
5. Ken Nigro, "Stone New Big Bird With Martinez Hurt," *The Sporting News*, April 19, 1980: 27.
6. Ken Nigro, "Stone New Big Bird With Martinez Hurt," 27.
7. Ken Nigro, "Singleton HR lifts Birds over Tigers by 5 to 3," *Baltimore Sun*, May 24, 1980: B6.
8. Baltimore Sun Staff Correspondent, "Stone lauds Koufax and Veeck for helping career," *Baltimore Sun*, July 8, 1980: C5.
9. Ross Newhan, "Stone Loses No-Hitter but Wins His 20th Game, 5–2," *Los Angeles Times*, August 20, 1980: 3–12.
10. Ken Nigro, "Stone Wins No. 20, Loses No-Hit Bid," *The Sporting News*, September 6, 1980: 28. By "Orioles history" we mean from when they moved from St. Louis, rather than when the club started playing, and we're not counting other clubs with the same name.
11. "Stone Loses No-Hitter but Wins His 20th Game, 5–2," 3–12.
12. "Cy Young Award Voting," *Baltimore Sun*, November 13, 1980: C15. Each first place vote is worth five points, second place three points and one point for a third place vote. Each member of the Baseball Writers Association of America (BWAA) voted for three pitchers.
13. Kent Baker, "Stone Captures Cy Young Award," *Baltimore Sun*, November 13, 1980: C11.
14. Baker, "Stone Captures Cy Young Award," C11.
15. Kit Stier, "Norris Plans Cy Young Assault," *The Sporting News*, December 6, 1980: 52.

Table 1. 1980 Regular Season Comparision

Player	I.P.	Wins	Losses	Runs	Earned Runs	Comp. Games	Shutouts	Strikeouts	Walks	ERA
Steve Stone	250.2	25	7	103	90	9	1	149	101	3.23
Mike Norris	284.1	22	9	88	80	24	1	180	83	2.53

Table 2. 1980 American League Cy Young Voting

Player	1st Place Votes	2nd Place Votes	3rd Place Votes	Total
Steve Stone	13	10	5	100
Mike Norris	13	7	5	91
Rich Gossage	2	7	6½	37½

Billy Martin and the Baltimore Brawls

John J. Burbridge, Jr.

The Yankees headed to Baltimore for a three-game series beginning on September 20, 1985. They had just lost three games in Detroit while being outscored, 24–6, and their losing streak was now seven games. While still in second place in the American League East, they had trailed the Blue Jays for much of the season and were still 5½ games behind them.

The series against the Orioles would be remembered more for what occurred off the field than what happened on it. Billy Martin, the Yankees manager, was involved in two incidents at the Cross Keys Inn where the Yankees were staying, one on Friday night, one on Saturday. The Saturday night incident involved Eddie Lee Whitson, a Yankees pitcher.

BILLY MARTIN

Billy Martin was born in Berkeley, California, and played for Oakland in the Pacific Coast League under Casey Stengel. The Yankees acquired him and he excelled in both the 1952 and 1953 World Series. In the seventh game of 1952, he made a game-saving catch of a wind-blown pop fly off the bat of Jackie Robinson. In the following year, he was honored with the Babe Ruth Memorial Award honoring the best player in the World Series.[1]

While outstanding in those postseasons, Martin will forever be remembered in Yankees lore for incidents like the one at the Copacabana where he and his Yankees teammates got into a skirmish that made headlines, or his fights with Clint Courtney and Jimmy Piersall.[2] In 1957 the Yankees decided that Martin was not a good influence on other Yankees (particularly Mickey Mantle) and traded him to the Kansas City Athletics. He finished his career bumping around midwest teams: Detroit, Cleveland, Cincinnati, Milwaukee. In 1960 came what might be his most infamous fight as a player. After a suspected beanball, Martin punched Chicago Cubs pitcher Jim Brewer in the face, causing significant damage. The incident resulted in Brewer suing Martin for one million dollars. After years of litigation, the suit was settled for $10,000.[3]

Following the conclusion of his playing career, Martin managed the Minnesota Twins, Detroit Tigers, Texas Rangers, and the Yankees. His brawls continued even then. While managing the Twins, Martin got into a fight with his own pitcher, Dave Boswell. He inflicted serious damage to Boswell's face.[4] In 1977 he and Reggie Jackson almost came to blows in a nationally televised game at Fenway Park. And, of course, there was the knockout of marshmallow salesman Joseph L. Cooper in Minnesota.[5]

While such antics should have discouraged teams from hiring Martin, his reputation for being able to turn teams into winners proved very attractive to owners and general managers. Both Detroit and Minnesota made the playoffs with Martin at the helm. In 1977 he led the Yankees to a World Series victory over the Los Angeles Dodgers. When asked about Martin's managerial prowess, Casey Stengel said, "He's a good manager. He might be a little selfish about some things he does and he may think he knows more about baseball than anybody else and it wouldn't surprise me if he was right."[6]

Prior to the 1985 season, Martin had managed the Yankees on three occasions. He was fired by George Steinbrenner each time. In all of Martin's managerial stints, he was somewhat successful, but his abrasive personality often resulted in issues. The Yankees hired Martin for a fourth time when Steinbrenner fired Yogi Berra shortly after the beginning of the 1985 season.

While the Yankees did improve under Martin's leadership in 1985, they were obviously struggling as they headed to Baltimore. The seven-game losing streak was clearly taking a toll on Martin, a man who detested losing.

EDDIE LEE WHITSON

Whitson was signed by the Yankees during the 1984–85 off-season. A native of Tennessee, he was originally signed by the Pittsburgh Pirates in 1974. His major league career began with the Pirates in 1977. During the 1979 season he was traded to the San Francisco Giants. While with the Giants, he was involved in a fight before a game with Giants reserve infielder

Roger Metzger. Supposedly Metzger commented that Whitson needed to refine his bunting skills. Whitson, 6'3" and weighing 205 pounds, knocked out Metzger, attesting to his pugilistic ability.[7] Whitson was also skilled in the martial arts.

The Giants traded Whitson to the Cleveland Indians for Duane Kuiper after the 1981 season. He pitched for the Indians in 1982 but was traded to the San Diego Padres after the season. Whitson had a very good 1984 season with the pennant-winning Padres. After the Padres lost the first two games against the Chicago Cubs in the NLCS, he won game three in San Diego, pitching eight effective innings. San Diego won games four and five to capture the NL pennant, but lost to the Tigers in the World Series. Whitson was pummeled in his only start.

Whitson became a free agent after the 1984 season and signed a five-year, $4.5 million contract with the Yankees. After a few poor performances during the 1985 season, Yankees fans not only booed him relentlessly to the point of psychological duress, Whitson was finding his home driveway vandalized with nails and tacks and once was even pursued by a carload of drunken fans upon leaving the Stadium.[8] (By 1986, then-manager Lou Piniella would decide only to play him in away games, and even Whitson's family couldn't come to Yankee Stadium without suffering the wrath of fans.) His relationship with Martin was simultaneously deteriorating as Whitson was not happy with the control Martin exercised over his pitch selection. Whitson bounced back somewhat during the late summer months but gave up four runs in just two innings in a start against Toronto on Sunday, September 15.

THE CROSS KEYS INN

The Village of Cross Keys is in northern Baltimore City, fairly close to Pimlico Race Course. The Village was designed and developed by James Rouse, an entrepreneurial real estate developer who was also the architect of Baltimore's Inner Harbor complex, Faneuil Hall in Boston, and many other projects. He was also responsible for the development of the model city Columbia, Maryland.

Part of the Village of Cross Keys was a hotel: the Cross Keys Inn. Yankees traveling secretary, Bill "Killer" Kane, decided to house the Yankees at this hotel during their trips to Baltimore in 1985. Cross Keys was a more bucolic setting than downtown Baltimore. Kane may have thought he was keeping the Yankee players away from the downtown nightlife. In addition, the Inn was a bit closer than downtown to Memorial Stadium on 33rd Street.

Billy Martin during one of his stints as manager of the Yankees.

NATIONAL BASEBALL HALL OF FAME AND LIBRARY, COOPERSTOWN, NY

SEPTEMBER 20, 1985

Whitson was under the assumption he was to be the starting pitcher for the opening game of the series on September 20, having started the previous Sunday. However, Martin gave the start to Rich Bordi instead. Whitson was very unhappy with the move and expressed his displeasure in the clubhouse before the game.[9] While Bordi was somewhat effective, the Orioles sent the Yankees to their eighth consecutive loss, 4–2. After the game Martin and several Yankees coaches and players gravitated to the bar at the hotel where a wedding party was celebrating. Once he had a few drinks, Martin was in a jovial mood and bought the bride, groom, and others in the wedding party a bottle of champagne. He even danced with the bride.

Eventually, the couple left the bar for their hotel room, but minutes later the groom, still in his tuxedo and weaving unsteadily, reappeared at Martin's side. "Hey, Billy, we've got to talk," he exclaimed. "You told my wife she has a potbelly." Martin replied without any emotion, "I did not say she had a potbelly." He pointed at another woman at the bar with her husband and added, "I said this woman had a fat ass."[10]

While Martin had angered two individuals, the brief scuffle ended with no punches being thrown. When word of the incident reached Yankees' owner, George Steinbrenner, he wondered about the curfew he had supposedly put in place.

SEPTEMBER 21, 1985

The Yankees' losing streak finally ended with a 5–2 victory on Saturday afternoon. After the game, Bill Pennington, then the Yankees beat writer for the *Bergen Record*, found Eddie Lee nursing a long-necked Bud in the Cross Keys bar. A brief discussion of the previous night's skirmish occurred. Whitson then left the bar for dinner.

NATIONAL BASEBALL HALL OF FAME AND LIBRARY, COOPERSTOWN, NY

Ed Whitson was a target for fan ire in the Bronx.

As the dinner hour was approaching, several Yankees including Martin headed downtown to a crab place Martin enjoyed. Others went to Little Italy for dinner. By midnight almost all were back at the Cross Keys bar. Martin sat at the bar talking with Dale Berra, Yogi's son, and Dale's wife, Leigh. Whitson sat in a booth behind Martin; both had been drinking most of the night.

Next to Whitson, only a few feet away, was Albert Millus, an attorney from Binghamton, New York, who had tickets to the games in Baltimore. In an interview years later, Millus said, "Whitson was agitated and talking loudly about Billy Martin. A woman, I think Dale Berra's wife, came over to Whitson and was trying to calm him. But Whitson kept saying things like, 'That man won't pitch me' or 'That S.O.B. won't play me.'"[11]

Milius also said that Whitson turned and grabbed him by the throat, accusing Milius of eavesdropping. Finally, Martin came over to Whitson to intervene, saying something like "Eddie, you're drunk, you don't need this."[12] Whitson then turned his rage at Martin. A wrestling match ensued during which Whitson may have kicked Martin several times, once in the forearm.

As the two were separated, they were pulled from the bar into the hotel lobby. Whitson broke away and kicked Martin in the groin. A stunned Martin said to Whitson, "Now I'm going to have to kill you."[13] Whitson was finally corralled and taken outside. An incensed Billy wanted to continue the fight and tried to exit through a sliding glass door to get at Whitson. Yankees coaches tried to block his path. Martin got past them and the fight recommenced outdoors. Eventually, the two were separated and escorted back to their rooms.

SEPTEMBER 22, 1985

Once Martin reached his room in the early hours of Sunday morning, it became obvious he had injured his

arm. Realizing he had just lost a fight, he challenged Whitson to meet him in the parking lot to continue the fracas, but coaches and staff interceded so nothing further ensued. Bill Kane also called Steinbrenner to give him the details of the fight. Once again, a confused Steinbrenner wondered what happened to the curfew.

Finally, Martin was taken to the emergency ward at Union Memorial Hospital where the injury was diagnosed as a broken arm. His arm was put in a cast, and he returned to Cross Keys at approximately 4:00 AM.

It was also decided that Whitson should not be in attendance during the Sunday afternoon game. Kane arranged for him to be driven back to his home in Closter, New Jersey, on Sunday morning.

Martin managed the Yankees that Sunday to a 5–4 win. When spotted with his arm in a cast, he joked that he hurt it bowling.[14] After making this comment to the local reporter, Martin did discuss the fight with the eight beat writers from the New York area. He stressed that he was trying to be a peacemaker and accused his adversary of using his feet to win the fight. When asked if Whitson could still pitch for him, Martin responded:

I've always said I would play Adolf Hitler and Benito Mussolini if they could help me win. I don't have to like them. If he can help us win the pennant, I'll pitch him. And I'll yank him from the mound, too, if he has to be yanked. But I'll watch his feet.[15]

Steinbrenner made it known he would be investigating the incidents and said the following about any punishment, "Ed Whitson will not be suspended at this time, nor will Billy. I don't know how I could take action against one without taking action against the other."[16] Steinbrenner was also critical about players being in the bar after the 1:00 AM curfew.[17]

AFTERMATH

After the Sunday game in Baltimore, the Yankees lost a few games but then rallied while Toronto was faltering. The final three-game series of the year was in Toronto. The Yankees were now three games back and if they could sweep, there would be a playoff. Whitson started the Friday night game but was not still on the mound when the Yankees prevailed in dramatic fashion. However, they lost on Saturday, eliminating them from contention.

On October 27, Steinbrenner replaced Martin with Lou Piniella, making Martin a special assistant to

Steinbrenner. After the Yankees had two somewhat unsuccessful seasons, George once again asked Martin to manage the Yankees for the 1988 season with Piniella becoming general manager. While Steinbrenner had issues with Martin's off-field activities, his desire to win outweighed other concerns. Still, after several additional incidents, Martin was once again replaced by Piniella.

After being ousted as manager for the final time, Martin sought refuge with his new wife Jill in his recently bought lake house in the Binghamton area of New York. On Christmas Day, 1989, Martin and his close friend Bill Reedy went to a local bar. After a day of drinking, Martin was killed in an automobile accident on the slick, icy road leading to his home.[18]

Whitson's days with the Yankees were also numbered. Although he began the 1986 season with the team, he was traded mid-season back to the San Diego Padres. He had a few good seasons there and retired in 1991. He has resisted inquiries to give his version of his fight with Billy.

The Cross Keys Inn, now part of the Radisson chain of hotels, still stands as part of the Village of Cross Keys. As far as this author was able to determine, no one who currently works there remembers the tumultuous weekend in September 1985. ■

Notes

1. Jimmy Keenan and Frank Russo. "Billy Martin," SABR BioProject, https://sabr.org/bioproj/person/59c5010b
2. Michael Goodwin, "The Two Sides of Billy Martin: A Study In Contrast," *The The New York Times*, May 6, 1985, C6.
3. Jimmy Keenan and Frank Russo.
4. Bill Pennington, *Billy Martin: Baseball's Flawed Genius* (Boston New York: Houghton Mifflin Harcourt, 2015), 168–69.
5. Murray Chass, "Martin Denies That He Hit Man in Hotel," *The The New York Times*, Oct. 26, 1979, A23.
6. Jimmy Keenan and Frank Russo.
7. Mike Huber, "Ed Whitson", SABR BioProject, https://sabr.org/bioproj/person/c2fc4b97.
8. Murray Chass, "No Relief In Sight for Whitson as Ordeal Goes On," *The New York Times*, April 20, 1986, A.
9. Bill Pennington, 417.
10. Bill Pennington, 419–20.
11. Bill Pennington, 421.
12. Bill Pennington, 422.
13. Bill Pennington, 423.
14. Murray Chass, "Martin Jokes After Brawl," *The New York Times*, September 23, 1985, C1.
15. Murray Chass, September 23, 1985.
16. Murray Chass, "Yankees Planning No Punishment," *The New York Times*, September 24, 1985, B7.
17. Murray Chass, September 24, 1985.
18. Murray Chass, "Billy Martin of Yankees Killed in Crash on Icy Road," *The New York Times*, December 26, 1988, A1.

Lou Gehrig and Cal Ripken Jr.

Two Quiet Heroes

Norman L. Macht

As I write this, I am aware that I might be the only person alive who saw Lou Gehrig play and was present at Camden Yards the night Cal Ripken Jr. broke Gehrig's 2,130 consecutive game record. I was an eight-year-old fan when I saw Gehrig at the original Yankee Stadium in 1938. I was a stringer for *Sports Network* in the press box at Oriole Park on September 6, 1995.

That night I knew I wasn't the only person in the ballpark who had seen both men in action. Joe DiMaggio was there, too, overshadowing lesser celebrities like President Bill Clinton and Vice-President Al Gore.

Both Gehrig and Ripken had the same attitude toward their job: If you could walk you showed up for work. You took care of yourself, ate healthy foods, stayed in shape, and practiced assiduously to improve. Gehrig made himself into a capable first baseman. Ripken always seemed to be experimenting with his batting stance. Ripken once said, "The most fun I ever had in baseball was in the minor leagues. After that, it was a business."

Both were quiet men—not exactly aloof, but neither courting the spotlight. Both earned the respect and admiration of their teammates. In the Orioles' expansive clubhouse, Ripken had three lockers—those on either side of him vacant—in the farthest corner. In the pregame clubhouse you could chat freely with Elrod and the other coaches, or with Brady, Roberto, Rick, and Will, but you didn't approach Cal without a purpose or appointment. At least I didn't. I was a freelancer, not a beat writer. If I had some specific questions to ask him, I would request a time through the Orioles' PR man, John Maroon, then stand in the clubhouse, noticed but ignored, until Ripken beckoned.

Kids idolized both men. Kids also revered Babe Ruth, but youngsters saw him more as as a big kid himself, built for fun, more than as a hero. For my thirteenth birthday, I received an aptly-named book: *Lou Gehrig: A Quiet Hero*. But in the 1930s, how did we know anything about our heroes? There was no TV; no New York teams' games were broadcast on the radio. We knew them only through reading the sports

pages of the many New York newspapers, *The Sporting News*, and *Baseball Magazine*. I was 11 when Gehrig died, just two years after his last game. Millions wept, including me. The loss was beyond my understanding: old people died, not young athletes.

Cal Ripken Jr. is also a quiet hero. In his playing days, if a writer mentioned that he or she had talked to him, wide-eyed Baltimore youngsters would gasp, "You know Cal 'Wipken'?" Before games, Junior would be the last man standing at the box-seat railing, signing autographs for the kids and adults waiting in line.

Gehrig hadn't missed a game in nine years, but in the 1930s little attention was paid to obscure stats like that. The record of 1,307 consecutive games played, held by Yankees shortstop Everett Scott, had quietly ended on May 6, 1925, merely 3½ weeks before Gehrig's streak began. In 1933, when a New York sportswriter called to his attention that Lou was closing in on the record, Gehrig became very conscious of it. Gehrig broke Scott's record on August 17, 1933, and with each game he played until May 9, 1939, he extended his own record.

Sometimes he made token appearances to keep the streak going. On July 13, 1934, Gehrig awoke in Detroit with rheumatism in his back. He could hardly move. He singled his first time up, almost fell going to first, and left the game. The next day he felt worse. He asked manager Joe McCarthy to let him lead off. McCarthy listed him at shortstop, batting first. Gehrig singled, then left for pinch runner Red Rolfe, who played short.

He played through more ailments and broken fingers than Ripken, who had both good luck and the advantages of better, more professional trainers and facilities. In Gehrig's day, a rolling pin for kneading out muscle knots was standard trainer's equipment. He played through broken fingers, rheumatism, heavy colds, and his last full season with the early effects of the debilitating disease that would kill him three years later. In a midseason exhibition game one year, he was hit in the head by a fastball and knocked unconscious. No fracture, just a big bump. He insisted on playing the next day, lest he become gun shy at the plate.

Unlike Gehrig, Ripken ground it out, every inning every game until 1987, when O's manager Cal Sr., sat him down in the ninth inning of a game near the end of the season, after 8,264 consecutive innings. He was lucky, avoiding serious injury while playing the most demanding infield position except catching. The streak was important to Ripken, but not more important than playing to win. He played through ankle sprains and minor aches and pains, the worst when he twisted an ankle on June 6, 1993, in a 20-minute brawl sparked by O's pitcher Mike Mussina hitting Seattle's Bill Haselman with a pitch; seven players and Mariners' manager Lou Piniella were ejected.

Ripken's run-up to the record was ballyhooed to the hilt. For the preceding week, a banner hung on the side of the warehouse beyond right field, displaying Ripken's consecutive game count each day. In the fifth inning—when each game would become official—the new number was unfurled.

On the night of September 6, 1995, in front of an announced crowd of 46,272 fans, some of whom had paid scalpers $200 or more for upper deck seats (remember, this was 25 years ago) plus guests like Clinton, Gore, and DiMaggio—and a crowded press box were present for the historic game against the California Angels. In the bottom of the fourth Bobby Bonilla homered, Ripken homered, and the Orioles led, 3–1. In the top of the fifth, Orioles ace Mike Mussina had a quick three-up, three-down inning. It was as if nobody could wait for the game to become official. Then, the 2131 banner unfurled and the noise and fireworks began, the raucous crowd trying to overpower the fireworks. Calls came for Ripken to step out of the first base dugout and take a bow…No Ripken. The crowd's chant grew louder. Finally, teammates pushed him out and he began a 22-minute lap along the seats around the ballpark. Angels players stood in front of their dugout and applauded as he passed.

After the game, the clubhouse-level concourse beneath the stands was bustling. Ted Koppel, host of the popular *Nightline* TV show, surrounded by cameramen and flunkies, pushed his way into the clubhouse past an unnoticed Joe DiMaggio, who was patiently signing autographs. Reporters scurried to an auxiliary clubhouse for a Ripken press conference. Long after midnight people were still milling around; there was no effort to shoo them out.

Both men ended their consecutive-game records without ceremony or fanfare, as low-key as the men who had achieved them. As the Yankees breezed to another world championship in 1938, Gehrig began

Cal Ripken, Jr.

Lou Gehrig

to feel sluggish. He still hit 29 home runs and drove in 114, but his batting average dipped below .300 for the first time since his rookie year. He had four hits—all singles—in the four-game World Series. That winter he felt tired, often stumbling while walking. But he thought he'd bounce back in the hot weather of spring training. He didn't. He couldn't pick up ground balls, couldn't hit with any power, almost fell when he ran. To get up the steps between the dugout and clubhouse, he had to grip the railing and pull himself up. His teammates were bewildered: what was wrong with Lou? But no one suggested he sit down or take a rest. They had too much respect for him.

After opening at home against Boston, the Yankees went to Washington for three games, in which he had one hit. A 14-year-old fan from the Eastern Shore, Gil Dunn, was at one of those games. Fifty years later he recalled:

After the game I was outside the stadium and Gehrig came out and brushed right by the boys asking for autographs and got into a taxi. He was alone, and he looked so dejected. He was walking bent over like an old man, graying at the temples, and I had never seen a man who looked so downhearted. I stood there and I felt sorry for him. Here he was one of the great heroes of baseball and I was feeling sorry for him.

Gehrig had four hits—all singles—in the first eight games when they headed to Detroit. But it wasn't his weak hitting that prompted his decision. The last straw for him came when he had made a routine play in the field and his teammates overdid it with their effusive "great play!" pats on the back. On the morning of May 2, he went to manager Joe McCarthy's room and said, "I need a rest. I'm not doing the team any good." He knew it was the end of the streak, but he didn't know he'd never play again. The Iron Horse had run his last 90 feet.

Although still able to play, Cal Ripken decided to relieve the constant speculation over when and how his streak would end by ending it himself near the end of the 1998 season. By then he had so far surpassed Gehrig's record, the count was rendered unimportant. Nobody in the future was likely to come close, and if they did, more power to them. He was 38 and knew he was no longer an everyday player. In 1997 he had switched to the less demanding third base position. The Orioles were a .500 team. Ripken wanted no ballyhoo, no ceremony, no fuss. The last home game of the season was Sunday night, September 20, 1998, against the Yankees. Before the game he told manager Ray Miller he wanted out of the lineup. And that was it: game 2,632. None of the reported 48,013 fans who filled Camden Yards knew what they were about to witness until the public address announcer, reading the lineup, said, "Batting sixth, the third baseman, Ryan Minor." Minor was a 6-foot-7 rookie who had made his debut as a pinch hitter on September 13. (Great trivia question: who replaced Cal Ripken the day his streak ended?) The next night in Toronto Cal Ripken was back in the lineup. He played in about half the games in the next two seasons. Then, in 2001, at age 40, he appeared in three-quarters of the Orioles games before quietly retiring—but not from baseball. He remains active as a minor league club owner and benefactor of youth baseball.

Two quiet heroes whose achievements will not be forgotten. ■

Retrosheet Begins in Baltimore

Jay Wigley

We baseball fans want the truth. Some of us want to know how well Duke Snider hit in 1957. We want to look it up. And some of us, once we've answered that question, begin to wonder if the Duke could hit lefties as well as righties, or not. Then we wonder, perhaps, how much of Duke's difference makes a difference when it comes to winning games. So, a handful of fans—asking such questions and knowing that data would be needed to search for the truth—began work in the 1970s that brought us to where we are today: baseball data heaven.

We modern fans have trouble imagining how no one had any landscape of baseball data in the 1970s. To provide any answer beyond the *Baseball Encyclopedia*'s simple totals and averages, we needed play-by-play information. The Elias Sports Bureau had that sort of data, the *official* data.[1] But Elias's data were certainly not available to satisfy fans' curiosity. Elias worked for their own pleasure (both personal and financial) and for their patrons, the league offices of the major leagues.

In short, Elias did not share with "just anyone," at least not publicly.

Beginning in the 1970s, SABR's Statistical Analysis Committee had more than a few members who wanted access to that quality of play-by-play data. Pete Palmer, Dick Cramer, and David Smith (co-chairs of the committee) wanted to know who did what, and when they did it. Not satisfied with the counting stats and career totals provided by the Baseball Encyclopedia, these studious, serious fans needed play-by-play data for their rigorous baseball analysis.

The first effort to gather such data began in 1983 when Bill James organized an army of volunteers in an effort he dubbed "Project Scoresheet."[2] His idea was to gather play-by-play data through volunteers dedicated enough to record every play of every game and send in their scoresheets. "The Project," as veterans of that effort still call it, generated enough data and made enough money to collapse eventually under the weight of its success. By the early 1990s, the remaining volunteers ended the Project. But some of them, under the leadership of David Smith, saw potential beyond anything James had imagined.

At a late 1978 SABR (Philadelphia chapter) meeting, Smith had met Carl Lundquist, a retired UPI sportswriter who had saved his professional scorebooks from 460 New York games (all three teams) 1949–56. Lundquist shared copies of all of them with Smith. Working with David Nichols (another Scoresheet volunteer) in 1988, Smith successfully entered a single Lundquist-scored game into a modified version of the Project Scoresheet software, to prove older games could be captured and coded using the same data format as modern seasons. While James's original vision had not included computerization of the data, Smith correctly reasoned that if he could aggregate as many games as he could find in a common data format already proven useful, the analysis possibilities would be limitless.

Smith's personal motives went beyond the desire for simply more data. For Smith, capturing the seasons of the past in an organized way, and making them available for both reflection and analysis, was and is "hugely important. To catalog the basic events of the national game [is] something of a moral obligation."[3] As Jayson Stark sees it, Smith's idea for Retrosheet eventually made today's "Baseball-Reference.com and their Play Index possible. It fuels the research that literally thousands of us do every week of every year. And it's an invaluable resource in every way, the gift that never stops giving."[4]

But to get his idea off the ground, Smith needed more scoresheets, lots of them.

Bill James's public approach had alienated both the insular major league teams and their official statisticians (Elias) so Smith began with a more personal appeal. Smith began contacting other SABR members and Project Scoresheet volunteers, hoping to fill file cabinets with scoresheets for eventual translation into computer data, to be shared via floppy disk. One of the first to reply was Pete Palmer, who promptly introduced Smith to Eddie Epstein.[5] This moment was a true breakthrough for Retrosheet because Epstein knew about "the stash." And Eddie soon learned that his new friend Dave Smith wanted it. Specifically, Dave wanted to *copy* it.

The stash was a collection of scoresheets for every Baltimore Orioles game since 1954. It wasn't Eddie's to share, but he knew how to pitch the idea to the Orioles front office. An early believer in the power of analytics, Epstein had come to work for the Orioles as a consultant in the mid-1980s, using his economics training to help the team make smart contract offers during player salary negotiations. So, while not in the public relations department himself, Eddie knew who was in charge of keeping up "the books." He knew it was the public relations department who cared about that history and used it to create daily game notes for the broadcast teams and more in-depth articles for all kinds of Orioles profiles and pieces.

Eddie began with the assistant public relations director, Rick Vaughn, asking him to open the Orioles' books to an outsider. Vaughn, who began with Baltimore in 1984, remembers being "extremely excited" when Eddie first told him about Smith's project, which would soon have a name: Retrosheet. Vaughn remembers that his boss, Bob Brown, head of Orioles public relations, was also excited, as both men loved the historical aspects of the game. Rick was happy to ask Brown for permission to share all his "working copies" of the scoresheets with Smith. Part of Vaughn's responsibilities in those days was "to make sure we copied the scoresheet after every game and put it in the loose-leaf binder we had for that season. They were kept in a bookshelf in [Vaughn's Memorial Stadium] office. The loose-leaf notebooks held up much better than the original scorebooks, but we had those as well. [The original scorebooks] were kept in Bob Brown's office, and eventually moved to a larger research area at Camden Yards."[6]

Vaughn cautions that while he was personally enthusiastic, nothing would have been shared between the team and Retrosheet without Bob Brown's endorsement. Brown was already an Orioles legend, having joined the team in 1958, alternating as traveling secretary and public relations director during his (eventual) 35-year Oriole career. Brown was chosen as the second recipient of the Robert O. Fishel Award for public relations excellence in 1982 (the first winner after Fishel himself), and there were few PR men in the game with more clout.[7] Vaughn remembers, "When I started, I was living in Virginia, and I drove 61 miles each way to Memorial Stadium. The primary reason I took the job was to work under Bob Brown. No one worked harder or cared more about baseball than

Bob."[8] By 2000, the Camden Yards press box would be renamed after Brown.[9]

Vaughn remembers that the mechanics of maintaining and collecting Orioles scoresheets went something like this: "The current [season] book was kept in the PR bag that we had with us for home and road games. Before the PR staff started traveling (in 1988 during the 0–21 start), the traveling secretary would maintain the scorebook on the road. I was the primary user because I was responsible for the game notes. I referred to them daily, but Bob and others used them as well, just not as much. We maintained it that way because that is not a project you want to get behind on. It just made sense to make a copy of the scoresheet and file it after every game. That was how thorough Bob was."[10]

According to Vaughn, Smith had "someone" come by and borrow all 30 binders during the 1988–89 off-season. Smith recalls, "The person who came by to borrow the binders was me. I drove to Baltimore in a huge rainstorm and collected all 30, brought them back to Delaware and copied them, returning them in about a month. [My wife] Amy still talks about seeing the binders on our coffee table and marveling at them, since she had always been an Orioles fan."[11]

And so just like that, for only the asking, Retrosheet had over 4,700 games to begin translating into the computer. Smith recruited volunteers to use a new Retro-version of the software by David Nichols and Tom Tippett, based on what they originally created for Project Scoresheet. The benefit of Retrosheet beginning with Baltimore would be evident for years to come, as Bob Brown proved influential with other major league teams reluctant to open their archives to outsiders. Slowly, many of the same teams who had rebuffed James years before would respond to Retrosheet's more personal approach, and to Bob Brown's professional reputation, as he vouched for them directly with the front offices and public relations departments of the Phillies, Padres, Tigers, and Mets.[12]

The Orioles data would serve other purposes as well. Retrosheet volunteers over the years became experts on one Orioles game in particular: the June 27, 1982, contest at Baltimore's Memorial Stadium against the Tigers. Smith selected the Baltimore play-by-play in that game to serve as training material for any volunteer wanting to enter data using the Retrosheet format.[13]

Years later, Bob Brown's choice to help Retrosheet with data would *cost* his team a little money. A Retrosheet volunteer discovered a discrepancy in the RBI totals for the 1961 season, resulting eventually in a revision to the official record. Instead of a single winner of the RBI crown that season (Roger Maris of the

Yankees), there were in truth *two*, the other being Oriole Jim Gentile. Gentile remembered his contract negotiations with Orioles GM Lee MacPhail the following season, with MacPhail telling him that if he had won the RBI race, his contract would have been "worth $5000 more." The Orioles made it right, when then-GM Andy MacPhail (Lee's son) delivered Gentile the money at a Camden Yards ballgame in the summer of 2010.[14]

David Smith wouldn't have an Eddie Epstein in every baseball club's front office. He would request the support of the president of the National League and even the Commissioner of Baseball in years to come, but ultimately it would be his success with the Orioles, parlayed into introductions to nearly every other team, that enabled Retrosheet to create and deliver the treasure trove of detailed play-by-play baseball data that is available, all for free, at their web site today. ∎

Notes

1. As Leonard Koppett reminded us, official means "of the office," not necessarily *correct*. See Koppett's article, "BACKTALK: Official is a Relative Term, and It Always Will Be" *The New York Times*, April 25, 1993, Section 8, page 9.
2. Bill James, "Introducing Project Scoresheet," *The Baseball Analyst*, Issue 8 (October 1983): 5–6.
3. David Smith, email to the author, November 2, 2018.
4. Jayson Stark, email to the author, July 11, 2019.
5. Smith, a professor in the University of Delaware's Biology department, had never met Epstein, though Eddie was a Delaware graduate (with a Master's degree in Economics), until Pete Palmer introduced them. A friendship began between Smith and Epstein, one further enhanced when Smith realized that Eddie's Delaware advisor was one of Smith's faculty friends.
6. Rick Vaughn, email to the author, September 18, 2018.
7. John Steadman, "Brown: Peerless among PR men, pride of O's," *Baltimore Sun*, April 30, 2000.
8. Vaughn, email.
9. Steadman, "Brown: Peerless…".
10. Vaughn, email.
11. David Smith, email to the author, February 10, 2020.
12. Smith, email.
13. Smith chose a 13–1 Orioles victory, unintentionally but completely appropriately. Visitors to the Retrosheet website today can view the training material for new volunteers at "Example Scoresheet," Retrosheet.org, https://www.retrosheet.org/ex-sheet.htm.
14. Mike Dodd, "Ex-Oriole Jim Gentile lost $5,000 over error giving Roger Maris RBI crown," *USA Today*, July 30, 2010.

Itchy Xu

From Chinese Sports Trailblazer to Baltimore Orioles Prospect

Eric Robinson

group of boys hung over their dorm's balcony railing, hardly believing that their hero was playing catch in the courtyard below with some of their schoolmates. The tall, rangy man throwing the ball to some of the older students was barely in his twenties, moving with the strong but casual grace common to athletes.[1] His name is Xu Guiyan (pronounced "shoo GEE-win"). To the students at the MLB baseball academies in China he is a star, but to sports fans in America, he was just another unknown name on the Baltimore Orioles rookie league team roster.

In July 2015, 19-year-old Xu was signed by scouts Brett Ward and Mike Snyder of the Baltimore Orioles. This signing made him the first player signed out of the MLB academies in China by an MLB team.[2] He was born January 29, 1996, and grew up in Shenzhen, China, a large city in the country's southeast that shares a border with Hong Kong.[3] He began playing baseball at the age of 10, joining his older brother on their school team. His skills quickly developed, and four years later he was invited to enroll at an MLB development center in Wuxi. This meant a move of over a thousand miles for the teenager, but it provided him with the best opportunity in the nation to improve his baseball skills.[4]

The MLB development centers, or academies, were first opened in 2009 in the cities of Nanjing and Wuxi. They were created to both increase the profile of baseball in the country of 1.4 billion people and to develop baseball talent.[5] The development centers behave like typical schools during the day, following a standard Chinese curriculum. Once classes end, the students then head to the baseball fields for hours of specialized practice. The coaches at these development centers include former major league managers, coaches, and ex-players from the professional and college ranks.[6]

Xu was fourteen years old when he reported to the development center in Wuxi in 2010 as a left-handed pitcher. After arriving, a coach asked the teenager what name he preferred to be called. He replied "Ichiro" after Ichiro Suzuki, his favorite player. The coach informed him that there were already too many students

calling themselves Ichiro and asked if instead, he wanted to be called "Itchy." Xu replied yes and only later found out what the English word itchy means. The nickname stuck, and that is still what his friends and those in the baseball world call him.[7]

To observers in Wuxi, Itchy stood out as a hard worker, dedicated to improving his skills.[8] As he spent time practicing under the guidance of the staff, they noticed that he had more ability to make contact and hit for power than the other students, and he converted to playing elsewhere than the mound. While he played multiple positions, his skills as a first baseman emerged. The players at the academy did more than just play against each other year after year: They traveled and played against other teams in Asia, and the Chinese National Team.[9] During this time Xu established himself as the best player in the Chinese development pipeline and the scouts from MLB teams began to consider signing him.[10]

In 2015 this happened when the Baltimore Orioles scouts Mike Snyder and Brett Ward visited the Development Center in Wuxi as part of their travels in Asia and the Pacific Rim. They were curious about the talent they would find there. A player had not been signed from the country in eight years, despite the fact that MLB and the Chinese government were increasing resources into player development.[11] They had seen videos of some of the talented players, but one thing that stood out to them was Xu's swing. Snyder felt "Xu had a beautiful swing that was capable of power."[12]

Their optimism was tempered by the fact Xu had started baseball later than most US prospects and had faced a lower level of competition. They saw he was "raw, but with skills that had a chance for a quick progression."[13]

Once the pair of scouts saw the players in person, Snyder felt that "it was clear that he was the one and while we had some interest in others that he was definitely the one."[14] Xu was put through a series of workouts, in which he performed well. Next, they wanted to see how he handled game at-bats, so a game was scheduled. As Snyder recalled:

It was around the 4th or 5th inning—he'd had 3 at-bats but had walked each time. Clearly, he had good plate discipline and could get on base, but we needed to see if he could actually hit. It was a scrimmage that was put on for our benefit, so we asked if Itchy could just lead off each half inning. We pulled him aside and explained the new arrangement through the interpreter. Brett then pointed to an apartment building, 500 or 600 feet away, and only half-jokingly told Xu we wanted him to hit it there—an impossible task. Itchy went up to bat and, I swear this is true, on his second pitch he hit a deep home run out towards the apartment building, easily clearing the fences though clearly not coming close to the building. As he crossed the plate, Brett feigned disappointment, saying, "we told you to HIT the building!" Without missing a beat, Itchy shot back in perfect English, "Next time!"[15]

Snyder and Ward had seen what they needed to and on July 20, 2015, the Orioles announced they had signed Xu, making him the first player from the MLB Development Centers to be signed by an MLB team. At the time of the signing, he received a $10,000 bonus.[16] The following March he reported to Sarasota, Florida, home of the Orioles spring training facility and rookie league team.

A film crew lead by *Baltimore Sun* reporter Jeff Barker, and filmmakers Kenneth Eng and Mark Hyman, who had been working on a documentary about Chinese baseball, was waiting for Xu at the airport to document his first days in America. This was just part of what made him stand out compared to the other long-shot prospects in the Gulf Coast League. Xu was not only far from his home and family, but he was the only Chinese player in American professional baseball at the time. He would have to learn how to get by in a new culture while trying to succeed in the competitive environment of professional baseball. Xu's situation was isolating but the team took steps to ease his adjustment, including hiring a trainer who could speak Chinese as well as using someone from the area who was born in China to help on occasion.[17]

Team officials knew from the beginning that Xu's development lagged behind others his age, expecting him to be rawer and less polished given his background, but they were quickly impressed with his desire to improve and his work ethic. His first GCL game was on June 25, 2016, and he began his career with a hot bat, getting 15 hits in his first 11 games. However, he soon began to have problems at the plate.

Xu Guiyuan was the first prospect signed out of the MLB academy in Wuxi.

BALTIMORE ORIOLES

The cold streak weighed on the young player. Barker noted, "Itchy was not only frustrated with his own performance but he felt a lot of pressure as the only player from China and as a representative of the MLB academies."

He experienced reduced playing time in games as a result of these problems, hindering the development that needed to occur through game at-bats. Still, Orioles' coaches and scouts continued to appreciate his grit and focus.[18] Following his initial hot streak, Xu only had 5 more hits over the remaining 22 games of the season. He finished with a slash line of .247/.271/.284 in 85 plate appearances.

Off the field, Xu would Skype his parents frequently, and while his English was good when he arrived, he worked to improve it. He also missed having regular Chinese food but did fall in love with one American restaurant, Chipotle Mexican Grill. The documentary crew was able to catch many moments of Xu joking around and having fun with his teammates, just like any 20-year-old would.

In March 2017, Xu played in front of the largest crowds he had seen when he represented China in the World Baseball Classic. He was excited to play for the national team on such a large stage. "I was just so proud to play for Team China. Before, I played for the province or city. Now, I play for China, for the country. It's very different."[19]

China played three games at the Tokyo Dome against Japan, Australia, and Cuba. The team lost all three games, scoring one total run in the process. The on-field highlight for Xu came in front of 40,053 fans as he hit a single in their third game against host country Japan. He was then picked off first base. After the series, team manager John McLaren, former skipper of the Seattle Mariners and Washington Nationals, said about Xu, "He had only played a few games in rookie league, and to jump up on the world stage like that is a little overwhelming for anybody." He continued,

"Being there in Japan in front of [40,000] people, that's pretty overwhelming. But he did fine. He didn't get excited. He was well-grounded."[20]

Xu returned to Sarasota in 2017, still putting pressure on himself to perform at a high level to meet not just his own expectations, but to serve as an inspiration to the baseball community in China. Unfortunately, he was still dealing with confidence issues in finding his swing.

The team had Xu split his time between the outfield and designated hitter rather than first base, where he got most of his innings in 2016. He made 45 plate appearances over 15 games and finished the season with a slash line of .179/.267/.256. During his second season, GCL Orioles hitting coach Milt May said about Xu and his struggles, "The speed of the game is something that he has improved on. It's still a work in progress, but he's made great strides along those lines."[21]

The Orioles promoted Xu to the Aberdeen IronBirds, the team's Class A affiliate, for his third professional season in 2018. The team played in the New York Penn League with 13 other teams including Brooklyn, Staten Island, Connecticut, and Vermont. Xu enjoyed the change and said, "All the new cities and the bigger crowds are exciting for me, especially New York, where we play in Brooklyn. I really like the night games, too. Some of the bus rides are very long, but I love to talk to my teammates to improve my English. Sometimes I have a beer with them, but American beer is much too bland for me."[22]

Despite his excitement for the step up and the getting to travel to new cities, his problems at the plate continued. IronBirds manager Kyle Moore spoke of Xu's difficulty adjusting to the new, harder-throwing pitchers he was not used to seeing. "Making the adjustment to better pitching is his biggest challenge, but he's definitely going in the right direction…He's facing some big college kids who can throw 95 miles per hour, and when you've never seen that kind of speed before, it can be pretty intimidating."[23]

The 2018 season produced similar results to Xu's 2017 numbers. He finished the year .167/.250/.222. It would be his final season with the Orioles. That winter, he played in the Australian Professional Baseball League with the Auckland Tuatara, a team based in New Zealand.[24] Xu appeared in all but five of Auckland's 40 games and had his best professional season to date. He finished with a line of .264/.343/.319, and the second best batting average on his team among hitters with more than 11 at-bats.

In 2019 Xu continued his pursuit of a career in baseball with the Kochi Fighting Dogs of Japan's Shikoku Island League Plus, a team best known to fans in the US for signing a 45-year-old Manny Ramirez. Xu was excited to play in the home country of his hero, Ichiro Suzuki. "After learning the American way, I think Japanese baseball can provide great benefits for me. Ichiro is my idol and playing in his homeland only doubles my inspiration."[25]

Even though Itchy may never make it to the major leagues, Mike Snyder feels like he will have a productive career in baseball. "He has grit and good make-up," the Orioles director of professional scouting said, "he will have a future in the game."[26] ▪

Source

Baseball-Reference.com – all statistical and game information

Notes

1. Jeff Barker, Mark Hyman, Kenneth Eng, "The Great China Baseball Hunt," Vimeo video, 2:42, posted by The Great China Baseball Hunt, https://chinabaseballfilm.com.
2. Kirstie Chiappelli, "Orioles Sign 'Itchy' Xu, First Player from Chinese Development Program," The Sporting News, https://www.sportingnews.com/us/mlb/news/orioles-free-agent-trades-signings-chinese-development-itchy-xu/3pl9rofouki31i5h3d1ag16ax. Date accessed January 31, 2020.
3. Thomas Neuman, "Xu Guiyuan is Itching to be a Trailblazer as MLB's first Chinese Player," ESPN, https://www.espn.com/mlb/story/_/id/17350633/xu-guiyuan-baltimore-orioles-prospect-china-itching-mlb-trailblazer, Accessed January 12, 2020.
4. Neuman, "Itching to be a Trailblazer."
5. "Major League Baseball opens 2nd development center in China," Global Times, http://www.globaltimes.cn/content/675299.shtml, Accessed February 20, 2020.
6. Jimmy Johnson, in person interview, July 2018.
7. Neuman, "Itching to be a Trailblazer."
8. Jeff Barker, telephone interview, February 7, 2020.
9. Brett Snyder, telephone interview, February 15, 2020.
10. Barker, interview.
11. Snyder, interview.
12. Snyder, interview.
13. Snyder, interview.
14. Snyder, interview.
15. Snyder, interview.
16. Chiappelli, "Orioles Sign 'Itchy' Xu," The Sporting News.
17. Snyder, interview.
18. Snyder, interview.
19. Thomas Neuman, "Orioles Prospect Xu Guiyuan Resumes MLB Quest after WBC," ESPN, https://www.espn.com/mlb/story/_/id/19026455/after-playing-china-wbc-stage-baltimore-orioles-prospect-xu-guiyuan-resumes-mlb-quest, Accessed February 16, 2020.
20. Neuman, "Orioles Prospect Xu Guiyuan Resumes MLB Quest."
21. Neuman, "Orioles Prospect Xu Guiyuan Resumes MLB Quest."
22. Mo Hong'e, "Xu's road to glory has speed bumps," ECNS.com, http://www.ecns.cn/news/feature/2018-07-20/detail-ifywhfmh2714628.shtml, Accessed February 17, 2020.
23. "Xu's road to glory."
24. Christopher Reive, "Auckland Tuatara sign Baltimore Orioles prospect Xu Guiyuan," NZ Herald, https://www.nzherald.co.nz/sport/news/article.cfm?c_id=4&objectid=12152753, Accessed February 17, 2020.
25. Yang Xinwei," Whole new ball game for 'Itchy'," China Daily, http://www.chinadaily.com.cn/a/201905/29/WS5cedde8da3104842260be621.html, Accessed February 17, 2020.
26. Snyder, interview.

When Sam Malone Faced Boog Powell

David Krell

Baltimoreans strolling on Eutaw Street outside Oriole Park before a home game may stop for a bite to eat and kibbitz with owners of the establishments. It's not an unusual sight. But one owner happens to be a civic icon—John Wesley Powell. Boog. The slugger who bashed 339 home runs in the majors does more than serve up mouth-watering food at Boog's BBQ, though. He's also an ambassador of good will. "I'm like, the official greeter at the ballpark," said Powell in 2017. "People come looking for something positive, a confirmation about their own lives—and they find a guy standing there, smiling, and trying to make them happy. I want you to feel good when you leave me."[1]

Powell saw the births of division playoffs and the designated hitter during his 1961–77 career, which ended with a .266 batting average and .462 slugging average. But for popular-culture buffs, Powell has the distinction of being a key part of a storyline in a first-season episode of *Cheers*.[2] It involves a retelling of an Orioles-Red Sox doubleheader in 1972. But could events really have happened the way they're explained in the dialogue?

Cheers aired on NBC from 1982 to 1993, focusing on the goings-on at a Boston bar owned by fictional former Red Sox relief pitcher Sam "Mayday" Malone. It used the famed Bull & Finch Pub for exterior shots. Adored by women in his "little black book" and idolized by men for his romantic exploits, Sam is a minor celebrity and a reformed alcoholic who suffers a relapse or two throughout the show's run. Later in the series, he's revealed to be a sex addict.

Sam's career with the 1970s Red Sox occasionally becomes a topic of conversation in early episodes for the bar's regular characters: wisecracking waitress Carla Tortelli, know-it-all postman Cliff Clavin, beer-guzzling accountant Norm Peterson, former pitching coach and good-natured but slightly unintelligent Ernie Pantusso, and high-brow waitress Diane Chambers. In the episode "Sam at Eleven," Sam recounts a memorable day in 1972, when he saved both games of a doubleheader against the Orioles on seven pitches.

Boston was five games out of first with eight to play. They couldn't afford to lose a game. Malone retired Powell on a 5–3 grounder with two men on base and a one-run lead to end the first game. He faced the iconic slugger again in the bottom of the ninth with Don Buford on first base. Though the scene ends before a full recounting, it's implied that Powell was not successful against "Mayday."[3]

Indeed, a Baltimore-Boston doubleheader took place toward the end of the 1972 schedule. The Red Sox had 15 games left and a predicament more dire than the one Sam described—at the time, Boston was 76–64, Detroit was 77–66, and Baltimore was 77–66. After that, the resemblance to the fictional account quickly fades.

Neither game required a Red Sox reliever—Marty Pattin and Luis Tiant each pitched a complete game. Pattin was a formidable hurler in 1972, compiling a 17–13 record with 13 complete games and four shutouts.

In the first game, Powell left in the seventh inning; Terry Crowley moved from right field to take over first base. Unlike Sam's tale, there was no significant danger for the Red Sox—they won the game, 9–1. Veteran shortstop Luis Aparicio had one RBI and scored two runs, and rookie Dwight Evans went 2-for-4 with two RBIs; Carlton Fisk went 3-for-4 with three RBIs; and Pattin tossed a five-hitter. Boston escalated the pounding in the fourth inning, when they tagged Jim Palmer—a 21–10 pitcher in '72—for two runs and extended the lead to 4–1.

Roric Harrison replaced Palmer and let in five runs (two charged to Palmer); Bob Reynolds came into the inning with one out and ended the destruction when Pattin grounded into an infield double play.[4]

In the second game, Tiant pitched a four-hit shutout and struck out seven Orioles in the 4–0 win. It was an emblem of an outstanding season—Tiant led the major leagues with a 1.91 ERA. The Sox were scoreless until the fifth inning, when Doug Griffin singled, Tiant advanced him with a sacrifice bunt, and Tommy Harper singled him home. Boston added two more runs in the

Boog Powell appeared on *Cheers* **in name only, but he can be seen at Orioles home games at Boog's BBQ.**

seventh inning and another in the eighth. Four runs tallied on five hits.

Powell struck out to lead off the ninth. It was his last at bat of the doubleheader.[5]

Despite batting .252 in 1972, Powell was an apt selection for Malone's story: four-time All-Star, 1970 American League MVP, runner-up for 1969 AL MVP, and hitter of 21 home runs in 1972. He began his pro career with the Orioles' Appalachian League team in Bluefield in 1959, playing in 56 games and batting .351. The O's moved him to the Three-I League in 1960, where his batting average was .312 for the Fox City Foxes.

In 1961, he thrashed International League pitching with the Rochester Red Wings for a .321 batting average. The Orioles elevated the slugger to Baltimore, where he played four games that year. From 1962 onward, he was a charm for Chesapeake Bay, until departing for the Indians in 1975–76. He ended his career in the National League with the Dodgers in 1977.

The AL East had a tight pennant race at the end of 1972. In early September, Powell reflected that the Orioles should have been ahead. "But look, I'm not hitting what I should, Donny Buford is only hitting .210, and Dave Johnson is batting only .224," said Powell. "With the great pitching we are getting, if we were hitting like we should, we'd be out in front like always. That's the only difference from last year."[6]

Powell bashed a three-run homer in the Orioles' 3–1 win against the Yankees on September 15. Complemented by "a vital relief lift from Grant Jackson and the defensive heroics of Bobby Grich," the first-inning blast gave legendary hurler Jim Palmer his third straight 20-win season. Yankees pitcher Mel Stottlemyre walked Don Buford and Rich Coggins to begin the game, then got Grich out before the cleanup hitter and future food impresario tagged him for a 425-foot home run. Powell was on a streak—it was his third round tripper in four games.

Ultimately, the Tigers won the AL East pennant, beating the Red Sox by half a game and the Orioles by five games. And these days, Boog greets his regulars at Boog's BBQ and cracks out the occasional story about his playing days, no fictionalizing needed. ∎

Notes

1. Mike Klingaman, "Fans still wait to rub elbows with former slugger Boog Powell at his BBQ stand," *Baltimore Sun*, https://www.baltimoresun.com/sports/orioles/bs-sp-boog-20170329-story.html, April 3, 2017 (accessed February 24, 2020).
2. *Cheers*, "Sam at Eleven," Paramount Television, NBC, directed by James Burrows, written by Glen Charles & Les Charles, October 21, 1982.
3. "Sam at Eleven."
4. Boston Red Sox 9, Baltimore Orioles 1, Setpember 20, 1972, https://www.retrosheet.org/boxesetc/1972/B09201BOS1972.htm (accessed February 24, 2020).
5. Boston Red Sox 4, Baltimore Orioles 0, September 20, 1972, https://www.retrosheet.org/boxesetc/1972/B09202BOS1972.htm (accessed February 24, 2020).
6. Phil Fuhrer, "Orioles Calm Despite Clustered Field," *The Sun-Telegram* (San Bernardino, CA), September 4, 1972: 20.
7. Lou Hatter, "Orioles shade Yankees," *Baltimore Sun*, Scptcmbcr 16, 1972. 21.

Promising Flight of Baby Birds

Francis Kinlaw

Other than finishing a season in first place,
Nothing is more exciting than a first pennant race;
In 1960 reborn Orioles chased their first flag,
In the preceding six seasons their standing did lag.

After the Browns moved east in '54
Hopes and optimism in Birdland failed to soar;
Absent each year from the league's first division,
Challenging of contenders was hard to envision.

In '59, the O's trailed Bill Veeck's Pale Hose
With an offense that was, too often, comatose;
But the following year a fresh era began
When Paul Richards emerged as a man with a plan.

Richards' young hurlers had quickly matured,
With them on the mound fewer runs were assured;
Barber, Estrada, Fisher, Walker, and Pappas—
All had strong arms to throw pitches with class.

"Skinny" Brown and Hoyt Wilhelm (relative "dinosaurs")
Gave firm support to this fine "Kiddie Korps";
The first baseman, free-swinging slugger Jim Gentile,
Injected power to an offense that finally was real.

The left side of the infield was in splendid hands
With a rookie shortstop and a third sacker so grand;
Ron Hansen and Brooksie were coming of age,
With valued contributions that were easy to gauge.

With Jackie Brandt acquired late the previous year
The lineup was set as the first pitch grew near;
Brandt played center, leading off more often than not,
Displaying personal traits tending to "stir the pot."

Marv Breeding was at second almost all of the time
And Triandos, at catcher, was still in his prime;
Gene Woodling, in left, was aging a bit
But, with a very good average, he could still hit.

Al Pilarcik covered right, though not every day
For Gene Stephens also needed a position to play;
The latter was acquired in June in a trade
After Willie Tasby had failed to make the grade.

Off the bench came Clint Courtney, Jim Busby, and Walt Dropo…
Each had performed many years and quite well as a pro;
Dave Nicholson originally seemed to have power to spare
But too often he left home plate in despair.

Occasionally the club had to call on reserves:
Triandos had surgery for a pinched nerve;
For five weeks Courtney filled in with his usual grit,
And on the 27th of May broke in a large catcher's mitt!

The mitt was designed to improve poor Clint's chances
Of corralling Wilhelm's knuckler with its dips, turns, and dances;
He did well enough, with help from his mates,
That in June the Birds hovered around first place.

The first of two All-Star Games provided relief
After five straight losses had caused momentary grief;
The All-Star Games, in KC and the House of Babe Ruth,
Served as a showcase for the Orioles' youth.

Hansen was the shortstop for the American League's team,
Al Lopez picked Estrada, fulfilling one of Chuck's dreams;
Brooks relieved Malzone at the hot corner,
And Gentile got a hit as a benchwarmer.

Eight wins in a row, a few weeks after the break,
Were followed by losses that made spirits shake;
Four games were dropped, two to Casey's strong crew—
Both by a run, one on a Courtney miscue.

But September began with the Yanks in the Orioles' park,
And good results gave the Birds an encouraging spark;
Pappas bested Ford on Friday for a shutout win,
And the next day Fisher froze Bombers' bats again.

Estrada and Wilhelm closed the series, allowing two runs,
But the Orioles scored six—more fun in the sun!
With seven wins in a row, the Birds jumped into first place,
And on Labor Day night they still led the race.

After losing three of four games, they dropped down one spot,
Cooling off somewhat as the Yankees got hot;
In mid-September the contenders were virtually tied—
A series in the Bronx would decide whose hopes were denied.

Four games were played, pinstripes prevailed in them all—
Oriole fans were covered with dread and a pall;
Experience in pennant chases had come to the fore,
And the Yanks were prepared to shut the O's door.

The Bombers blocked the path to the pennant with force—
Disappointed in '59, they reversed their course;
They closed the season by winning 15 games straight,
And the Birds finished second, trailing by eight.

But Baltimore had turned a corner and was prepared to contend,
The next few years would see its fortunes ascend;
And six years later dreams attained realization
When a sweep of the Dodgers brought celebration.

Contributors

BRUCE ADAMS co-founded Bethesda Community Base Ball Club (1998), Cal Ripken Collegiate Baseball League (2004), and Fields of Dreams after-school program in Washington, DC (2002). A SABR member since 1990, Bruce was selected as a member of the inaugural class of the Cal Ripken Collegiate Baseball League Hall of Fame.

DR. JOHN J. BURBRIDGE, JR. is currently Professor Emeritus at Elon University where he was both a dean and professor. He is also an adjunct at York College of Pennsylvania. While at Elon he introduced and taught *Baseball and Statistics*. He has authored several SABR publications and presented at SABR Conventions, NINE, and the Seymour meetings. He is a lifelong New York Giants baseball fan. The greatest Giants-Dodgers game he attended was a 1–0 Giants' victory in Jersey City in 1956. Yes, the Dodgers did play in Jersey City in 1956 and 1957. John can be reached at burbridg@elon.edu.

ALAN COHEN has been a SABR member since 2010. He serves as Vice President-Treasurer of the Connecticut Smoky Joe Wood Chapter and is datacaster (MiLB First Pitch stringer) for the Hartford Yard Goats, the Double-A affiliate of the Colorado Rockies. His biographies, game stories and essays have appeared in more than 40 SABR publications. Since his first *Baseball Research Journal* article appeared in 2013, Alan has continued to expand his research into the Hearst Sandlot Classic (1946–65) from which 88 players advanced to the major leagues. He has four children and eight grandchildren and resides in Connecticut with wife, Frances, their dog, and three cats.

STEPHEN W. DITTMORE, PHD is a professor of sport management and assistant dean at the University of Arkansas. A lifelong Dodgers fan born in Redondo Beach, California, Dittmore is co-author of a Sport Public Relations textbook now in its third edition and has more than 40 peer-reviewed publications. He has been a SABR member since 2018.

ED EDMONDS is Professor Emeritus of Law at the Notre Dame Law School. He is the former law library director at William & Mary, Loyola New Orleans, St. Thomas (Minnesota), and Notre Dame. With Frank Houdek, he is co-author of *Baseball Meets the Law* (McFarland 2017). He taught sports law for 35 years, and he has published law review articles on labor and antitrust issues involving baseball and salary arbitration.

GORDON J. GATTIE is an engineer for the US Navy. His baseball research interests include ballparks, historical trends, and statistical analysis. A SABR member since 1998, Gordon earned his PhD from SUNY Buffalo, where he used baseball to investigate judgment performance in complex dynamic environments. Ever the optimist, he dreams of a Cleveland Indians-Washington Nationals World Series matchup, especially after the Nationals' 2019 World Series championship. Lisa, his wonderful wife who roots for the Yankees, and Morrigan, their beloved Labrador retriever, are looking forward to resuming their cross-country travels visiting ballparks and other baseball-related sites. Gordon has contributed to several SABR publications, including *The National Pastime* and the Games Project.

STEVEN M. GLASSMAN has been a SABR member since 1994 and is a frequent contributor to *The National Pastime*. His article in this volume is his sixth. He graduated with a Bachelor of Science Degree in Sport and Recreation Management from Temple University and currently lives in Warminster, Pennsylvania.

BOB GOLON is a retired manuscript librarian and archivist, Princeton Theological Seminary Library, Princeton, New Jersey. He also spent three years as labor archivist at Rutgers University Special Collections and University Archives. He is a member of the Mid-Atlantic Regional Archives Conference and past-president of the New Jersey Library Association History and Preservation section. Prior to getting his MLIS from Rutgers University in 2004, Bob spent 18 years in sales and marketing for the Hewlett-Packard Company. A baseball historian and SABR member, Bob has been a contributor to numerous publications, can be prominently seen on the YES Network's "Yankeeography—Casey Stengel," and is the author of *No Minor Accomplishment: The Revival of New Jersey Professional Baseball* (Rivergate Books/Rutgers University Press, 2008).

BILL HICKMAN chaired SABR's Pictorial History Committee for ten years, and currently maintains the "near major leaguers" database on the SABR website. Bill co-founded the Rockville (MD) Baseball Hall of Fame and is the historian for the Bethesda Big Train Collegiate Baseball Team.

JIMMY KEENAN has been a SABR member since 2001. His grandfather, Jimmy Lyston, and four other family members were all professional baseball players. A frequent contributor to SABR publications, Keenan is the author of the following books; *The Lystons: A Story of One Baltimore Family & Our National Pastime*, *The Life, Times and Tragic Death of Pitcher Win Mercer*, *The Lyston Brothers: A Journey Through 19th Century Baseball*. Keenan is a 2010 inductee into the Oldtimers Baseball Association of Maryland's Hall of Fame and a 2012 inductee into the Baltimore's Boys of Summer Hall of Fame.

HERM KRABBENHOFT, a SABR member since 1981, is a retired research chemist (organic synthesis and polymer chemistry). Over the years his baseball research has been published in *Baseball Digest*, *The Sporting News*, *Baseball America*, *Baseball Weekly*, and several SABR publications, including *The Baseball Research Journal*, *The National Pastime*, *By The Numbers*, *The Inside Game*, and *Nineteenth Century Notes*. He has also described his research in 26 oral presentations at SABR National Conventions. His 2012 *BRJ* article, "Lou Gehrig's RBI Record: 1923–39," was selected for inclusion in SABR 50 at 50: The Society of American Baseball Research's Fifty Most-Essential Contributions to the Game. Herm's recent baseball research endeavors have encompassed five-tool players, quasi-cycles, and day-in/day-out double-duty diamondeers.

DAVID KRELL is the editor of the anthologies *The New York Mets in Popular Culture* and *The New York Yankees in Popular Culture*. He's also the author of *Our Bums: The Brooklyn Dodgers in History, Memory and Popular Culture*. David's contributions to SABR's Baseball Biography Project include Johnny Podres, Bucky

Dent, Joe Pepitone, Kurt Russell, and Harry Sinclair. David is the chair of SABR's Elysian Fields Chapter (Northern New Jersey).

NORMAN L. MACHT has written more than 35 books, the latest being *They Played the Game*, oral histories of 47 players—including nine Hall of Famers—whose careers ranged from 1912 to 1981. His website, normanmacht.com, will soon include articles written by him over the past half century.

KEITH SPALDING ROBBINS has been a SABR member since 2013. His family's baseball story is an open book for all, especially if you read John Thorn, Peter Levine, or Mark Lampster. He was named after his father's uncle, whose namesake building catches its fair share of home runs hit at Cal Tech. Keith has been published in the 2013–2014 Cooperstown Symposium and *NINE* and his research interests include old-timers games and international baseball tours.

ERIC ROBINSON has been a member of SABR since 2013 and is currently co-chair of the Asian Baseball Committee. In that time he has given presentations at SABR 44, regional SABR meetings, public schools, NPR and Nerd Nite. He has also written articles that have appeared in various SABR journals and *The Hardball Times*. He lives in Fort Worth, Texas, and for more information check out www.lyndonbaseballjohnson.com.

GARY A. SARNOFF has been an active SABR member since 1994. A member of SABR's Bob Davids chapter, he has contributed to SABR's Bio and games projects, and to the annual *National Pastime* publication. He is also a member of the SABR Negro Leagues committee and serves as chairman of the Ron Gabriel Committee. In addition, he has authored two baseball books: *The Wrecking Crew of '33* and *The First Yankees Dynasty*. He currently resides in Alexandria, Virginia.

WILLIAM SCHNEIDER has been a baseball fan since opening his first pack of baseball cards in 1974. An engineer by trade, he has a particular interest in the strategic and team-building aspects of the game. He has contributed articles to several SABR publications.

DAVID W. SMITH joined SABR in 1977 and in 2005 he received SABR's highest honor, the Bob Davids Award. In 2012 he was honored with the Henry Chadwick award. He is a past co-chair of the statistical analysis committee and the recipient of the first SABR Special Achievement award. He is also the founder and president of Retrosheet, a non-profit organization dedicated to the collection, computerization, and free distribution of play-by-play accounts of major league games. He is an Emeritus Professor of Biology at the University of Delaware.

DENNIS SNELLING is a three-time Casey Award finalist for Best Baseball Book of the Year, including for *The Greatest Minor League: A History of the Pacific Coast League*, and *Lefty O'Doul: Baseball's Forgotten Ambassador*, which was runner-up for the award in 2017. He was a 2015 Seymour Medal finalist for *Johnny Evers: A Baseball Life*. Snelling is an active member of the Dusty Baker and Lefty O'Doul SABR chapters in Northern California, and is an Associate Superintendent for a school district in Roseville, California.

WAYNE TOWERS is a retired SeaWorld San Diego educator and a retired college professor. Prior to retiring, he also worked as a data analyst for the *Oklahoman and Times* daily newspaper and for multiple business research firms. His published work includes "World Series Coverage in the 1920s" (Journalism Monographs).

THOMAS E. VAN HYNING covered the 2020 Caribbean Series in San Juan, Puerto Rico. His research helped Buster Clarkson and Bob Thurman to be recently inducted into the Caribbean Series Hall of Fame. Tom authored *Puerto Rico's Winter League* and *The Santurce Crabbers*. He is published in beisbol101.com, *The National Pastime*, *Baseball Research Journal*, and writes SABR BioProject biographies. A charter member of SABR's Cool Papa Bell (Mississippi) Chapter, Tom is Tourism Economist/Data Analyst, Mississippi Development Authority. His BBA is from the University of Georgia.

DAN VANDEMORTEL became a Giants fan in upstate New York and moved to San Francisco to follow the team more closely. He has written extensively on Northern Ireland political and legal affairs. His baseball writing has appeared in *The National Pastime*, San Francisco's *Nob Hill Gazette*, and other publications. His article "White Circles Drawn In Crayon" won the 2020 McFarland-SABR Baseball Research Award. Feedback is welcome at giants1971@yahoo.com.

A SABR member since 1999, **CORT VITTY** grew up in New Jersey and has been a fan of the New York Yankees since 1959, subsequently making numerous trips to Yankee Stadium. Articles authored by Vitty are posted on the SABR website and included in numerous SABR publications. Vitty and his wife Mary Anne reside in Maryland, with Sparkle, their affable goldendoodle.

JOSEPH WANCHO resides in Brooklyn, Ohio. He has been part of the editing team for two BioProject Books: *Pitching to the Pennant: The 1954 Cleveland Indians* and *The Sleeping Giant Awakes: The 1995 Cleveland Indians*. Currently, he serves as the vice chair for the Baseball Index Project.

JAY WIGLEY first joined SABR in 1999 after discovering Retrosheet in 1996. His earliest baseball memory is of the scoreboard animations at the Astrodome during a game in the early 1970s. Jay lives in Knoxville, Tennessee, where he works in the medical device industry as a Quality professional.

A native of Boonsboro, Maryland, **MARK ZEIGLER** has researched minor league baseball since 1996. A graduate of Salisbury University in Maryland, Mark spent 20 years in professional baseball with the Philadelphia Phillies, Baltimore Orioles and Texas Rangers minor league affiliates, primarily with the Orioles, Advanced A, Carolina League affiliate, Frederick Keys. He has extensively researched the early years of the Class D Blue Ridge League, and his research can be found on his website at www.blueridgeleague.org. More recently, he has been researching the Class D Potomac League, which played less than one full season in 1916. Mark is a Realtor in the Eastern Panhandle of West Virginia, and lives with wife, Margaret, and his two children, Gracie and Jacob, in Kearneysville.

Friends of SABR

You can become a Friend of SABR by giving as little as $10 per month or by making a one-time gift of $1,000 or more. When you do so, you will be inducted into a community of passionate baseball fans dedicated to supporting SABR's work.

Friends of SABR receive the following benefits:
- ✓ Recognition in This Week in SABR, SABR.org, and the SABR Annual Report
- ✓ Access to the SABR Annual Convention VIP donor event
- ✓ Invitations to exclusive Friends of SABR events

SABR On-Deck Circle - $10/month, $30/month, $50/month

Get in the SABR On-Deck Circle, and help SABR become the essential community for the world of baseball. Your support will build capacity around all things SABR, including publications, website content, podcast development, and community growth.

A monthly gift is deducted from your bank account or charged to a credit card until you tell us to stop. No more email, mail, or phone reminders.

Josh Gibson

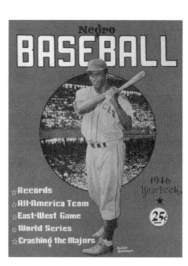
Jackie Robinson

Cool Papa Bell

Join the SABR On-Deck Circle

Payment Info: __Visa __Mastercard __ Discover

Name on Card: _____

Card #: _____

Exp. Date: _____ Security Code: _____

Signature: _____

- ○ $10/month
- ○ $30/month
- ○ $50/month
- ○ Other amount _____

Go to sabr.org/donate to make your gift online